Frans Wijsen

Christianity and Other Cultures

Frans Wijsen

Christianity and Other Cultures

Introduction to Mission Studies

LIT

Bibliographic information published by the Deutsche Nationalbibliothek
The Deutsche Nationalbibliothek lists this publication in the Deutsche Nationalbibliografie; detailed bibliographic data are available in the Internet at http://dnb.d-nb.de.

ISBN 978-3-643-90579-6

A catalogue record for this book is available from the British Library

Klosbachstr. 107
CH-8032 Zürich
Tel. +41 (0) 44-251 75 05 Fax +41 (0) 44-251 75 06
E-Mail: zuerich@lit-verlag.ch http://www.lit-verlag.ch

Distribution:

In the UK: Global Book Marketing, e-mail: mo@centralbooks.com
In North America: International Specialized Book Services, e-mail: orders@isbs.com
In Germany: LIT Verlag Fresnostr. 2, D-48159 Münster
Tel. +49 (0) 2 51-620 32 22, Fax +49 (0) 2 51-922 60 99, E-mail: vertrieb@lit-verlag.de

In Austria: Medienlogistik Pichler-ÖBZ, e-mail: mlo@medien-logistik.at
e-books are available at www.litwebshop.de

Foreword

Although I was nominated as a professor of mission studies in 2000 and have published various books since then, I have not published an introduction to mission studies thus far. Rapid changes in this field of study prevented me from doing so. Dissatisfied with and complaining about readers that I compiled for post-graduate seminars over successive years, which seemed to lack cohesion, MA and PhD students challenged me to produce a selection of my own work. With the help of some student assistants, I selected a number of articles previously published which might be helpful for their further studies. Out of a multiplicity of themes that I dealt with over the past fifteen years, I choose one, namely, inculturation and syncretism in African Christianity. I do not intend to give an overview of my entire work, but only to introduce one topic which seems to me missing: 'how to do' mission studies. I find it striking that in most introductions to mission studies there is no chapter on methods. The chapters included here cover a period of ten years. I did not change the contents. However, I did write a new introduction from the perspective of 'how to do' mission studies. I am grateful that at the fifteenth anniversary of my professorship in mission studies, this introduction to mission studies is published, and I thank the publishers of the original articles (the sources are given at the end) for their permission to reproduce them in this book.

Nijmegen, 2015

Table of Contents

Introduction My 'pilgrimage' in mission studies

In my doctoral dissertation I quote a conversation between an old man (*mzee*) and a Dutch missionary who worked in Sukumaland, Northwest Tanzania, the area where I conducted the fieldwork for my doctoral research. The old man said:

> Padre, you trouble yourself for nothing. I will never agree to join your religion. All people have their own religion. The Germans were here and they had their own religion. The British came; they also had their own religion. The Protestants at Ng'wagala also have their own religion. The Ba-Swahili (Muslims) of Shanwa have their own religion. You Padres also have your own religion. And we the black people have also our own religions. Our religion is the one of Masamva (Ancestral spirits). All religions are good.[1]

"All people have their own religion" and "all religions are good". The attitude of the old man is not only the attitude of most people in Sukumaland, and in other parts of Africa, but in most parts of the world. Just as most modern people in contemporary Europe the Sukuma have a "do it yourself religion" and a "cash and carry culture". The old man continued:

> Father, your religion has Christ as your ancestor. I know Christ was a European. Your forefathers tortured him. He died through beating. He died a very bad death, hanging from a tree, as you have been showing me the pictures. This man has turned into a very fierce ancestor. He has tortured you very much. You kill yourselves by wars. You are not at peace because of this ancestor. For years you have tried to appease him through your sacrifices and prayers. I think you need us to help you to appease your own ancestor when you want us to become Christians.[2]

---

[1] F. Wijsen, *There is only one God. A Social-Scientific and Theological Study of Popular Religion and Evangelization in Sukumaland, Northwest Tanzania*, Kampen 1993, 79.
[2] Wijsen, *There is only one God*, 221.

"I think you need us to help you". Whereas the Dutch missionary thought that he had come to Africa to help the Africans, to save them from eternal damnation, the old man reversed the traditional mission thinking. This is what missiologists would currently call 'co-evangelisation', a shift from mission *ad gentes* to mission *inter gentes*, or from mission as conversion to mission as conversation.

The old man rejects Christianity, an attitude which he shares with the overwhelming majority of the Sukuma people until now. Most Sukuma people are indigenous believers. There has not been a massive conversion to Christianity or Islam in Sukumaland as has happened in other parts of Tanzania, and Africa in general. Nevertheless, there has been quite some appropriation of Christian or Islamic symbols and ideas from which the Sukuma borrow freely. Examples are the notion of a Supreme Being, which the Sukuma had not known before as they venerated nature as a whole, and the copper bracelets which the Sukuma who went as porters of goods to the Indian Ocean coast returned home with. These bracelets of Arab origin were considered to be Sukuma amulets.

From the very beginning of my academic career my knowledge guiding interest has been to understand the acculturation processes that people go through when they encounter new cultures, be they European missionaries encountering Africans in Africa, Africans encountering European missionaries in Africa, or African immigrants encountering Europeans in Europe.[3] In these processes there is quite some asymmetry and domination, but also borrowing and conversation.

I see Christianity as a culture, just as any other culture. For this reason I speak about 'Christianity and other cultures', not about 'Christianity and cultures', as other missiologists do. I do not define culture in a classical way as a 'shared meaning system' or 'software of the mind', but as 'imagined community' or 'organisation of diversity' as Ulf Han-

---

[3] F. Wijsen, Mission and Multiculturalism. On Communication between Europeans and Africans, in: *Exchange. Journal of Missiological and Ecumenical Research* 32(2003)3, 260-277.

nerz says.[4] I define mission as 'cross-cultural Christian communication', or 'cross-cultural communication of Christian faith', and missiology as theory of mission (or in terms of a practice, theorizing about mission). In this book (which is a compilation of earlier published works covering a decade) I use the terms 'missiology' and 'mission studies' as equivalents.

Mission as 'cross-cultural Christian communication' covers both the communication within Christianity between Western and non-Western Christians (or members of 'old' and 'new' Churches, 'sending' and 'receiving' Churches, also called 'ecumenical studies') and communication between Christians and non-Christians (better called the believers of other faiths). I have resisted the trend to call the former field of study 'intercultural theology', and the latter 'comparative theology', although I clearly see the reasons why some of my colleagues prefer to do so.

In my doctoral dissertation I classified four attitudes of Sukuma people towards cultural contact.[5] And this classification runs throughout my entire work:[6]

- Some people keep a foot in two systems, leaving them as they are, taking spiritual and material help from both sides. They are Christians on Sunday and believers of the indigenous religion on other days of the week.
- Other people reject completely one of the two systems, sticking strictly to the Christian-European civilisation or (returning) to the 'path of the ancestors'.

---

[4] Quoted in F. Wijsen, *Seeds of conflict in a haven of peace. From religious studies to interreligious studies in Africa,* Amsterdam and New York 2007, 19.

[5] Wijsen, *There is only one God*, 98.

[6] F. Wijsen, Inculturation or Syncretism? Popular Christianity in East Africa, in: A. Kalliath (ed.), *Pilgrims in Dialogue. A new configuration of Religions for Millennium Community*. Bangalore 2000, 253.

- Again others reject both systems, which is the attitude of African intellectuals who adhere to African socialism or humanism and have a secular world view.
- However, a large number create an intermediate set of beliefs and practices which offers a synthesis between African religion and Christian message.[7]

In harmony with the idea that Christian mission can be defined as cross-cultural Christian communication,[8] and that missiology therefore is a communication science,[9] I developed the idea that missiology has four perspectives. Missiology studies how cross-cultural Christian communication was (historical perspective) and is practiced (empirical perspective), and how it should (normative perspective) and could (strategic perspective) be practiced. Seen as such, missiology has four sub-disciplines, namely anthropology, history, theology and pedagogy of mission.

Although missiology is often classified as the broadest theological discipline, and the four perspectives distinguished above could justify that classification, I have always understood missiology to be part of practical theology.[10] In principle the discipline of missiology could be placed in departments of historical or systematic theology. However, when I make historical analyses and theological reflections I do that in view of a (better) practice.

---

[7] F. Wijsen, Intercultural Theology and the Mission of the Church, *Exchange. Journal of Missiological and Ecumenical Research* 30(2001)3, 225.

[8] Wijsen, *There is only one God*, 22.

[9] Wijsen, *There is only one God*, 243; Wijsen, Mission and Multiculturalism, 260.

[10] Wijsen, *There is only one God*, 22; F. Wijsen, New Wine in Old Wineskins? Intercultural Theology instead of Missiology, in: M. Frederiks, M. Dijkstra and A. Houtepen (eds.), *Towards an Intercultural Theology,* Zoetermeer 2003, 47.

In my doctoral dissertation I used the so called pastoral circle[11] which I later developed as the practical-theological spiral.[12] Although some of my publications are more descriptive and analytic, and other publications are normative and strategic, they always need to be seen against the background of this spiral. The four stages and their development in my work can be described as follows:

- The objective of the first stage of the practical-theological spiral is to acquire knowledge of the practice that is experienced as problematic. The question at this stage is: What practice is problematic for whom? With respect to the method in this stage there has been a shift from participant observation to participatory objectification. I have always favoured research from within (emic) and from below (inductive), but I have become less naïve and more self-critical as a researcher.
- The objective of the second stage of the practical theological spiral is to gain insight into the practice that is experienced as problematic. The question at this stage is: Why is the practice experienced as problematic? With respect to the method in this stage there has been a shift from ethnography of speaking to critical discourse analysis. I have always been concerned with language. But my views of language have shifted from informative to constitutive.
- The objective of the third stage of the practical-theological spiral is to give an evaluation of the practice. The question at this stage is: What do I think of the practice and where do my norms

[11] Wijsen, *There is only one God*, 11-13; F. Wijsen, The Pastoral Circle in the Training of Church Ministers, in: *African Ecclesial Review* 39(1997)4, 238-250.

[12] F. Wijsen, The Practical-Theological Spiral. Bridging Theology in the West and the Rest of the World, in: F. Wijsen, P. Henriot and R. Mejía (eds.), *The Pastoral Circle Revisited. A Critical Quest for Truth and Transformation*, New York 2005, 108-126; F. Wijsen, The practical-theological spiral revisited. From social to discursive analysis, in: R. Setio, W. Wibowo and P. Widjaja (eds.), *Teks dan Konteks yang Tiada Bertepi*, Semarang 2012, 73-91.

come from? With respect to the method in this stage there has been a shift from correlation to confrontation. There is a continuity, but also a discontinuity between Christian culture and other cultures.

- The objective of the fourth stage of the practical-theological spiral is to demonstrate conditions for the possibility of an innovation of the situation. The question is: What could a better practice be and how can we go there? With respect to the method in this stage there has been a shift from a community based to an evidence based approach. Using the example of cattle raiding as God-given practice I demonstrated that a community based approach can become naïve and romantic.[13]

Looking back at my own 'pilgrimage' in mission studies I clearly see a continuity and change of insights.

- In my anthropology of mission there is a shift from an essentialist to a constructivist view of culture.[14] In my doctoral dissertation I was eager to "grasp the native's point of view", in harmony with the classical understanding of ethnography. However, I now recognise that "the native's point of view" as such does not exist and is always related to social positions and specific interests, influenced by power relations.
- In my historical study of mission there is a shift from a focus on active participation of receivers of messages in communication processes to power relations and resistance. I resisted the 'fatal impact' theory and emphasised the 'invention of tradition' theo-

---

[13] Wijsen, The Practical-Theological Spiral, 221.

[14] F. Wijsen and R. Tanner, *'I am just a Sukuma.' Globalization and Identity Construction in Northwest Tanzania*, Amsterdam and New York 2002; Wijsen, Mission and Multiculturalism, 275-276; Wijsen, New Wine in Old Wineskins?, 43; Wijsen, *Seeds of conflict*, 19-20.

ry.[15] Perhaps my experience in Sukumaland, where colonial oppression was limited, was generalised too rapidly. It was after I conducted case studies in Indonesia that I looked more from the perspective of victims of history. My shift to critical discourse analysis as method helped to emphasise peripheral voices.

- In my theology of mission there is a shift from pluralism to universalism.[16] In my earlier work I stressed that God's revelation in African religion is independent from God's revelation in Christianity, leading to particularity. In my later work I stress that both revelations are interdependent and that there is a common ground.
- In my pedagogy of mission there is a shift from mission as inculturation to mission as interculturation.[17] In my earlier work I described inculturation as to "abide by the Otherness of Africa and the Africans".[18] Later I understood that this was quite naïve and that critical interrogation is needed.

Although missiology at Nijmegen has been characterised as empirical missiology,[19] I have never been in favour of a pure empirical missiology without critical reference. Some try to save missiology for academia by limiting themselves to description and analysis and refraining from making normative statements or recommendations for

---

[15] F. Wijsen, Beyond the Fatal Impact Theory, in: M. Amaladoss (ed.), *Globalization and its victims as seen by its victims,* Delhi 1999, 130.

[16] F. Wijsen, Interkulturelle Theologie und Religionswissenschaft, in: *Interkulturelle Theologie. Zeitschrift für Missionswissenschaft* 40(2014)2-3, 219-229; F. Wijsen, What is intercultural about Intercultural Theology?, in: *Gema Teologi. Jurnal Fakultas Theologia Universitas Kristen Duta Wacana*, 2014, 185-192.

[17] F. Wijsen, Intercultural Theology and the Mission of the Church, *Exchange. Journal of Missiological and Ecumenical Research* 30(2001)3, 218-228; F. Wijsen, Mission in a new key. From inculturation to interculturation, in: *SMA Bulletin*, June 2007(125), 41-53.

[18] P. Turkson and F. Wijsen (eds.), *Inculturation. Abide by the Otherness of Africa and the Africans,* Kampen 1994.

[19] Wijsen, *Seeds of conflict*, 49.

practice. Just as we expect economists to say what is good for the economy, and medical specialists what is good for our health, missiologists can make statements about just and authentic communication practices.

I see mission as a religious phenomenon, present in most religions. I argued that mission is even present in African indigenous religions.[20] If people are deeply convinced of something they try to spread their convictions. Just as one can practice religious studies from a mission studies perspective, as was done in the past and is still done in some evangelical circles, one can also practice mission studies from a religious studies perspective, using methodological agnosticism as a principle. Whereas these are two models, I always practice a third one. I see religious studies and mission studies as different disciplines, which collaborate with each other without mixing them. In this sense I have become reluctant to accept an intra-disciplinary approach.[21]

Over the past thirty years I dealt with various issues, namely syncretism and inculturation in African Christianity;[22] Muslim-Christian relations in Tanzania[23] and Indonesia;[24] religion and development issues, in

---

[20] Wijsen, Mission in a new key, 158.

[21] Wijsen, *There is only one God*, 22.

[22] F. Wijsen, "The Gold and the spirits are close". Popular Religion and social transformation in Sukumaland, North-West Tanzania, in: *Exchange. Journal of Missiological and Ecumenical Research* 24(1995)1, 45-60; F. Wijsen, "All People See the Same Sun". Liturgy in Africa between Inculturation and Syncretism, in: *Questions Liturgiques* 77(1996)1-2, 77-95; 'I have all kinds of medicines.' Dialogue and syncretism in African Christianity, in: W. Valkenberg and F. Wijsen (eds.), *The Polemic Dialogue*, Saarbrücken 1997, 123-145; Wijsen, Inculturation or Syncretism?.

[23] F. Wijsen, 'Strive in competition for good deeds'. Christians and Muslims in Tanzania, in: *Studies in Interreligious Dialogue* 7(1997)2, 158-167; F. Wijsen, 'When two elephants fight the grass gets hurt...' Muslim-Christian Relationships in Upcountry Tanzania, in: F. Wijsen and P. Nissen (eds.), *'Mission is a Must.' Intercultural Theology and the Mission of the Church*, Amsterdam and New York 2002, 235-248; F. Wijsen and B. Mfumbusa, Seeds of Conflict. Muslim-Christian Relations in Tanzania, in: J. Gort, H. Janssen and H. Vroom (eds.), *Religion, Conflict and reconciliation. Multifaith Ideals and Realities*, Amsterdam and New York 2002, 316-326; F. Wijsen,

particular health, justice and environment;[25] global Christianity[26] and migration,[27] particularly African[28] and post-colonial[29] immigrants; in-

---

Religionism in Tanzania, in: A. Borsboom and F. Jespers (eds.), *Identity and Religion. A Multidisciplinary Approach*, Saarbrücken 2003, 121-137; F. Wijsen, and T. Ndaluka, Ujamaa is still alive. A sign of hope for Africa?, in: A.J. Bwangatto (ed.), *Africa is not Destined to die. Signs of hope and renewal*. Nairobi 2012, 240-253; F. Wijsen, "Keep the conversation going". Regulating Islamic Revivalism in Tanzania, in: T. Ndaluka and F. Wijsen (eds.), *Religion and state in Tanzania revisited. Reflections from 50 years of independence*, Münster 2014, 198-205.

[24] F. Wijsen and F. Husein, Dakwah and mission. Muslim - Christian encounters in Indonesia, in: C. Sterkens, M. Machasin and F. Wijsen (eds.), *Religion, Civil Society and Conflict in Indonesia*, Zürich and Berlin 2009, 135-152; F. Wijsen, and G. Singgih, Regulation on Houses of Worship. A Threat to Social Cohesion?, in: Sterkens, Machasin and Wijsen, *Religion, Civil Society*, 87-97; F. Wijsen and S. Cholil, 'I come from a Pacasila Family'. Muslims and Christians in Indonesia, in: V. Küster and R. Setio (eds.), *Muslim Christian Relations Observed. Comparative Studies from Indonesia and The Netherlands*, Leipzig 2014, 29-46.

[25] F. Wijsen, Indigenous Spirituality and Sustainable Development. A Critical Appraisal of African Renaissance Rhetoric, in: J. Gort, H. Jansen and H. Stoker (eds.), *Crossroads Discourses between Christianity and Culture*, Amsterdam and New York 2010, 275-300; F. Wijsen, Religion, Development and Security. A Mission Studies Perspective, in: *Exchange. Journal of Missiological and Ecumenical Research*, 40(2011) 2, 274-287; F. Wijsen and S. Marcos, Indigeneity and sustainability. An introduction, in: F. Wijsen and S. Marcos (eds.), *Indigenous Voices in the Sustainability Discourse. Spirituality and the struggle for a better quality of life*, Münster 2010, 9-30.

[26] F. Wijsen, The resurgence of religion in today's world, in: F. Stenger and J. Wandera (eds.), *Christian-Muslim Co-Existence in Eastern Africa*, Nairobi 2008, 41-58; Global Christianity. A European Perspective, in: *Exchange. Journal of Missiological and Ecumenical Research* 39(2009) 2, 147-160; F. Wijsen and R. Schreiter, *Global Christianity, Contested Claims*. Amsterdam and New York 2007.

[27] J. Castillo Guerra, F. Wijsen, M. Steggerda, *Een gebedshuis voor alle volken. Kerkopbouw en kadervorming in room-katholieke allochtonengemeenschappen*, Zoetermeer 2006; J. Castillo Guerra and F. Wijsen, Katholieke Migranten tussen folklore en het recht om bestaan, in: E. Burgmans and P. Minderhoud (eds.), *Mythen en misverstanden over migratie,* Nijmegen 2007, 274-308; J. Castillo Guerra, F. Wijsen, Multiculturele of interculturele liturgie? In: D.

tercultural theology[30] and interreligious studies;[31] popular religion and missionary presence in my hometown, Maastricht;[32] language and translation[33] and theory and method in the study of religion and mission.[34]

Broersen, G. Smit, H. Luyten (red.), *Ik loop hier stage*, Heeswijk 2005, 85-102.

28 F. Wijsen, "Een vreemdeling is twee dagen gast ...". Afrikaanse Katholieken in Nederland en hun uitdaging aan theologie en pastoraat, in: L. Boeve and J. Haers (eds.), *God ondergronds,* Averbode 2001, 161-174; F. Wijsen, 'The future of the church is in our hands'. Christian migrants in the Netherlands, in: J. Haers and N. Hintersteiner (eds.), *Postcolonial Europe in the Crucible of Cultures. Reckoning with God in a World of Conflicts*, Amsterdam and New York 2007, 99-110; F. Wijsen, "...op zondag willen wij vooral onszelf zijn". Allochtone Christenen in Nederland, in: C. Hermans (ed.), *Is er nog godsdienst in 2050?*, Budel 2003, 92-111.

29 F. Wijsen and J. Vos, 'This is how we are at home'. Indonesian Muslims in The Hague, in: V. Küster and R. Setio (eds.), *Muslim Christian Relations Observed. Comparative Studies from Indonesia and The Netherlands*, Leipzig 2014, 15-28.

30 Wijsen, Intercultural Theology; Wijsen, Interkulturelle Theologie; Wijsen, What is intercultural about Intercultural Theology?; F. Wijsen and P. Nissen (eds.), *'Mission is a Must.' Intercultural Theology and the Mission of the Church*. Amsterdam and New York 2002.

31 F. Wijsen, *Seeds of conflict in a haven of peace. From religious studies to interreligious studies in Africa*, Amsterdam and New York 2007; F. Wijsen, From Religious to Interreligious Studies in East Africa, in: I. Mwase and E. Kamaara (eds.), *Theologies of Liberation and Reconstruction*. Nairobi 2012, 249-268.

32 F. Wijsen, Missionair pastoraat in de stad Maastricht, in: *Wereld en Zending. Tijdschrift voor missionaire informatie en bezinning* 14(1981)1, 48-54; F. Wijsen, Geloof in een volksbuurt van Maastricht, in: M. Van Uden and J. Pieper (eds.), *Bij geloof. Over bedevaarten en andere uitingen van volksreligiositeit*, Hilversum 1991, 163-188; F. Wijsen, Volksreligiositeit in Maastricht. Een semiotische analyse, in: J. Pieper, P. Post and M. Van Uden (eds.), *Bedevaart en pelgrimage*, Baarn 1994, 155-200; F. Wijsen, *Geloven bij het leven. Missionaire presentie in een volkswijk*. Baarn 1997.

33 R. Tanner and F. Wijsen, Christianity in Usukuma. A working misunderstanding, in: *Neue Zeitschrift für Missionswissenschaft* 49(1993)3, 177-193; F. Wijsen and R. Tanner, The Limitations of an Ecumenical Language. The case of Ki-Swahili, in: *Anthropos. International Review of Anthropology and Linguistics* 103(2008)2, 549-554; F. Wijsen, and H. Tullemans (eds.), *Dic-*

In this introduction I have no wish to be exhaustive and cover my entire work, but rather focus on one topic. I have always advocated a practice–oriented type of research[35] and I am struck by the fact that in most handbooks of missiology a chapter on 'methods in missiology' is missing. Therefore the main aim of this introduction is to show 'how to do' mission studies. In my view, methods of mission studies can be learned best, not in a skills lab, but by looking at how others conducted mission studies. I choose one of the issues that I dealt with, the one that I started with, syncretism and inculturation in African Christianity.

I combine a professorship in mission studies with a professorship in practical religious studies. This is in harmony with the tradition of empirical missiology in Nijmegen. Standing in this tradition I draw upon another tradition, namely that of missiological anthropology of the Society of the Divine Word which has been present in my faculty since the foundation of its Institute of Missiology in 1948.[36]

Looking back I see my work as a reflection of the *duplex ordo* system in the Netherlands. As my esteemed colleague Jan Platvoet once remarked, my work is multidisciplinary, a combination of social science and theology, without mixing the two, standing in the tradition of religious studies and mission studies.[37]

---

tionary of Literary Swahili by Jan Knappert and Leo van Kessel, Lewiston 2010.

[34] F. Wijsen, Discourse Analysis in Religious Studies. The Case of Interreligious Worship in Friesland, in: *Anthropos. International Review of Anthropology and Linguistics* 105(2010)2, 539-553; F. Wijsen, 'There are radical Muslims and normal Muslims': an analysis of the discourse on Islamic extremism, in: *Religion* 43(2013)1, 70-88; F. Wijsen, *Religious Discourse, Social Cohesion and Conflict. Studying Muslim-Christian Relations,* Oxford 2013; F. Wijsen, Theology as religious studies. A plea for methodological conversion, in: J. Mugambi (ed.), *Endless Quest. The Vocation of an African Christian Theologian*, Nairobi 2014, 290-302.

[35] Wijsen, Mission in a new key; Wijsen, The Practical-Theological Spiral; Wijsen, The practical-theological spiral revisited.

[36] Wijsen, *Seeds of conflict*, 50.

[37] Quoted in Wijsen, *Seeds of Conflict*, 53 n.76.

Going back to the one who many Dutch scholars of religion consider to be the 'real' founding father of science of religion, the Leiden based professor of religious studies Cornelius Tiele, one can see missiology as part of an 'applied science of religion', without using the term 'applied'.[38] However, I have never been convinced of a 'science' of mission, detached from practical issues. In this sense my work is closer to Wilfred Cantwell Smith and Mircea Eliade, who practice religious studies in view of humanistic goals. Also Harold Turner went beyond the history and phenomelogy of religion, shifting to normative and strategic issues.[39] Just as the pastoral circle in practical theology, practical religious studies can use the practical spiral, comprising four stages or better tasks: observation, interpretation, evaluation, innovation.

In this sense I classify my work as 'dialogical missiology'. Here, I do not mean a missiology that promotes dialogue,[40] but a missiology that is based on a dialogical research, where subjects and objects of research are in constant conversation. This is in harmony with Richard Rorty's notion of 'conversation' which recently influences my work.[41] I advocate a shift in mission (studies) from 'conversion' to 'conversation'.

A recent development in my work is the influence of the Dialogical Self Theory.[42] Looking at myself from this perspective I see myself as a 'polyphonic self'; a bit Dutch, although a typical 'Southerner'; a bit Tanzanian, although more a Sukuma than a Chagga; and a bit Indonesian, although more Javanese than a Batak, to generalise. I have often been asked if I see a contradiction or even a conflict in positioning myself as missiologist or scholar of religion. I have always answered 'no'. I now understand the missiologist and the scholar of religion in me as 'I positions' of my 'multiple identity'.

---

[38] Wijsen, Theology as religious studies, 303; Wijsen, Interkulturelle Theologie, 227.
[39] Wijsen, *Seeds of conflict*, 54-55.
[40] Wijsen and Nissen (eds.), *'Mission is a Must.'*
[41] Wijsen, "Keep the conversation going".
[42] Wijsen, *Religious Discourse*; Wijsen, Interkulturelle Theologie; Wijsen, What is intercultural about Intercultural Theology?

The following chapters cover all perspectives of mission studies. Although there is some overlap, as most chapters have historical, empirical, normative and strategic aspects, they have a clear focus. The first chapter discusses the present trend to replace mission studies by intercultural or comparative theology and opts for maintaining mission studies as a separate field of study. The second chapter introduces the practical-theological spiral as an appropriate method to conduct mission studies.

The third chapter studies the main topic from an anthropological point of view. It uses ethnographic semantics as a research method. The fourth chapter looks at the encounter of cultures from a historical point of view. It shows how Christianisation and Europeanisation were equated during the colonial era, and how it was and still is resisted by revival movements, popular religiosity being one of them.

Chapter five gives a theological reflection on syncretism and inculturation, opting for a theology 'from below', taking seriously the *sensus fidelium* as a locus theologicus, and advocating study of empirical methods in theological training programme. Chapter six offers a reflection on the future of mission from a strategic point of view. It advocates a shift from inculturation to interculturation, making room for unity in diversity and untranslatable translatability, or translatable untranslatability of cultural (including religious) orientations.

In the conclusion I once again focus on the object of mission studies, namely cross-cultural Christian communication, and add a new line: the significance of mission studies in the southern hemisphere for migration studies in Europe, and the reversed mission of non-Western immigrants in Europe, including foreign priests. This is a new field for mission studies, yet to be developed further. In the epilogue I reflect on what this study is all about: the method of mission studies, or the practical-theological spiral.

The chapters cover everything a beginning scholar needs to practice mission studies. After two introductory chapters on the object (chapter one) and the method (chapter two) of mission studies, the subsequent chapters introduce the four perspectives which we distinguished above:

the anthropology (chapter three), the history (chapter four), the theology (chapter five) and the pedagogy of mission (chapter six).

All the chapters, except this introduction, were published previously. Although they cover a decade, they focus on one topic and form a more or less coherent whole. Except some slight changes in the wording, I did not change the contents. In some instances I added a footnote. The original sources are given at the end of this study. For better comprehension each chapter closes with further readings and questions. The further readings do not pretend to be exhaustive. They tend to focus on the more general (not contextual) and classical (not necessarily the best) ones, and have a bias on Catholic studies (without excluding Protestant ones) which seem relevant to the Western European (Dutch) context.

Further readings on mission studies as discipline

- D. Becker and A. Feldtkeller (eds.), *Es begann in Halle ... Missionswissenschaft von Gustav Warneck bis heute*, Neuendettelsau 1997.
- G. Buono, *Missiology. Theology and praxis*, Nairobi 2000.
- I. Daneel, C. van Engen and H. Vroom (eds.), *Fullness of Life for All. Challenges for Mission in Early 21st Century*, Amsterdam and New York 2003.
- K. Müller (ed.), *Dictionary of Mission. Theology, History, Perspectives*, Maryknoll, New York 1997.
- S. Skreslet (ed.), *Comprehending Mission. The questions, methods, themes, problems and prospects of missiology*, Maryknoll, New York 2012.

Questions for better comprehension

1. What does the author mean by “mission as cross-cultural Christian communication”? According to him, what is the difference between ‘conversion’ and ‘conversation’?

2. Do you think that positioning missiology within practical theology is a wise choice? If yes, why? If not, why not?
3. What are the four perspectives of mission studies which the author distinguishes? Explain their difference in your own words.
4. According to the author, what is the relation between mission studies and religious studies?
5. Why does the author speak about "Christianity and other cultures", not just "Christianity and cultures"?

Chapter 1 Intercultural theology instead of missiology?

1.1 Introduction

In 1978 the Münster-based pastoral theologian, Adolf Exeler, wrote a 'provocative' article in which he proposed developing a comparative theology instead of missiology.[1] He argued that the end of political colonialism meant there was no room anymore for a paternalistic missiology that was at home only in the North Atlantic region.[2] The Second Vatican Council, moreover, said clearly that mission should be a dimension of all theological disciplines and that local churches should develop their own theologies. To the extent that both these precepts of the Second Vatican Council are realised, missiology becomes a doubtful enterprise and comparative theology should work on 'the issue that is at stake in missiology'.[3]

Exeler's proposal was neither the first nor the last attempt to rename missiology or to replace it with something else. The *Missionwissenschaftliches Institut Missio* at Aachen has had a lengthy discussion on renaming the institute an Institute of Contextual Theologies, following

---

[1] Cf. A. Exeler, Vergleichende Theologie statt Missionswissenschaft? Provozierende Anfrage eines nichtfachmannes, in: H. Waldenfels (ed.), *"...denn ich bin bei euch"*, Zürich 1978, 199-211. It is noteworthy that the author first speaks about comparative theology instead of missiology (205). Later on he says that comparative theology will not push aside missiology but broaden it to fulfil its proper task (211).

[2] The presuppositions that missiology is 'paternalistic' and 'only at home in the North-Atlantic region' emerge throughout the article, although the author is aware that at the time he wrote the article missiology had already become missiology on "six continents" (208).

[3] Exeler, Vergleichende Theologie, 199. The author does not explain what this issue is, nor whether and to what extent the challenges of the Second Vatican Council were met. See further T. Kramm, Was ist von einer 'vergleichende Theologie' zu erwarten?, in: *Zeitschrift für Missionswissenschaft und Religionswissenschaft* 68(1984)69-73; T. Kramm, Vergleichende Theologie statt Missionswissenschaft, in: *Zeitschrift für Missionswissenschaft und Religionswissenschaft* 70(1986)101-111.

its well-known bibliography *Theology in Context*.[4] At the theological faculty at Tilburg missiology became development studies,[5] and at the theological faculty at Nijmegen it was known as Third World theology up to 1992, when my predecessor Rogier van Rossum was appointed to the chair of missiology.[6]

Nowadays some scholars prefer to speak of intercultural theology rather than missiology. At the Theological University of Kampen a new chair of "cross-cultural theology" was established "in the framework of missiology/ecumenism", as the advertisement for this chair read. The Faculty of Theology at the University of Nijmegen has recently started new master's and doctoral programmes in intercultural theology "in co-operation with the Nijmegen Institute for Missiology", and the chair of ecumenism at the University of Utrecht will be renamed the chair of intercultural theology.[7] The main question that concerns us here is whether this is just another freak of fashion – observable in other disciplines as well: intercultural philosophy, transcultural psychology, transcultural pedagogy, intercultural communication, and so on – that is to

---

[4] Cf. L. Wiedenman, Missionswissenschaft oder kontextuelle Theologie?, in: M. Pankoke-Schenk and G. Evers (eds.), *Inkulturation und Kontextualität. Theologien im Weltweiten Austausch*, Frankfurt am Main 1994, 231-240; J. Estermann, Missiological Instititute Missio, in: S. Karotemprel et al., *Promoting mission studies*, Shilling 2000, 43-73.

[5] See V. Neckebrouck, *De stomme duivelen. Het anti-missionair syndroom in de westerse kerk*, Brugge 1990, p. 63; V. Neckebrouck, *Westerse weerstanden tegen de kerkelijke leer over missie en ontwikkeling in kensociologisch perspectief*, in: J. Bulckens, P. Cooreman (eds.), Kerkelijk leven in Vlaanderen anno 2000, Leuven 1989.

[6] My predecessor always opposed the tendency to reduce missiology to theology of liberation or theology of dialogue and fought for missiology as an independent discipline. See F. Wijsen and P. Nissen (eds.), *'Mission is a must'. Intercultural theology and the mission of the church*, Amsterdam and New York 2002, p. 3-10.

[7] At the same time the Inter-university Institute for Missiology and Ecumenical Research is to be renamed the Centre for Intercultural Theology, Interreligious Dialogue, Mission and Ecumenism.

say, old wine in new wineskins? Or is the latest attempt to rename missiology more fundamental than that?[8]

Since this chapter does not aim at introducing intercultural theology in itself, it does not deal with its history extensively. The main question, which was raised above, is subdivided into some sub-questions. In the first section of this chapter we ask what intercultural theology is all about and whether it can replace missiology. We argue that it cannot. In the third section we ask what a contemporary missiology that takes into account the concerns of intercultural theology could look like.

The term 'intercultural theology' was first propagated by Walter Hollenweger in 1979, who regarded missiology and ecumenism as a coherent whole,[9] studying the common witness of formerly divided churches amid rapid development of church and theology in the 'third world' and the emerging gospel of the newer Pentecostal, Evangelical and Independent Churches. "*Das eben ist das Thema der interkulturellen Theologie (früher Missionswissenschaft genannt), nämlich dass der kulturelle Kontext ausserhalb unsere Gesichts-, Kultur- und Bildungskreisen für unsere Theologie wichtig ist*".[10] This is exactly where my problem starts.

---

[8] The fact that some journals have recently changed their (sub)titles – '*Theology in Context*' is now '*Chakana. Intercultural Forum of Theology and Philosophy*' and '*Wereld en Zending. Oecumenisch Tijdschrift voor missiologie en missionaire praktijk*' is '*Wereld en Zending. Tijdschrift voor interculturele theologie*' – makes me apply a 'hermeneutics of suspicion'. Is this what Germans would call just *Etikettenschwindel*? And if so, what is the interest behind this *Schwindel*?

[9] Without going into detail, this must be seen against the background of the complex relationship between mission, church and world and of the incomplete integration of the missionary and ecumenical movements. See L. Hoedemaker, The people of God and the ends of the earth, in: F. Verstraelen (general editor), *Missiology. An ecumenical introduction*, Grand Rapids 1995, 157-171.

[10] W. Hollenweger, Kultur und Evangelium, Das Thema der interkulturellen Theology, in: *Jahrbuch Evangelische Mission*. Band 17, 1985, 56.

1.2 What's in a name?

To start with, by intercultural theology we mean the theology of intercultural encounter in the context of multicultural societies and a globalising world. The present author was asked to write about the variety of words that are used and the terminological confusion in the debate on intercultural theology. We will adhere strictly to the terms of this request and concentrate on the components of the term 'intercultural theo-logy'. Taking these components, we present contemporary trends in the debate, mainly in Roman Catholic theology, and give a critical appraisal of intercultural theology. We then ask whether this theology can replace missiology.

1.2.1 Inter

As far as we know, the world has always been 'multicultural' in the sense that there were many cultures; we leave aside the theory that it was only the experiment of the tower of Babel that led to cultural diversity.[11] There were also early contacts between cultures, evidenced, for example, by the 'Indonesian complex' in Africa and the 'Indian Ocean trading complex' with links between the East African coast and India, extending to China and probably dating back to some decades before Christ. What is new is the extent and the intensity of this phenomenon, as indicated already by Richard Friedli in his monumental book *Fremdheit als Heimat*, which introduced 'cultural circulation' as a new context for theology.[12]

Various terms have been used to refer to this reality, and their meaning is not always clear. The prefix 'multi-' simply means 'having many of'. When we speak about a 'multicultural society' we refer to a society in which there are many cultures. 'Inter-' means 'between', 'from one

---

[11] Cf. F. Barth, *Ethnic groups and boundaries. The social organization of difference*, London 1969.

[12] Cf. R. Friedli, *Fremdheit als Heimat. Auf der Suche nach einem Kriterium für den Dialog zwischen den Religionen*, Zürich 1974.

to the other'. Intercultural communication refers to communication between (members of) two or more different cultures. 'Cross-' means more or less the same as 'inter-', but in theoretical studies, the term 'cross-cultural' seems to refer to generalisations that are made about intercultural relations. 'Trans-' means 'across' or 'beyond'. Transcultural hermeneutics moves beyond the existence of particular cultures, or culture as such. Consequently one can state that 'cultures do not exist'.[13]

The term 'intercultural' is also understood differently, not as 'between cultures' but as a 'culture-in-between', an intermediate or 'meta-' culture which provides the mediator with an interface.[14] Interpreted thus it is equivalent to the 'he' or 'outsider' perspective in the theory that stresses the need for a switch and coordination of perspectives. Like intercultural philosophy, intercultural theology then becomes a cultural no man's land, a free space where two or more inculturated theologies can meet and interact but without reducing either of them to the other.[15]

Some people say that 'inter-cultural theo-logy' has no future. Our world is becoming one through the process of globalisation and homogenisation of cultures. Thus intercultural theology is just an in-between stage. Instead of intercultural theology it is better to speak of

---

[13] Cf. W. Van Binsbergen, *'Culturen bestaan niet'. Het onderzoek van interculturaliteit als een openbreken van vanzelfsprekendheden*, Rotterdam 1999; R. Keesing, Theories of culture revisited, in: R. Borofsky (ed.), *Assessing cultural anthropology*, New York 1994, 301-312; R. Brightman, Forget culture. Replacement, transcendence, relexification, in: *Cultural Anthropology* 10(1995)4, 509-546.

[14] Cf. W. Van Beek, The culture in-between. Anthropologist and missionary as partners, in: R. Bonsen, H. Mark and J. Miedema (eds.), *The ambiguity of rapprochement. Reflections of anthropologists on their controversial relationship with missionaries*, Nijmegen 1990, 109. For 'meta-culture' see Van Binsbergen, *Culturen bestaan niet*, 34.

[15] Cf. Van Binsbergen, *Culturen bestaan niet*, 34. For the 'he' perspective see J. Habermas, *Theorie des kommunikativen Handeln* II, Frankfurt 1982, 53-56. Later on Habermas modifies this position by distinguishing between neutrality and impartiality.

'universal', 'world', or 'global' theology.[16] Others expect a revival of cultures and even a 'clash of civilisations', 'jihad' instead of 'McWorld'.[17] Thus there is a need for a theory (theology) of intercultural encounter and understanding, just as there is a theory (theology) of interreligious dialogue. This is what intercultural theology is all about, carefully balancing between the unity and diversity of cultures.[18]

1.2.2 Cultural

By referring to the 'McDonaldisation thesis' we are already entering into a second debate, namely: What is cultural? What is culture? Over the past century innumerable definitions of culture have been formulated. Yet we still do not know what culture is, or even whether it exists. One thing is clear: if cultures exist – and given the dialectical relation between reality and the mental representation of reality we believe they do – people's understanding of culture has changed considerably.

Inspired, among other things, by the 'linguistic turn', many anthropologists saw cultures as monolithic blocks, characterised by coherence (integrated wholes) and continuity (more or less static), a shared knowledge that is learnt by the members of a group and used by them

---

[16] See W. C. Smith, *Towards a world theology*, Philadelphia 1981; D. Krieger, *The new universalism. Foundations for a global theology*, Maryknoll, New York 1991; H. Küng, *Global responsibility. In search of a new world ethic*, New York 1991; P. Knitter, *One earth many religions. Multifaith dialogue and global responsibility*, Maryknoll, New York 1995, to mention just a few.

[17] Cf. B. Barber, *Jihad vs. McWorld*, New York 1995; G. Ritzer, *The McDonaldization of society*, Thousand Oaks 1993; G. Ritzer, *The McDonaldization thesis. Exploration and extension*, London 1997; S. Huntington, *The clash of civilizations and the remaking of the world order*, New York 1996

[18] What is needed is a shift from inculturation (or contextualisation) as the main paradigm to interculturation. Intercultural theology is the theory of interculturation. See F. Wijsen, Intercultural theology and the mission of the church, in: *Exchange. Journal of Missiological and Ecumenical Research* 30(2001)3, 221; H. Waldenfels, On the hermeneutics of intercultural encounter, in: *Studies in Interreligious Dialogue* 2(1992)1, 31-50; T. Tosolini, H. G. Gadamer and E. Levinas. Two philosophical approaches to the concept of dialogue, in: *Studies in Interreligious Dialogue* 12(2002)1, 37-62.

to interpret experience and generate behaviour; a meaning system that is simply there, doing things on its own, independently of the actor. It was fashionable to speak about *the* Nuer worldview, *the* Ndembu inside view, *the* Javanese culture.[19]

Gradually anthropologists came to understand cultures as complex wholes. They no longer described culture in terms of a shared meaning system but in terms of "organisation of diversity".[20] They became aware that cultures are not homogeneous but diverse, that cultural knowledge is not only shared by the members of the group but that there is also a great variety of interpretations within groups. Cultures are not only coherent and integrated but also ambiguous and inconsistent, not timeless (static) but dynamic (flexible), not closed but open to outside influences and capitalised on in various power struggles. Cultures are not 'simply there', but depend on the actors.

The understanding of culture has considerable implications for a theory (theology) of intercultural encounter. If cultures are seen as exclusive, well-defined wholes, understanding another culture and communication between cultures seem almost impossible. Multicultural society becomes a tragedy.[21] When cultures are seen as open and flexible, intercultural communication is possible. Multicultural societies in this case are not to be seen as a mosaic or a patchwork quilt, but as a cultural mix or cocktail for which creole languages serve as metaphors. Multiculturalism is not considered to be a feature of societies but of

---

[19] Cf. E. Evans-Pritchard, *Nuer religion*, Oxford 1956; V. Turner, *The ritual process*, London 1969; C. Geertz, *The religion of Java*, London 1960.

[20] For culture as shared knowledge see: J. Spradley (ed.), *Culture and cognition*, San Francisco 1972; for an understanding of culture that stresses diversity: U. Hannerz, *Cultural complexity. Studies in the social organization of meaning*, New York 1992, 19.

[21] As some of the proponents of the 'multicultural tragedy' or 'multicultural illusion' theory say. See P. Cliteur, *Moderne Papoea's. Dilemma's van een multiculturele samenleving*, Amsterdam 2002; C. Huinder, P. Schnabel, R. Gowricharn and R. Mok, *De multiculturele illusie. Een fikse ruzie waard*, Utrecht 2000.

people who share a multiplicity of cultural orientations. Viewed thus intercultural understanding and communication are possible.[22]

1.2.3 Theo

Our next question is whether intercultural theology is really theology or whether it has become science of religion. The relation between the two disciplines is complex due to the emancipation of science of religion from faculties of theology. From a theological point of view the difference between the two disciplines has been described in terms of their material object (ultimate concern versus ultimate Reality) and of their objectives (description and analysis versus evaluation and innovation of religious beliefs and practices).[23] Here I would like to take up a debate within science of religion. In this discipline a distinction is made between religionist, positivist and empiricist theories. Without going into detail, I would say that theology has stuck to the religionist theory, whereas science of religion has become increasingly positivist or empiricist.[24]

Theology starts from the presupposition of the truth of the religion that it studies (in this regard there is no difference between Christian theologians and those of other religious traditions), that is to say, the conviction that a Reality (in the Christian tradition called *theos*) corresponds with the religious concepts or practices (representations) that are being studied. Most scientists of religion no longer make this as-

---

[22] The dilemma between essentialism and constructivism reflects the earlier debate between structuralism and action theory. We expect that this debate will fizzle out, as the debate on action theory and structuralism did. See A. Borsboom and F. Jespers (eds.), *Religion and identity*, Saarbrücken 2003.

[23] See, among others, P. Tillich, *Systematic theology*. Vol. 1, Chicago 1951; W. Pannenberg, *Wissenschaftstheorie und Theologie*, Frankfurt 1973. See also T. Sundermeier, *Was ist Religion? Religionswissenschaft im theologischen Kontext*, Gütersloh 1999; K. Hock, *Einführung in die Religionswissenschaft*, Darmstadt 2002.

[24] See J. Platvoet and A. Molendijk (eds.), *The pragmatics of defining religion*, Leiden 1999; W. Van Beek, *The culture in-between*, 101-109.

sumption. They proceed from methodological atheism (positivists) or methodological agnosticism (empiricists).[25] Does its starting point make theology less scientific? I do not think so. Following Edward Schillebeeckx I would say that a theologian considers the religious conviction to be a hypothesis that has to be tested against human experience. In so doing theologians operate in essentially the same way as other scientists.[26] I could agree to the term 'theological science of religion' if the distinctive starting point of theology and its difference from (other) sciences of religion remain clear. In practice, however, such terminology leads to confusion and ambiguity in the scientific study of religion. This is exactly what happens in several studies in intercultural theology.

Very often scholars who feel embarrassed about the mistakes of mission in the past, and therefore want to replace missiology with something else, not only exchange missiology for comparative or intercultural theology, but exchange theology as a whole for science of religion.[27] Several theologians in Europe are convinced that in the secularised European context there is little room left for theology except maybe at seminaries. At some universities this has already led to a shift from a Faculty of Theology to a department in a Faculty of Religious Studies or a Faculty of Human Sciences.[28]

---

[25] Historically speaking the positivist position came first, more or less as a result of the Enlightenment, and hence marks the beginning of secularisation. The religionist position was a reaction to it.

[26] Cf. E. Schillebeeckx, *Geloofsverstaan: interpretatie en kritiek*, Bloemendaal 1972, 214; E. Schillebeeckx, *Jesus. An experiment in christology*, New York 1979, 617-619.

[27] Cf. R. Friedli, Mission, Religionen, Religionswissenschaft. Erfahrungen mit universitären Neukompositionen, in: D. Becker (ed.), *Mit dem Fremden Leben*, Erlangen 2000, 185-191; W. Ustorf, Rethinking missiology, in: A. Houtepen and A. Ploeger (eds.), *World Christianity reconsidered*, Zoetermeer 2001, 67-78.

[28] Cf. J. Van der Ven, Theologie beoefenen binnen een Instituut der Religiewetenschappen, in: *Tijdschrift voor Theologie* 42(2002)3, 244-267. Of course, one must take into account that the situation in faculties with a *duplex*

Sometimes intercultural theology is no more than a branch of comparative science of religion, in the sense of historical and empirical studies of the theologies of the world religions and their interactions with other religions.[29] It is no longer a critical and thus normative reflection on what these theologies say or what is going on in these interactions, as would be the case in a theology of (world) religions or a theology of interreligious dialogue. Exeler already said that his aim was dialogue between theologies, not an assessment of theologies.[30] According to others, it is a rather vague, if not boring, enterprise simply to describe and analyse missionary practices without asking critically: what do we think about these practices, are they good or bad?[31]

At many universities in the southern hemisphere (except the confessional ones) there are departments of religious studies but their professors, be they Christian or Muslim, start from the presupposition of their faith and consider themselves theologians. So there is a remarkable imbalance here. In the Western world there are faculties of theology, but their professors consider themselves to be scientists of religion; in the southern hemisphere there are departments of religious studies, but their professors consider themselves to be theologians.[32]

---

ordo system is very different from that in faculties with a *simplex ordo* system.

[29] Cf. F. Clooney, The emergent field of comparative theology, in: *Theological Studies* 56(1995), 521-550. Clooney's comparative theology of world religions is not to be confused with the comparative theology proposed by Adolf Exeler.

[30] Cf. A. Exeler, *Vergleichende Theologie*, 205-208; A. Exeler, Wege einer vergleichenden Pastoral, in: L. Bertsch and F. Schlösser (eds.), *Evangelisation in der dritten Welt*, Freiburg 1981, 103-107.

[31] Cf. T. Witvliet, Reponse to Werner Ustorf, in: Houtepen and Ploeger (eds.), *World Christianity reconsidered*, 80.

[32] Examples are Mercy Amba Oduyoye, University of Legon, Ghana; Jesse Mugambi, University of Nairobi, Kenya; Felix Wildfred, University of Madras, India.

1.2.4 Logos

If it is agreed that intercultural theology is indeed theology and not science of religion, the next question that arises is: what kind of theology? It is well known that the Greek word *logos* has various meanings, but two meanings are basic: 'reason' and 'word'. From this we may infer two forms of theo-logy, one based on reasoning, the other on narrating.

More or less in keeping with our previous observation concerning the tendency to reduce intercultural theology to comparative (historical and/or empirical) studies of religion, some advocates of intercultural theology reduce theology to one specific form of logic, namely propositional logic or searching for truth by reasoning. Many Third World theologians claim that there is also another type of logic, namely, existential logic: discovering the truth that shows itself in everyday life, in storytelling and arts. They claim that reasoning is necessary, but not sufficient. Reality is intelligible and morally right behaviour is the most reasonable behaviour. But reason, all by itself, cannot lead us to it. We need reason integrally considered: reason nourished by imagination.[33]

So we must ask: How intercultural is intercultural theology? Do the advocates of intercultural theology really accept other forms of theology and rationality, or are they 'mono-logical'? Often European theologians eagerly take up contextual theologies from Africa, Asia and Latin America but they do not change their Western outlook and view of theology. They treat Third World theologies as if they are exotic fruits to supplement their traditional European dishes.[34]

---

[33] Cf. Mercy Amba Oduyoye, *Daughters of Anowa. African women and patriarchy*, Maryknoll, New York 1995; C. Van Engen, N. Thomas and R. Gallagher, *Footprints of God. A narrative theology of mission*, Monrovia 1999; I. Phiri, D. Govinden and S. Nadar (eds.), *Her-stories. Hidden histories of women of faith in Africa*, Pietermaritzburg 2002; A. Shorter, *Christianity and the African imagination*, Nairobi 1999, 15-20.

[34] Cf. F. Weber, *Mission. Gegenstand der Praktische Theologie*, Frankfurt am Main 1999, 22. See also T. Schreijack (ed.), *Religionsdialog im Kulturwandel.*

Theologies that are based on narrative, not to mention preaching and confession, are not highly esteemed in the West. This was one of the reasons for starting the Ecumenical Association of Third World Theologians in 1976. Thus speaking about intercultural theology can mask a conflict between Western and non-Western theologies. For this reason some non-Western theologians are suspicious of 'cross-cultural' theology.[35] We will return to this debate in the third section.

1.2.5 Conclusion

The aim of this second section was to give a critical appraisal of intercultural theology and to investigate whether it can replace missiology. We have shown that the discussion underlying the plea for intercultural theology is an old one. But this discussion has become more radical and concerns not only the place of missiology, but the place of theology as a whole in the academic institutions and secularised societies of Western Europe.

Can intercultural theology replace missiology? Just like Exeler, who did not define 'the issue that is at stake in missiology', various theologians who answer the question in the affirmative do not say what missiology is. Sometimes they say what mission is; most of the time they say what mission used to be, not realising the tremendous changes within the missionary movement world-wide and mission within the world religions.

In this chapter missiology is understood as the theory (*logos*) of intercultural communication of religious meanings (*missio*). Missiology has much in common with intercultural theology and can contribute to

---

Interkulturelle und interreligiöse Kommunikations- und Handlungskompetenzen auf dem Weg in die Weltgemeinschaft, Münster 2002.

[35] This suspicion surfaced repeatedly during the consultations on intercultural theology organised by the Institute of Missiology at Aachen. See M. Amaladoss (ed.), *Globalization and its victims as seen by its victims*, Delhi 1999; P. Kanyandago (ed.), *Marginalized Africa. An international perspective*, Nairobi 2002. See for example Laurenti Magesa's criticism of Robert Schreiter, in: Amaladoss, *Globalization*, 188-189.

it, as it does to liberation theology or theology of religions, but it cannot be equated with it.[36] Although missiology was the first theological discipline to take the pluralism of theologies seriously, missiologists cannot claim intercultural theology as their specialist field as if they were *the* experts in it. Intercultural theology is a new perspective in theology that is used in several of its disciplines, for example ethics and exegesis.[37]

Besides, there is no need for missiology to be renamed or replaced with intercultural theology. There is more missionary activity in this world than ever before,[38] both in the missionary movements proceeding from Christian churches in the southern hemisphere and those from the non-Christian world religions – missions that call for thorough study and critical reflection.[39] If we limit ourselves to our own field of study, namely religious dynamics in East Africa, we cannot ignore the 'thirst for souls' among the as yet unconverted indigenous believers on the part of Christian and Islamic revivalist movements, as well as the battle between them.[40]

It is better to study these missions critically in a discipline that specialises in this field than to abandon this discipline in the hope that its

---

[36] Cf. Wijsen and Nissen (eds.), *'Mission is a Must'*, 1-2.

[37] Cf. B. Adeney, *Strange virtues. Ethics in a multicultural world*, Downers Grove 1995; T. Okure (ed.), *To cast fire upon the earth. Bible and mission in today's multicultural global context*, Pietermaritzburg 2000; J. Ukpong et al., *Reading the Bible in the global village*, Cape Town 2002.

[38] Frans Verstraelen noted that after the "moratorium on mission" formulated at the conference on World Mission and Evangelism at Bangkok in 1973 there was an "explosion of interest in mission". Cf. F. Verstraelen, *Christianity in a new key. New voices and vistas through intercontinental communication*, Gweru 1996, 211.

[39] Cf. O. Degrijse, *Going forth. Missionary consciousness in Third World Catholic churches*, Maryknoll, New York 1984. The mission of non-Christian religions is almost completely neglected in present-day missiology.

[40] Cf. F. Wijsen and B. Mfumbusa, Seeds of conflict. Christian-Muslim relations in Tanzania, in: J. Gort, H. Jansen and H. Vroom (eds.), *Religion, conflict and reconciliation*, Amsterdam and New York 2002, 316-326; F. Wijsen, Religionism in Tanzania, in: A. Borsboom and F. Jespers (eds.), *Identity and religion*, Saarbrücken 2002.

task will be taken over by others. It makes no sense to reduce missiology to a historical and empirical study of the boundary-crossing activities of religions, as this is being done already by, for example, historians of religion and anthropologists.[41] It is the perspective of the dialectical relation between what missionary practice is and what it should be that makes missiology a discipline in its own right. This perspective motivates us to practice missiology within the department of empirical theology.[42]

1.3 What's the game?

What we have said so far shows that the attempt to replace missiology with intercultural theology is closely related to the debate on secularisation.[43] This, however, is primarily a European debate and it is noteworthy that positions in it are shifting. Various scholars are realising that anti-Christian and anti-mission sentiments are closely linked with a generation that feels embarrassed by the excessively expansionist mission during the era of decolonisation. Those who trained after the fall of the Berlin Wall see mission more neutrally or regard it as an interesting phenomenon found in almost all religions.

---

[41] Cf. A. Borsboom and J. Kommers, *Anthropologists and the missionary endeavour*, Saarbrücken 2002. See also R. Bonsen et al. (eds.), *The ambiguity of rapprochement*.

[42] One of my predecessors proposed doing missiology in a more empirical way as far back as 1972! See A. Camps, Vier sleutelbegrippen voor een meer empirische missiologie, in: *Vox Theologica* 42(1972), 218-231. It has become a hallmark of the missiology in Nijmegen. See J. Van Engelen, *Langs een andere weg. Zoektocht naar een empirische missiologie van het Rijk Gods*, Nijmegen 1996; J. Van Engelen, *Van kerk naar rijk Gods. Naar een empirische missiologie*, Nijmegen 2003.

[43] It goes without saying that the debate should also be seen in the context of economic scarcity and that it is part of the ordinary conflict of interests that governs not only our societies but also our universities. It has little to do with theoretical scientific discourse and a lot to do with rationalisation of resources.

There is a lively discussion about a new missiology in Europe (both east and west) among members of the International Association of Mission Studies and the International Association of Catholic Missiologists.[44] Following from the discussion in the second section our question in this third section is: what could a missiology, which takes into account the insights gained from intercultural theology but is not reduced to intercultural theology, look like? As mentioned already, missiology is the theory (*logos*) of intercultural communication of religious meanings (*missio*), but it has to be developed further to overcome its weaknesses and realise its claims.[45] Here again I will explain and elaborate on the words used.

1.3.1 Theory

It goes without saying that missiology as an academic discipline must be theory-oriented. Seen from this perspective one must admit that in the past missiology was too descriptive, either historically or phenomenologically.[46] If one looks at the major missiology handbooks and introductions that have appeared in recent decades one cannot but conclude that there has been little theorising in missiology. This is partly why it has been easy to remove this discipline from universities.

If one takes methodology as an indicator of the maturity of an academic discipline, discussion on methods in missiology is manifestly deficient. David Bosch's *Transforming mission* does not contain one

---

[44] During the 1996 IAMS conference in Buenos Aires Jan Jongeneel proposed to have a European IAMS meeting. That meeting took place in 1998 in Stavanger. The second European IAMS meeting was held in 2002 at Halle. The major concern of these meetings is to strengthen European missiology.

[45] See W. Biernatski, *Roots of Acceptance. The Intercultural Communication of Religious Meanings*, Rome 1991, and other Working Papers on Living Faiths and Cultures of the Faculty of Missiology, Pontifical Gregorian University, Rome.

[46] Cf. J. Jongeneel, Is Missiology an academic discipline?, in: *Exchange. Journal of Missiological and Ecumenical Research* 27(1998)3, 1-14. With anthropology missiology shares a neglect of more fundamental research.

section on methodology; in his *Philosophy, science and theology of mission* (comprising two parts), Jongeneel devotes only eight pages to 'methods of missiology'; in the *Ecumenical introduction* the 'working method' is explained in a mere two pages, resulting in "a variety of sketches for a theology of mission".[47] So instead of replacing missiology with another discipline there is a challenge for missiologists to make missiology more academic in the sense of methodical and theoretical.

In the past missiology has been largely practice-oriented. One reason was that the aim was to train missionaries. Another reason was that many missiologists shared with Third World theologians the 'primacy of praxis' as an epistemological principle. But one must ask, humbly and respectfully, whether this principle does anything to develop missiology as an academic discipline. There are theories (theologies) on various levels: first order, second order and third order theories or, to use the Boff brothers' terms, popular, pastoral and professional theology.[48] Academic missiology naturally strives for scientific theories, but it does so in interaction with first order and second order theories.

Instead of the 'primacy of practice' I would like the stress the *real dialectic* between theory and practice,[49] that of moving from practice-oriented to more theory-oriented research. This leaves open the ques-

---

[47] Cf. D. Bosch, *Transforming mission*, Maryknoll, New York 1992; J. Jongeneel, *Philosophy, Science and Theology of Mission*, Frankfurt am Main 1995, 175-183, Verstraelen (general editor), *Missiology*, 5-6.

[48] Cf. H.-G. Ziebertz, Normativity and Empirical Research in Practical Theology, in: *Journal for Empirical Theology* 15(2002)1, 5-18; L. Boff and C. Boff, *Introducing liberation theology*, Maryknoll, New York 1987, 12-16. Whereas Boff and Boff speak about professional theology as third order theory, I would like to reserve the term 'professional' for practice-theories, second order theories. Third order theories are to be labelled 'scientific' or 'academic'.

[49] The founding fathers of academic missiology (Warneck, Schmidlin) in the beginning of the 20th century were theorists in the sense of being remote from missionary practice. Against this background the 'primacy of practice' principle was an enormous step forward. Now the time has come to become more theory-oriented again in the sense of a real dialectic between theory and practice.

tion whether missiology must opt for a theory-testing or a theory-generating research strategy. Because of its preoccupation with non-Western issues, and consequently its close cooperation with anthropology, missiology has had a preference for a grounded theory approach or exploratory research, but this is not inevitable. At all events, I conclude that academic missiology is theory-oriented (theory in the sense of academic theories), or it is not academic.

1.3.2 Intercultural

One of the things that distinguishes missiology as a theological discipline is its formal object: the intercultural perspective. All theological disciplines deal with the communication of faith to some extent. But what distinguishes missiology is that it deals with communication of faith across the boundaries of one's own cultural meaning system, the communication of the Christian faith to non-Christians, traditionally referred to as 'pagans' or 'gentiles', 'all peoples everywhere' (Mt. 28:19), 'to the ends of the earth' (Acts 1:8).[50] Missiology has been described, not without reason, as the study of the church's boundary-crossing activity – meaning boundaries in both a temporal and a geographical sense. Nowadays one may add that missiology studies any boundary-crossing activity, not only by Christianity but also by other world religions and ideologies.[51]

In its latest 'Assessment of research quality' the Association of Universities in the Netherlands noted that there is an 'overly introspective

---

[50] Cf. G. Collet, *'Bis an die Grenzen der Erde'. Grundfragen heutiger Missionswissenschaft*, Freiburg 2002. In this sense the conventional distinction between pastoral theology and missiology remains valid. See K. Müller, Missiology, in: S. Karotemprel (ed.), *Following Christ in mission*, Bombay 1995, 21-36. Gentes, however, is no longer to be seen in a geographical sense but in a sociological sense.

[51] Cf. L. Rütti, *Theologie der Mission*, München 1972, 132-133; V. Tirimanna, The church and the crossing of boundaries, in: F. Wilfred and O. Beozzo (eds.), Frontier Violations. *Concilium* 2(1990), 80-89; W. Ustorf, *Rethinking missiology*, 75-76.

Eurocentrism' in Dutch theological practice.[52] Our experience in the master's and doctoral programmes in intercultural theology shows that this is indeed the case. Again and again our students complain about the staff's lack of interest in extra-European issues and perspectives, albeit with some exceptions. Since most missiologists are experts in religion, church and theology in at least one context other than their own, they have a role to play in theological faculties. It is naïve to think that other theologians will pick up 'the issue that is at stake in missiology', as Exeler expected them to do. The facts show that this has not happened in the past twenty-five years.[53]

Interculturality in the present context is neither a fragmented particularism nor a stifling universalism. Missiologists, who have lived and worked in more than one culture, generally accept that human potential is universal, which is not to say that all people are the same. Intercultural hermeneutics balances between universality and particularity. In this regard missiology safeguards the differentness of people and views every claim to universality with a hermeneutics of suspicion, whether the claim is made by the central doctrinal authority or by modern rationality.

1.3.3 Communication

For a long time mission was understood mainly in terms of communication and the science of communication was embraced as a major ancillary science of missiology.[54] Given the right packaging of the contents and using the correct channels, the 'message' was sure to reach the 'recipient'. Studies of, and reflections on, intercultural and interreligious dialogues, however, have revealed a 'communication crisis'.

---

[52] Cf. Association of the Universities in the Netherlands, *Assessment of research quality*, Utrecht 2000.

[53] Cf. Weber, *Mission*, 22.

[54] Whereas Jongeneel says that missiology has been too theological, Hesselgrave noted that (Evangelical) missiologists were more interested in the social sciences. Cf. Jongeneel, *Is missiology an academic discipline?*, 217; E. Rommen and G. Corwin, *Missiology and the social sciences*, Pasadena 1996, 1-3.

Consequently several missiologists advocated the return of hermeneutics to missiology.[55]

But the return of hermeneutics should not be exaggerated. After all, mission is not just a matter of understanding the other but also of transmitting the faith.[56] Communication relates to faith from the perspective of the sender, hermeneutics relates to faith from the perspective of the recipient. Communication is not concerned with senders and recipients but with participants in a process. Hence communication and hermeneutics refer to two sides of the same coin. In our department of empirical theology, therefore, we see hermeneutic-communicative practice as our overall object of study, that is to say the interpretation of written and spoken texts and their verbal and nonverbal communication.[57]

Cooperation with cultural anthropologists and communication scientists in the field of intercultural communication can give missiology a solid basis. Missiology has a long tradition in this field, which has produced its finest and most appreciated studies.[58] One may refer to the ongoing work of the Divine Word Missionaries worldwide; *Communi-*

---

[55] It is to Theo Sundermeier's credit that he made this point. Cf. T. Sundermeier, *Konvivenz und Differenz. Studien zu einer verstehende Missionswissenschaft*, Erlangen 1995; *Den Fremden Verstehen. Eine praktische Hermeneutik*, Göttingen 1996; T. Sundermeier and W. Ustorf, *Die Begegnung mit dem Anderen. Plädoyer für eine interkulturelle Hermeneutik*, Gütersloh 1991.

[56] For the same reason missiology cannot be equated with intercultural theology. See Collet, *"...bis an die Grenzen der Erde"*, 56. See also H. Balz, Krise der Kommunikation – Wiederkehr der Hermeneutik?, in: T. Sundermeier (ed.), *Die Begegnung mit dem Anderen*, 39-65; R. Friedli, Kultur und kulturelle Vielfalt, in: T. Sundermeier (ed.), *Die Begegnung mit dem Anderen*, 29-38.

[57] Cf. J. Van der Ven, *Practical theology. An empirical approach*, Louvain 1998, 41-59; *Education for reflective ministry*, Louvain 1998, 116-125.

[58] An example of such a study is E. Nida, *Message and mission*, New York 1960. It was one of my predecessors, Alphons Mulders, who introduced anthropology and linguistics as disciplines at the Institute for Missiology at the University of Nijmegen. Now these disciplines are taught by separate departments in other faculties.

catio Socialis, the journal of the Gesellschaft Katholischen Publizisten Deutschlands; *Media Development*, the journal of the World Association of Christian Communication; the Institute for Missiology and Communication in Pune; and the chair of intercultural pastoral theology and missiology in Innsbrück, which focusses on theme-centred interaction.[59]

1.3.4 Religious

It may be questioned whether it is adequate to speak about intercultural communication of religious meanings. Would it not be better to speak about intercultural and interreligious communication? Is religion not being reduced to a cultural system? Is religion not a reality in itself, that exists *sui generis*? Without discussing various theories of religion in detail,[60] I think missiologists, more than other theologians, have discovered that religion is always inculturated or, as anthropologists put it, that religion is a cultural system.[61]

It should be noted straightaway that 'religion' is itself a Western concept, based on a division between the secular and sacred domains. To most people in Africa, and in the world for that matter, this division does not exist.[62] To them the material and the spiritual are one, some-

---

[59] See F.-J. Eilers, *Communicating between cultures*, Manila 1987; M. Scharer and B. Hilberath (eds.), *Kommunikative Theologie*, Mainz 2002. In our country I refer to the work of Anne van der Meiden, with his doctoral dissertation on mission as communication, and Cees Hamelink, professor for Theology and Communication at the Free University of Amsterdam.

[60] See Platvoet and Molendijk, *The pragmatics of defining religion*; D. Pals, *Seven theories of religion*, Oxford 1996; T. Idinopulos and B. Wilson, *What is religion?* Leiden 1998; T. Sundermeier, *Was ist Religion?* Gütersloh 1999.

[61] Cf. E. Hillmann, *Many paths*, Maryknoll, New York 1989, 1-23; C. Geertz, *The interpretation of cultures*, New York 1993, 167-186; *Available light. Anthropological reflections on philosophical topics*, Princeton 2000, 167-186.

[62] Cf. F. Wijsen, "I have all kinds of medicines", in: W. Valkenberg and F. Wijsen (eds.), *The polemical dialogue*, Saarbrücken 1997; D. Westerlund, The study of African religions in retrospect from Westernization to Africanization,

thing which modern Europeans manifestly find hard to grasp, considering the ongoing debate on secularisation. The 'culture Catholicism' of the person who says "I am a Catholic, but I don't do anything about it" is considered nonreligious.[63] By the same token European scholars created a religion called Hinduism from various data that they gathered in India.

It is an illusion to think that if one strips away all the cultural overlays, one will be left with pure religion and that this will enable one to compile a list of key concepts of religion that can then be operationalised and measured by means of questionnaire research. This is not to deny – on the contrary, it is fully accepted – that religions and cultures have certain essential characteristics. But these are always spatiotemporally determined, or they become so generalised as to be practically meaningless.

In some faculties of theology missiology was equated with liberation theology or development studies. This was based, among other things, on a reduction of religion to (social and political) ethics, leaving the problem of the plurality of religions unsolved. The first stage of liberation theology in Latin America illustrates the point. The worldwide growth of the Evangelical and Pentecostal movements shows that this was a mistake. Without ignoring the issues of liberation, justice and peace, ecology and feminism, the plea for missiology as the theory of the intercultural communication of religious meanings wants to do justice to the revival of religion as a major force to be reckoned with in the 21st century.[64]

---

in: J. Olupona (ed.), *Religious plurality in Africa*, Berlin and New York 1993, 43-66.

[63] See the ongoing debate on 'popular' versus 'official' religion. Very often, 'popular' religion is seen as 'just folklore', nonreligious or pseudo-religious. See my book *Geloven bij het leven. Missionaire presentie in een volkswijk*, Baarn 1997, 198-199.

[64] See among others P. Berger, *The desecularization of the world. Resurgent religion and world politics*, Grand Rapids 1999; H. Cox, *Fire from heaven. The rise of Pentecostal spirituality and the reshaping of religion in the twenty-first century*, London 1996; F. Wijsen, "...op zondag willen wij vooral onszelf

1.3.5 Meanings

To study communication entails much more than studying the relation between stimulus and response. It means studying the creation of a message out of signs and understanding its meaning from the respective signs. As happened in other disciplines, the focus of the missiological study of Christian communication shifted from functions to meanings. In this regard Victor Turner, a devout Catholic, and Clifford Geertz had great influence.[65] Turner's multi-perspective and poly-methodical approach, distinguishing meanings on the exegetical, positional and operational levels, helped to resolve the tensions between functionalism, structuralism and action theory.

It is striking that many adherents of comparative or intercultural theology pay little or no attention to power relations and conflicts of interests. They deal with dialogue, mutual assistance of theologians, open-ended communication, exchange, learning from each other, and so on.[66] Anyone who is really involved in the dialogue between North and South, Western and non-Western, Christian and non-Christian theologians, 'the West and the rest of us', knows that this dialogue is polemical and conflictive. As the theory of intercultural communication of

---

zijn". Allochtone Christenen in Nederland, in: C. Hermans (ed.), *Is er nog godsdienst in 2050?*, Budel 2003.

[65] The present author was trained in this way of looking at cultural meaning systems by Aylward Shorter at the Catholic University of Eastern Africa. See A. Shorter, Symbol, ritual and history. An examination of the work of Victor Turner, in: T. Tanger and I. Kimambo (eds.), *The historical study of African religion*, London 1979, 139-150.

[66] Cf. K. Piepel, *Lerngemeinschaft Weltkirche. Lernprozesse in Partnerschaften zwischen Christen der Ersten und der Dritten Welt*, Aachen 1993; V. Küster, *The many faces of Jesus Christ. Intercultural Christology*, London 2001; R. Schreiter, *The new Catholicity. Theology between the Global and the Local*, Maryknoll, New York 1997.

religious meanings, contemporary missiology cannot avoid studying religion's contribution to the breakdown of communication.[67]

Pierre Bourdieu, who did his fieldwork in Algeria during the liberation struggle there, sees society as an arena where actors or groups of actors try to serve their own interests, partly in coalition and partly in competition with others. He gives a theoretical orientation on *die Sache, um die es die Missionswissenschaft geht*: boundary-crossing, inclusion and exclusion, vision and di-vision of the world. Understanding the meaning of (political or religious) utterances requires rigorous reconstruction of the fields in which these utterances are produced and reproduced, and of the links between the positions and agents within them.[68]

The reference to Bourdieu brings us to a feature of the academic discourse in Western Europe that explains, more than anything else, the marginalisation of missiology in faculties of theology. The main problem is not method and perspective, but the view of science. Science in the Western world has become predominantly positivist.[69] Since missiology has on the whole maintained a critical-emancipatory view of science it no longer seems to be at home in Western universities. In our view, however, it is not 'conservative' to stick to an interpretation of theology as a 'science of liberation'.[70]

---

[67] Cf. J. Gort, H. Janssen and H. Vroom, *Religion, conflict and reconciliation*, Amsterdam and New York 2002; W. Valkenberg and F. Wijsen, *The polemical dialogue; Chinweizu, The West and the rest of us. White predators, black slaves and the African elite*, Lagos 1987.

[68] Cf. P. Bourdieu, *Ce que parler veut dire*, Paris 1992, 135-148; P. Bourdieu, *Ein soziologischer Selbstversuch*, Franfurt am Main 2002. Bourdieu assumes a fundamental link between actions and interests. This applies also to science. He criticises the 'myth of an interest-free science'.

[69] For the debate on methodology see: P. Verschuren, *Dogma's en ontwikkeling in wetenschap en methodologie*, Nijmegen 2002; H.-G. Ziebertz, Komplementarität von Forschungsmethoden, in: J. Van der Ven and H.-G. Ziebertz (eds.), *Paradigmenentwicklung in der Praktischen Theologie*, Kampen 1993, 225-260.

[70] Cf. E. Schillebeeckx, Theologie als bevrijdingskunde, in: *Tijdschrift voor Theologie* 24(1984)4, 388-402; E. Borgman, Theology as the art of liberation.

1.4 Epilogue

In this chapter we asked what intercultural theology is all about and whether intercultural theology can replace missiology. In the second section we concluded that it cannot. From attempts to rename or replace missiology with intercultural theology we inferred a challenge for missiology to become more academic so as to prevent it from being ousted from universities. But there is another problem. At the beginning of this chapter we quoted the 'founding father' of intercultural theology, Walter Hollenweger, who said that the main concern of intercultural theology is that it takes into account the 'other' cultural context in doing theology. This is in fact the strongest argument against the attempt to rename or replace missiology with intercultural theology. Maybe this attempt makes sense from a mainline perspective in our Western cultural context. But we would be completely misunderstood by our Pentecostal and Third World colleagues, since for most of them mission is the heart of the matter. It is noteworthy that new institutes and even new faculties of missiology are mushrooming in the southern hemisphere.

Is the attempt to rename or replace missiology in itself not an expression of Eurocentric thinking? Do we not isolate ourselves from the international theological discourse, most of whose participants no longer live in the Western world? Are not our Evangelical and Pentecostal colleagues the most eloquent proponents of missiology and do we not block scientific cooperation with them when we remove missiology from our institutions? From our experience at the Nijmegen Graduate School of Theology, which is training some fifty-five master's and doctoral students from Africa, Asia and Eastern Europe, we suspect that an

---

Edward Schillebeeckx's response to the theologies of the EATWOT, in: *Exchange. Journal of Missiological and Ecumenical Research* 32(2003)2. See also the debate on liberation theology: G. De Schrijver (ed.), *Liberation theologies on shifting grounds*, Leuven 1998; S. Schipani and A. Wessels (eds.), *The promise of hope*, Elkhart and Amsterdam 2002.

attempt to replace missiology with something else would block intercultural communication and understanding in theology rather than promote it.

1.5 Further readings on the object of mission studies

- G. Anderson, *Witness to World Christianity. The international association of Missions Studies, 1972-2012*, New Haven 2012.
- D. Dorr, *Mission in today's world*, Maryknoll, New York 2000.
- D. Hesselgrave and E. Stetzer (eds.), *Missionshift. Global mission issues in the third millennium*, Nashville 2010.
- K. Kim and A. Anderson (eds.), *Mission today and tomorrow*, Oxford 2011.
- J. Kroeger (ed.), *The gift of mission. Yesterday, today, tomorrow*, Maryknoll, New York 2013.
- V. Küster, *Mission revisited. Between mission history and intercultural theology*, Münster and Zürich 2011.
- M. Sievernich, *Die christliche Mission. Geschichte und Gegenwart*, Darmstadt 2009.
- A. Walls and C. Ross, *Mission in the twenty-first century. Exploring the five marks of global mission*, Maryknoll, New York 2008.
- F. Wijsen and P. Nissen (eds.), *'Mission is a Must'. Intercultural Theology and the mission of the church*, Amsterdam and New York 2002.

1.6 Questions for better comprehension

1. Why do some authors want to do away with the term missiology?
2. Why does the author of this book think that replacing missiology by intercultural theology is not a good idea?

3. Relate the notion of 'boundary-crossing' to the definition of missiology as theory of 'intercultural communication of religious meanings'.
4. Explain the difference between 'multicultural' and 'intercultural'. Relate these words to the unity and diversity of cultures.
5. What does the author of this book mean by theology as 'science of liberation'?

Chapter 2 The practical-theological spiral revisited

2.1 Introduction

As a lecturer in various teaching positions in Africa and Asia who also works with 'Third World' students in Europe, I am always struck by the fact that the research proposals and papers of these students are mostly aimed at promoting the transformation of church and society. This is understandable, of course, as the contexts in which they do theology are often marked by poverty, injustice, war, ecological and medical disasters. In Europe, on the other hand, theological practice is growing more and more detached from practical problems and has become a 'pure science'. This, too, is understandable in the context of highly secularised societies, where health and wealth are catered for by governments and churches are being largely marginalised. In Europe theology tries to justify itself by joining in academic debates and compensating for its seeming irrelevance by using unquestioned scientific methods.

Often the divide leads to tacit misunderstanding and even open conflict between theologians in the West and their counterparts in 'the Rest' of the world.[1] It appears that the gulf between the two ways of doing theology and their practitioners has widened over the past few decades. Some twenty or thirty years ago it was quite fashionable to deal with Third World theologies in European faculties of theology. The bibliographies of modules in Christology and ecclesiology often included authors from the southern hemisphere. This accorded with the critical climate that prevailed in Europe after the student revolts and the broad acceptance of an emancipatory view of science[2] in the 1970s and 1980s. There was lively interaction between 'political' theologians in Europe and 'liberation' theologians in the Third World. Some of them knew each other personally and had studied together, mostly at Europe-

---

[1] D. Becker, Der Westen gegen den Rest?, in: D. Becker (ed.), *Globaler Kampf der Kulturen*, Stuttgart 1999.
[2] J. Habermas, *Erkentnis und Interesse*, Frankfurt am Main 1968.

an universities. On the whole presuppositions were shared, although contexts differed. But the emancipatory interest at European universities fizzled out and science has once more become – to a large extent – positivist. By and large this applies to theology as well, with the possible exceptions of feminist theology and my own discipline, missiology.

The objective of this chapter is to help bridge the gap between European and Third World theologians with a view to better understanding and possible collaboration on common concerns, such as globalisation and the marginalisation of groups on the underside of societies worldwide.[3] Following, but also broadening, the basic intuition of Holland and Henriot[4] concerning the dialectical relation between experience and reflection, it will be argued that the dilemma between theory and practice – more specifically between theory-oriented and practice-oriented research – is a false dilemma. The practical-theological spiral is not just a pastoral method aimed at problem solving, but also a strategy for developing theories in the scientific sense of the word – a grounded theory approach to theology. In this chapter I will expand on previous ideas about the pastoral circle, which I have renamed the practical-theological spiral, by reflecting on my discussions with Third World theology students and using methodological insights gained from the works of the French philosopher and sociologist Pierre Bourdieu.[5]

These reflections stem from a specific local context: that of a European university, more particularly the Catholic University Nijmegen (renamed Radboud University Nijmegen in 2004) and its Graduate School of Theology. But they seek to be global in their outlook and relevant to the grass roots. Our students come from all parts of the world – mainly Africa, Asia and Eastern Europe – and their contexts differ greatly. Therefore I restrict myself to the construction of African

---

[3] M. Amaladoss (ed.), *Globalization and its victims*, Delhi 1999.

[4] J. Holland and P. Henriot, *Social analysis. Linking faith and justice*, Maryknoll, New York 1983, 8; P. Henriot, Grassroots analysis. The emphasis on culture, in: G. De Schrijver (ed.), *Liberation theologies on shifting grounds*, Leuven 1998, 340.

[5] P. Bourdieu, *Das religiöse Feld*, Konstanz 2000; Bourdieu, *Ein soziologischer Selbstversuch*, Frankfurt am Main, 2002.

theologies and the debate between European and African theologians. I hope to show that both parties can benefit by using the practical-theological spiral. It can make European theologians less reluctant to engage in practice by showing that this approach helps to develop grounded theories in theology. African theologians, on the other hand, may become less hesitant to accept scientific methods if they are shown that academic theology can be very 'practical' and relevant to the transformation of church and society.

My reflections are not only focussed on ivory tower debates at universities but also on everyday struggles for survival at the grassroots. Indeed, my aim is to show that the practical-theological spiral can help overcome this dichotomy, which is detrimental to both academics and activists. The 'academic' versus 'pastoral' dichotomy is overdrawn, say Holland and Henriot.[6] Nevertheless it appears in the debate between European and Third World theologians again and again. I prefer, therefore, to speak about the *practical-theological* spiral rather than the *pastoral* circle. I shall outline the four steps of the practical-theological spiral from the perspective of a grounded theory approach. But first let me describe my journey with the pastoral circle and the methodological and epistemological questions that arise from that journey.

2.2 The pastoral circle

I studied philosophy, theology and social sciences at Heerlen and Nijmegen in the late 1970s and early 1980s. At the time Edward Schillebeeckx dominated the debate in church and theology, not only at Nijmegen but throughout the Netherlands.[7] In those years Schillebeeckx embraced critical theory and there was a critical climate in the whole of society. The mass protests against nuclear weapons, called

---

[6] Holland and Henriot, *Social analysis*, 7; Henriot, Grassroots analysis, 339-340.

[7] W. Portier, Interpretation and method, in: R. Schreiter and M. Hilkert (eds.), *The praxis of Christian experience. An introduction to the theology of Edward Schillebeeckx*, San Francisco 1989.

'Dutch disease' or 'Hollanditis', are just one example. 'Political' and 'liberation' theologies were booming. After completing my studies I was sent as a lay missionary to Sukumaland, Northwest Tanzania in 1984. I had made quite a study of *ujamaa* socialism and Julius Nyerere's thoughts on development as a condition for peace were widely admired in the Netherlands as manifestations of that same critical spirit, so I was eager to go. But I soon learned that the situation on the ground was very different from what I had read in books. In retrospect I can say that this was where I became aware of the big difference between science and ideology,[8] between the official image of a society and what really goes on at the grassroots.

My further training as a missionary included a language course (Swahili) at the Danish Volunteer Training Centre at Arusha, Northeast Tanzania, and some seminars in cultural anthropology and pastoral theology at the then newly established Catholic Higher Institute (later renamed Catholic University) of East Africa in Nairobi, Kenya. Aylward Shorter[9] introduced me to the work of Victor Turner and his ideas about root metaphors. Rodrigo Mejía[10] introduced me to a new understanding of pastoral theology, using the pastoral circle. Later, when doing my doctoral research in Sukumaland, both introductions proved extremely useful. But in some ways I also found them unsatisfactory. Turner's multi-perspective and poly-method approach to studying the exegetical, positional and operational meaning of symbols, combining phenomenology, structuralism and action theory, helped me to understand Sukuma beliefs and practices. His analysis of what he called "the Ndembu inside view"[11] largely disregarded the researchers' own con-

---

[8] K. Mannheim, *Ideology and utopia. An introduction to the sociology of knowledge*, London 1960.

[9] A. Shorter, Symbolism, ritual and history. An examination of the work of Victor Turner, in: T. Ranger and J. Kimambo (eds.), *The historical study of African religion*, London 1972, 139-149.

[10] R. Mejía, The new understanding of pastoral theology, in: C. McGarry, R. Mejía and V. Shirima (eds.), A new light on our path, Nairobi 1993, 27-37.

[11] V. Turner, *The ritual process. Structure and anti-structure*, London 1969, 10-11.

tribution to the production of their research material. Consequently I broadened phenomenological analysis by including a hermeneutic slant, taking into account my pre-understanding and interest as a researcher and the influence of the production context on the research material – me being a white male intellectual and my informants black farmers.

When it came to the analysis of the positional meaning of symbols, Turner's "criss-crossing binary oppositions"[12] seemed rather arbitrary. Consequently I looked for a more 'objective' way of making a contrast analysis and found it in James Spradley's ethnographic semantics, as explained to me by Michael Kirwen at the then newly established Maryknoll Institute of African Studies in Nairobi. The analysis of the operational meaning of symbols also struck me as unsatisfactory. Although Turner presented rituals as anti-structure, he remained a functionalist in the sense that he saw rituals mainly as conducive to social harmony and cohesion. He did not take the conflict of interests and the division of power in Ndembu society sufficiently seriously. To overcome this omission I became interested in and used Bourdieu's theory of practice, which has influenced my further development as an academic to this day.

Mejía's introductions to pastoral theology in general and to the pastoral circle in particular greatly influenced my approach. I was inspired by his wide knowledge of both Latin American and African theology and his methodological thoroughness. The pastoral circle became the research design for my doctoral thesis, which was quite unique at that time.[13] In retrospect, what I tried to do was to make the pastoral circle, which is basically a practice-oriented approach, more theory-oriented. I wanted to make the pastoral circle a practical-theological research design. The debate about practical theology as empirical theology and the inauguration of the *Journal of Empirical Theology* at the University of

---

[12] Turner, *The ritual process*, 38.

[13] H. Janssen, Der pastorale Zirkel – eine Einführung, in: M. Pankoke-Schenk and G. Evers (eds.), *Inkulturation und Kontextualität*, Frankfurt am Main 1994, 221-230.

Nijmegen, where I defended my doctoral thesis in 1994, provided the methodological and theoretical framework for my research.[14]

After completing my doctorate I started using the pastoral circle in training missiology students in the Netherlands, preparing them for their overseas training programme in seminars on popular religion and evangelisation for major seminarians and native priests in Tanzania, and in a postgraduate practical theology programme for Protestant ministers in Indonesia. Apparently my approach attracted the interest of other researchers, as my working papers were published in the *African Ecclesial Review*[15] and the *East Asian Pastoral Review*[16] and were translated into German[17] and Bahasa Indonesia.[18]

My present context is the Nijmegen Graduate School of Theology, of which I am the director. The school offers a master's and a doctoral programme in intercultural theology. The advertisement for this school reads: "Intercultural theology. A challenge for the 21st century". The presupposition is that constructing local theologies was the main theological challenge for the 20th century, in which the decolonisation process took place. The construction of local theologies will undoubtedly continue on various continents. Economically and politically the decolonisation process may be complete,[19] but from a cultural and religious

---

[14] J. Van der Ven, Practical theology. From applied to empirical theology, in: *Journal of Empirical Theology* 1(1988)1, 7-27.

[15] F. Wijsen, The pastoral circle in the training of church ministers, in: *African Ecclesial Review* 39(1997)4, 238-250.

[16] F. Wijsen, The pastoral circle in the training of church ministers, in: *East Asian Pastoral Review* 34(1997)4, 325-336.

[17] F. Wijsen, Der Pastorale Zirkel in der Ausbildung im kirchlichen Dienst, in: H. Janssen (ed.), *Zeichen der Zeit. Pastoraler Zirkel, Gesellschaftsanalyse, Bibel-Teilen*, Aachen 1996, 45-56.

[18] F. Wijsen, *Lingkaran pastoral dalam pendidikan pelayanan*. Seri Pastoral 296, Yogyakarta 1999.

[19] J. Mugambi, *From liberation to reconstruction. African Christian theology after the Cold War*, Nairobi 1995; T. Maluleke, A rediscovery of the agency of Africans, in: P. Kanyandago (ed.), *Marginalized Africa*, Nairobi 2002, 165-190.

point of view it continues.[20] At the Nijmegen Graduate School of Theology we do not construct contextual theologies in the sense of local theologies (of course, the Faculty of Theology at Nijmegen will continue to do so for the European context). On the assumption that our students have been thoroughly trained in the contextual theologies of their home countries, we seek to facilitate interaction between inculturated theologies.

It is this intercultural context that raises epistemological and methodological questions. Is a theology divorced from action necessarily irrelevant or uncommitted? Is commitment a condition for adequate knowledge, as the inaugural statement of the Ecumenical Association of Third World Theologians seems to claim, or is the condition detachment? What is scientific knowledge? Do scholars in the West have a monopoly in methodology? Can they learn from scholars in the rest of the world? Or must scholars in the West stick to their own academic principles, and should non-Western students learn from them how to practise theology? Of course, it makes a big difference whether theology is studied at a university or a seminary, and differences between and within regions further complicate the picture. "The West" and "the Rest" are used as metaphors with a sly wink at Chiweizu.[21] They show how wide the divide is. My experience is that many intercultural misunderstandings and even conflicts arise from different perceptions of what scientific knowledge is all about.[22]

---

[20] L. Magesa, African Renaissance, in: P. Kanyandago (ed.), *Marginalized Africa*, Nairobi 2002, 13-27.

[21] Chinweizu, *The West and the rest of us. White predators, black slavers and the African elite*, Lagos, 1987.

[22] H. Fox, *Listening to the world. Cultural issues in academic writing*, Urbana, 1994.

2.3 A grounded theory approach

Methodology handbooks, in both Western and non-Western contexts, make a distinction between theory-oriented and practice-oriented research.[23] According to this classification, theory-oriented research is done at academic institutions and practice-oriented research at institutions for professional training. Put differently, academics primarily want *to know* (more) about things (knowledge development), not *to do* things (knowledge implementation). Making scientific research practical or, even worse, problem-solving is to lower its academic status. For a long time the ideal of science was to be 'pure', producing knowledge for its own sake and not for its usefulness. One can distinguish between various forms of theory. There are everyday or pre-scientific theories, reflected or practice theories, and third degree or meta-theories. Meta-theories offer reflections on reflected theories.[24] Consequently one can distinguish between popular, pastoral and professional theology.[25] When I referred to theory 'in the scientific sense of the word' above, I had the third category of theory in mind.

Many Third World theology students find such distinctions artificial, even unethical. For them, scientific research must serve the needs of the people, not the other way round. They tend to inquire suspiciously who is going to profit from theological investigations. They adhere to the 'primacy of practice' principle, or 'doing before knowing'.[26] These expressions, however, are often misunderstood. When early liberation theologians spoke about the primacy of practice and theology being (only) a second step, their main concern was to safeguard the social

---

[23] P. Verschuren and H. Doorewaard, *Designing a research project*, Utrecht 1999, 33; O. Mugenda and A. Mugenda, *Research methods*, Nairobi 2003, 4-5.

[24] H.-G. Ziebertz, Normativity and empirical research in practical theology, in: *Journal for Empirical Theology* 15(2002)1, 5-18.

[25] L. Boff and C. Boff, *Introducing liberation theology*, Maryknoll, New York, 1987, 11-21.

[26] G. Gutiérrez, *Theology of liberation*, Maryknoll, New York 1973; Boff and Boff, *Introducing liberation theology*.

struggle of the people as a secular or autonomous reality (trade unions should not be confused with basic Christian communities), and social analysis of this reality should not to be dictated by a (hidden or overt) theological agenda. Their point was that practical involvement is a necessary step, but not necessarily the first one. This is one source of disagreement between European and Third World theologians. To what extent is commitment a necessary step in constructing authentic and relevant theology? Most European theologians would accept that commitment is important, but a scientific theologian cannot be overly committed, for it would entail a risk that the practice will no longer be critically questioned. Thus, whereas Third World theologians stress involvement in practice, European theologians stress distance from practice. The task facing theology is to strike a balance between the two.[27]

In Third World contexts many methods have been developed for pastoral purposes, such as pedagogy of liberation[28] in Latin America, training for transformation[29] or the Lumko method in Africa,[30] and the integrated pastoral approach based on that method in Asia. From a European perspective it is said that, while these pastoral methods may meet the needs of the people, they are not very helpful in generating scientific theories. But there are various examples to the contrary, such as the use of the Asian integrated pastoral approach for constructing an Asian Christology,[31] the use of the pastoral circle for constructing a social theology in Indonesia[32] and the use of the Lumko method of Bible sharing in small Christian communities for constructing an African bib-

---

[27] V. Fabella and S. Torres, *The emergent gospel*. Maryknoll, New York, 1977, 269.

[28] P. Freire, *Pedagogy of the oppressed*, New York, 1971.

[29] A. Hope and S. Timmel, *Training for transformation*. Handbooks 1, 2, 3, Gweru 1984.

[30] F. Lobinger, *Towards non-dominating leadership. Aims and methods of the Lumko-series*, Delmenville 1983.

[31] J. De Mesa, Making salvation concrete and Jesus real, in: *Exchange. Journal of Missiological and Ecumenical Research* 30(2001)1, 1-17.

[32] J. Banawiratma and J. Müller, *Contextual social theology. An Indonesian model*, Manila 1999.

lical hermeneutics.[33] The point at issue, however, is not so much whether or not theology should be theory-oriented, as in what way it should be theory-oriented.

Methodology handbooks make a distinction between theory-developing and theory-testing research.[34] Each research strategy has its own type of concepts (operational versus sensitising) and design (linear versus cyclical). Whereas a theory-testing approach proceeds from defining a problem, formulating a hypothesis and providing operational definitions, to gathering and analysing data and drawing conclusions, a theory-developing strategy is iterative.[35] In such an approach the researcher can start wherever he or she sees fit; in every stage the researcher can move backwards or forwards; this approach sets no starting point or end, although the research must reach a conclusion somewhere. But the conclusion is open to fresh criticism. In my view the practical-theological spiral is best seen as a grounded theory approach to theology, based on a real dialectic relation between data sources (e.g., qualitative or quantitative empirical facts gathered through fieldwork) and knowledge sources (e.g., existing insights and theories developed previously by others that can be studied through secondary research).[36]

I consider the Judaeo-Christian tradition to be such a knowledge source, based on several thousands of years of human experience in the search for justice and liberation. In a book on theological method Edward Schillebeeckx[37] claims that, just like any other science, theology starts from a hypothesis, namely the truth of faith given in the Christian tradition, and that this hypothesis must be tested and possibly falsified by human experience. He later applied this methodological principle in

---

[33] P. Kalilombe, *Doing theology at the grassroots*, Gweru 1999.

[34] Verschuren and Doorewaard, *Designing a research project*, 33-36; Mugenda and Mugenda, *Research methods*, 198-201.

[35] J. Spradley, *Participant observation*, New York 1980, 26-28.

[36] Verschuren and Doorewaard, *Designing a research project*, 114-115.

[37] E. Schillebeeckx, *The understanding of faith. Interpretation and criticism*, London 1974.

his Christology.[38] From a social science point of view, James Spradley writes that the researcher infers a hypothesis about cultural knowledge from what people say, the way they act and the artifacts they use. This hypothesis must be tested over and over again until the researcher is relatively certain that this is indeed what people have in mind. Researchers can evaluate the adequacy of their knowledge by their ability to anticipate future behaviour of the people they investigated.[39]

In previous studies I spoke about the research object in terms of a social situation that is experienced as problematic.[40] A social situation is understood as people (actors) doing things (activities) in a physical setting or place.[41] In guiding students I discovered that the concept 'social situation' can easily lead to (excessively) broad research projects, so I narrowed down the research object to practice. I do not propose to elaborate on the concept of practice, as this has been done by others in some detail. Suffice to say that I take practice to be "reflection based on experience and experience based on reflection", as Holland and Henriot[42] defined it, following Paulo Freire. Probably 'praxis' would be a more appropriate term, as 'practice' has the connotation of application of theory. Praxis, by contrast, is understood as co-constituting theory.[43]

Definition of the research object helped me to clarify the research perspective. I am not primarily interested in ideas (beliefs), but in the dialectical relation between cognitive structures (e.g., cultural symbolism) and social structures (e.g., power relations). This focus brings the actor back into the study of religion and theology. It makes the practical-theological spiral quite different from a systematic-theological approach, which is primarily interested in the contents of faith, more particularly in a coherent interpretation of those contents.

---

[38] E. Schillebeeckx, *Jesus. An experiment in Christology*, New York 1979, 617-619.
[39] Spradley, *Participant observation*, 10.
[40] F. Wijsen, *There is only one God*, Kampen 1993, 12.
[41] Wijsen, *There is only one God*, 40; Spradley, *Participant observation*, 39-42.
[42] Holland and Henriot, *Social analysis*, 8; Henriot, Grassroots analysis, 340.
[43] Portier, Interpretation and method, 113.

2.4 Participatory objectification

The objective of the first stage of the practical-theological spiral is to acquire knowledge about the practice under investigation. The method (if it is a method) for this stage is called insertion.[44] Many approaches based on Joseph Cardijn's see, judge and act scheme do not make a clear-cut distinction between observation and analysis. They give detailed directions for data analysis but not for gathering the data. In my earlier work I replaced the first stage of the practical-theological spiral, which Boff and Boff call "the preliminary stage"[45] or "step zero",[46] with participant observation. The reason for this is that the researcher's involvement in the praxis differs from that of the other participants, in that is it more systematic and methodical, and has preconceived intentions. The researcher cannot deny his or her past history and 'second nature'.[47] I shall return to this point when I discuss theological reflection.

Participant observation as a scientific method is known to be hotly contested in academia. It is considered subjective and biased. One criterion of scientific knowledge is its objectivity and neutrality. The classical ideal of science is to refrain from involvement and commitment as far as possible. Hence a questionnaire survey is seen as more objective than participant observation. There are, however, various degrees of participation, from non-participation, through moderate and active participation to complete participation, with increasing degrees of commitment on the part of the researcher.[48] The point at issue is that of involvement (or its opposite: detachment) as a condition for the possibility of 'true' knowledge. By true knowledge I mean that the reality 'out there' corresponds to the mental representation of that reality.

---

[44] Holland and Henriot, *Social analysis*, 8.
[45] Boff and Boff, *Introducing liberation theology*, 22.
[46] Boff and Boff, *Introducing liberation theology*, 41.
[47] Wijsen, *There is only one God*, 21; The pastoral circle, 249.
[48] Spradley, *Participant observation*, 58-62.

A case in point that is fundamental to the construction of African theologies is the references to anthropological poverty in Africa. Most African students claim that missionaries and colonialists discarded African customs and traditions and replaced them with European and Christian values. Thus they speak about cultural schizophrenia in Africa, and even the cultural death of Africans. It seems to me that they use their own experience as African intellectuals, having trained for twelve years or more in a European seminary or university system, as a lens to observe the reality in Africa, without seriously analysing their own contribution to the production and reproduction of these statements. More detached research would stress the symbolic capital and even spiritual power that is alive as never before in African folk culture and popular religion, traditional medicine and customary law.[49]

According to Bourdieu, who started his academic career at the National Institute for Statistical and Economic Research of the University of Algiers, the idea of a neutral or disinterested science is one of the myths of our times.[50] From his own experience he knows that statistical research is no more 'objective' than participatory forms of research. One can manipulate – to a large extent – the product of statistical analysis, for instance by combining two or more variables. Disinterested practice simply does not exist. A field (or 'market') is always a site of struggles, where people try to serve their own interests (or make a 'profit'), using various resources (or forms of 'capital'), in coalition (inclusion) or in competition (exclusion) with others. Universities are not exempted from this struggle. Academics fight over scarce resources, not only to accumulate symbolic capital (honour and prestige) but also for financial gain (research assistants, computers or funds).

---

[49] G. Huizer, Research-through-action, in: G. Huizer and B. Manheim (eds.), *The politics of anthropology*, The Hague and Paris 1979, 395-420; F. Wijsen, Beyond the fatal impact theory, in: M. Amaladoss (ed.), *Globalization and its victims*, Delhi 1999, 122-131.

[50] Bourdieu, *Das religiöse Feld*; Habermas, *Erkentnis und Interesse*.

Bourdieu[51] classifies himself as a constructivist structuralist or a structuralist constructivist. He tries to overcome the classical distinction between subjectivism and objectivism, phenomenology and structuralism, by stressing the dialectical relation between reality and the representation of that reality in the mind. By conducting research, scientists not only discover what is 'out there', but to a large extent they construct what they try to discover. The 'creation' of ethnic groups by cultural anthropologists serves as an example. Bourdieu tries to reduce subjectivism through participatory objectification. By this phrase he understands the objectification of the subject of the objectification, that is, the researcher him/herself. The aim is not to analyse the researcher's experience but to analyse the societal conditions of that experience.[52]

2.5 Analysis of symbolic power

The objective of the second stage of the practical-theological spiral is to gain insight into the observed practice. The method here is social analysis. Holland and Henriot[53] stress the importance of symbolism. The language of technical social analysis is elitist, they say. Locked in the chains of technical language, it has little communicative power. "The alternative to this technical language is the symbolic dimension of popular culture. Thus we emphasise the need to explore the symbolism, myths, dreams, and visions of the ordinary people." Fully in harmony with the dominant form of liberation theology – at least dominant in the reception of this theology in the Western world in the late 1970s – Holland and Henriot emphasise the socio-economic aspects of their analysis. There was also another trend of liberation theology that has always been more interested in cultural symbolism and popular religiosity. This trend was developed mainly in the Argentinian school[54] and was

---

[51] P. Bourdieu, *In other words*, Cambridge, 1990, 123.
[52] Bourdieu, *Ein soziologischer Selbstversuch*.
[53] Holland and Henriot, *Social analysis*.
[54] J. Scannone, "Axial" shift instead of "paradigm shift". In: G. De Schrijver (ed.), *Liberation theologies on shifting grounds*, Leuven 1998.

shared by influential groups in Chile and Brazil. But it remained a minority position up to the 1980s.

The innovation in this second stage is the broadening and deepening of the social analysis by combining it with cultural analysis[55]. But there are various ways of making a cultural analysis and not all of them are helpful for the kind of theological research that I am advocating here. Surprisingly, among many African theology students it has become a fad to discover the people's world-view as a starting point for constructing contextual theologies.[56] A people's world-view is "their picture of the ways things in sheer actuality are, their concept of nature, of self, of society. It contains their most comprehensive ideas of order".[57] By analysing and reflecting on the proverbs or sayings of their people these African students try to construct 'ethno-theologies'. Often they analyse the past more than the present situation, and the ideal more than the real. In many instances they romanticise the past based on 'ideologies of home'.[58] I recall sometimes painful debates with students from Tanzania and Kenya about a 'theology of African Renaissance', based on nationalist ideologies of *ujamaa* or *harambee*, which they embrace in a rather naïve way. My critical questions concerning *ujamaa*[59] met with suspicion that I was an 'uncommitted' theologian. It takes these students quite some time to become more down-to-earth or empirical theologians. Maybe this applies more to Catholic students, who are thoroughly trained in neo-scholastic philosophy, than to mainline Protestant students, who have a solid background in biblical studies and are more inclined to protest.

---

[55] Wijsen, The pastoral circle; P. Henriot, Grassroots analysis. The emphasis on culture. In: G. De Schrijver (ed.), *Liberation theologies on shifting grounds*, Leuven 1998, 333-350.

[56] R. Schreiter, *Constructing local theologies*, Maryknoll, New York 1985.

[57] C. Geertz, *The interpretation of cultures*, London 1993, 127.

[58] R. Robertson, Glocalization. Time - space and homogeneity - heterogeneity, in: M. Featherstone, S. Lash and R. Robertson (eds.), *Global modernities*, London 1995, 25-44.

[59] F. Wijsen, and R. Tanner, *"I am Just a Sukuma". Globalization and identity construction in Northwest Tanzania*, Amsterdam and New York 2002.

Many theologians are trained in a form of cultural analysis derived from the Sapir and Whorf hypothesis. These American linguists maintain that language and culture are intrinsically connected. Thus they assume that one can study a culture just as one studies a language.[60] Based on a Saussurian or Chomskyan linguistics, making a distinction between language and speech, competence and performance, they claim that one can understand a culture by studying the cultural grammar that underlies ritual and symbolism and thus discover, for example, the basic structure of African thought.[61] In theology religiously oriented anthropologists such as Clifford Geertz and Victor Turner are quite influential. This is understandable, as they stress the autonomy of symbol systems independently of actors and social structures, a position held by theologians and phenomenologists of religion who say that religion exists *sui generis*.[62] The anthropologist Victor Turner[63] even said that he was looking for some evidence of ethno-philosophy or ethnotheology in Ndembu culture.

Bourdieu criticises this type of cultural analysis that remains purely internal, overlooking the fact that symbolic classifications fulfil not only cognitive but also practical functions and that they are always oriented to the production of social effects. To interpret religious (political, scientific or any other) speech acts requires not (only) the discovery of the cultural grammar underlying these acts, but (also) a thorough reconstruction of the field in which these speech acts are produced and reproduced, the interests that are served, and the (power) relations between the positions and agents in the field. He proposes that one should study the symbolism, myths, dreams and visions of the ordinary people as cultural capital that is used by (groups of) actors to serve their

---

[60] K. Tanner, *Theories of culture. A new agenda for theology*, Minneapolis1973, 3-24.
[61] M. Kirwen, *African cultural themes*, Nairobi and Minnesota 2004.
[62] Schreiter, *Constructing local theologies*, 56-73; V. Küster *The many faces of Jesus Christ*, London 2001, 3-4.
[63] V. Turner, *Revelation and divination in Ndembu ritual*, Ithaca and London 1975, 20.

own interests.[64] In particular he wants to know "how power creates religion".[65]

2.6 Correlation or confrontation?

The objective of the third stage of the practical-theological spiral is to evaluate the practice that has been observed and analysed. The method for this stage is theological reflection. Holland and Henriot have already corrected the misconception that the first stage is pre-theological[66] and that theological reflection is merely a second step.[67] The idea that theological reflection is merely a second step is often misunderstood by Western theologians. Holland and Henriot write: "None of these parts can be totally isolated; theology is not restricted to that moment explicitly called 'theological reflection'. In a wider sense, all the moments of the circle are part of an expanded definition of theology. All are linked and overlap."[68] Thus what this model presents as an orderly sequence of stages in a process often happen simultaneously in reality.

That is why I spoke about preconceived intentions in the first step of the practical-theological spiral. The choice to be committed and engaged in action is a theological option and not a 'step zero' or 'pre-theological'. I have already explained why early liberation theologians spoke about theological reflection being a second step. But they had a further reason to distinguish clearly between social analysis and theological reflection: they wanted to avoid being branded Marxists by ecclesiastic authorities. Marxism was just a tool used by (them as) sociologists. But there is a pitfall. Early liberation theology inclines towards a two-stage model: first there is socio-analytical mediation, fol-

---

[64] P. Bourdieu, *Das religiöse Feld*, Konstanz 2000.
[65] T. Asad, Anthropological conception of religion. Reflections on Geertz, in: *Man* 18(1983), 237-259.
[66] L. Boff and C. Boff, *Introducing liberation theology*, Maryknoll, New York 1987, 22.
[67] G. Gutiérrez, *Theology of liberation*, Maryknoll, New York 1973.
[68] Holland and Henriot, *Social analysis*, 13.

lowed by hermeneutic mediation.[69] In the department of empirical theology at the Radboud University Nijmegen we do not speak about interdisciplinary study but about intra-disciplinary study to show straight away that there is a dialectical relation between facts and norms.[70] Intra-disciplinary study refers to theologians using the methods of empirical sciences, just as biblical scholars use literary methods, church historians use historical methods and systematic theologians use philosophical methods. Of course, theologians' use of empirical methods must meet the standards of social scientists, which has to be confirmed and guaranteed by scholarly collaboration with them.

In keeping with the foregoing observations, my reflection on this stage of the practical-theological spiral concerns the theologian's 'commitment'.[71] Some students at the Nijmegen Graduate School of Theology are attracted to the Radboud University Nijmegen because they associate it with the hermeneutic method of Edward Schillebeeckx. In his later works Schillebeeckx[72] defined theology as an 'Art of Liberation'. He developed this art in dialogue with Third World theologians, in particular with Gustavo Gutiérrez, with whom he shared an admiration for the 'new theology' of French theologians such as Yves Congar and Marie-Dominique Chenu. But whereas Gutiérrez criticised Schillebeeckx for being too much of an academic theologian, too abstract and too detached from the poor, Schillebeeckx in his turn holds that Gutiérrez identifies too much with the poor and that his theological reflection becomes too much part of their struggle.[73]

Much the same debate goes on at the Nijmegen Graduate School of Theology. Whereas some of the Third World students say that the pro-

---

[69] C. Boff, *Theologie und Praxis. Die erkenntnistheoretische Grundlagen der Theologie der Befreiung*, München 1983.

[70] J. Van der Ven, Practical theology. From applied to empirical theology, in: *Journal of Empirical Theology* 1(1988)1, 7-27.

[71] Fabella and Torres, *The emergent gospel*, 269.

[72] E. Schillebeeckx, Theologie als bevrijdingskunde. In: *Tijdschrift voor Theologie* 24(1984)4, 7-24.

[73] E. Borgman, Theology as the art of liberation. In: *Exchange. Journal of Missiological and Ecumenical Research* 32(2003)2, 98-108.

fessors are too much theorists, the professors say that the students are too much activists. By being too committed they are no longer capable of critical reflection on the practice. Theology becomes a justification of the practice. Some of my African students think in terms of incarnation. They say that God was already present in Africa long before the missionaries came, working among Africans in mysterious ways. What the missionary does is to make explicit what had always been there. Incarnation theology undoubtedly fulfilled a liberating function, recognising the intrinsic value of African cultures, eliminating the pitfalls of the earlier adaptation theology that sought to jettison African culture and Christianise it from within. This theology served the interests of colonialists and missionaries, who wanted African people to adapt to their point of view. In this sense it was an ideology.[74] But it is unwise to combat one ideology with another. Incarnation theology was a necessary step to overcome cultural and religious oppression, but when applied too radically it becomes naïve.

Liberation theology never took root in Africa, except in South Africa (in the form of Black Theology) and in Cameroon, with outstanding scholars like Jean-Marc Ela and Fabien Eboussi Boulaga. In other countries they remained prophets in the desert, such as Laurenti Magesa in Tanzania. But these scholars were either silenced (by the government or the church) or they turned secular. This is understandable in the context of growing church control and dependence on outside funding.[75] At present the debate is no longer between liberation and inculturation, but between reconstruction and renaissance.[76] In general, my African students are very enthusiastic about the potential of popular wisdom and the possibility of going back to the 'path of the ancestors'. They praise the African community spirit (e.g., *ujamaa* in Tanzania or *ubuntu* in South Africa), and tend to see it as solution to (almost) all evils in society. But they tend to forget that *ujamaa* was not a great

---

[74] Mannheim, *Ideology and utopia*, London 1960.

[75] A. Hastings, *African Catholicism*. London and Philadelphia 1989, 122-137.

[76] Magesa, African Renaissance; S. Kobia, *The courage to hope. A challenge to the churches in Africa*, Nairobi 2003, 103-150.

success, and not only because of external influences.[77] Much the same applies to Benezet Bujo's *Ethical dimension of community*[78] and Laurenti Magesa's *Moral traditions of abundant life*.[79] However appealing these theologies may be, others feel they take the need to justify African traditions too far.[80] A similar debate on ideology and science may be found in African philosophy between ethno-philosophers and nationalistic philosophers on the one hand and professional or scientific philosophers on the other.[81]

Theological reflection is not just an evaluation of experience "in the light of living faith, scripture, church social teaching, and the resources of tradition", as Holland and Henriot seem to suggest.[82] The phrase "in the light of living faith" remains too much a one-sided procedure. Schillebeeckx says that there is a correlation between human experience and the Christian tradition, gospel and culture. And – as an adherent of social theory – he immediately adds that it is a critical correlation, hence not only mutually clarifying but also mutually critical. Along with African incarnation or inculturation theologians, he says that God and his kingdom are already present in Africa, but also yet to come. This is a condition for the possibility of negative contrast experiences, another basic category in Schillebeeckx's theological reflection. There is always a strong eschatological and thus prophetic strain in his theology. Besides the primacy of practice, the hermeneutics of suspicion – another principle of liberation theology – should be

---

[77] C. Schweigman, Ujamaa. A phantom, in: *Quest. International African Journal of Philosophy* 15(2001)1-2, 113-125.

[78] B. Bujo, *The ethical dimension of community. The African model and the dialogue between North and South.* Nairobi 1998.

[79] L. Magesa, *African religion. The moral traditions of abundant life.* Maryknoll, New York 1997.

[80] Maluleke, A rediscovery of the agency of Africans, 165-190.

[81] P. Hountondji, *African philosophy. Myth an reality*, London 1983; K. Gyekye, *Tradition and modernity. Philosophical reflection on African experience*, New York 1997; K. Appiah, *In my father's house. Africa in the philosophy of culture*, Oxford 1992; K. Wiredu, *Cultural universals and particulars. An African perspective*, Indiana 1996.

[82] Holland and Henriot, *Social analysis*; Henriot, Grassroots analysis.

applied to liberation and other emancipation theologies as well. In some African students' research projects commitment and identification with the people and popular wisdom go too far. I challenge them to balance commitment and criticism. There is continuity, but also discontinuity, between gospel and culture. Hermeneutic fusion of horizons must be complemented by a hermeneutics of differentiation.

2.7 Empowerment of the people

The objective of the fourth stage of the practical-theological spiral is to demonstrate conditions for the possibility of innovating the practice under investigation. The method for this stage is pastoral planning. In discussing the first stage of the spiral I referred to various types of participant observation.[83] In the last of these types (i.e., complete participation) there is no longer any distinction between the roles of observer and participant. The researcher has become an insider. This form is more aptly called action research.[84] Action research as a research strategy developed on the margins of academic studies and became a hallmark of a lot of Third World or liberation theology, where theologising serves as a means of empowering the people – especially the most marginalised – through adult education and community development. Here the methodological principles of learning by doing and doing before knowing are applied in their purest form. The presupposition is that the best knowledge comes from below and from within.

An interesting example of an observer who became a participant is a Dutch anthropologist who studied spirit mediums in Botswana. He identified with his informants to such an extent that he became a spirit medium himself.[85] He was prepared to trade his status as an anthropo-

---

[83] Spradley, *Participant observation*, 58-62.

[84] G. Huizer, *Folk spirituality and liberation in Southern Africa*, Bourdeaux 1991.

[85] W. Van Binsbergen, Becoming a sangoma. Religious anthropological fieldwork in Francistown, Botswana. In: *Journal of Religion in Africa* 21(1991)4, 309-344.

logical fieldworker for that of a religious specialist. Becoming a *sangoma* offered him the inside view which is not accessible to participant observers who, however committed they may be, remain to a large extent outsiders. The author, a respected anthropologist with over twenty years' experience, was no longer able to write an ethnography but only to tell his story. In a later publication the same author, who moved from cultural anthropology to intercultural philosophy, dissociates himself from his earlier romanticising of *sangoma* beliefs.[86]

Action research emerged in social psychology just before the Second World War as a strategy in which the researcher learns about group dynamics and change processes by participating in or manipulating certain aspects of these processes. Kurt Lewin, who coined the term 'action research' and was himself a Jewish refugee from Nazi Germany with a background in the *Frankfurter Schule*, once said: "If you want to know how things really are, just try to change them".[87] This type of research has been used in Third World contexts and elsewhere, in both urban industrial and rural agricultural settings, for the purpose of mobilising the group power of workers and farmers through a pedagogy of the oppressed[88] and training for transformation.[89] It has given rise to a tradition of research-through-action, stressing indigenous knowledge and spiritual power.[90] In general the presupposition is that development or change must be people-oriented or community based.

In line with my argument in the previous sections, such an approach can become naïve and uncritical. One of my doctoral students, who was interested in developing a people-oriented biblical hermeneutics among the Pokot in West Kenya, discovered that community based practice is not always good practice. To the Pokot stealing from their neighbours is evil. But according to their popular wisdom there is nothing wrong

---

86 W. Van Binsbergen, Sangoma in Nederland. Over integriteit en interculturele bemiddeling. In: M. Ellias and R. Reis (eds.), *Getuigen ondanks zichzelf*, Maastricht 1998, 1-29.
87 K. Lewin, *Resolving social conflicts*, New York 1948.
88 Freire, *Pedagogy of the oppressed.*
89 Hope and Timmel, *Training for transformation.*
90 Huizer, *Folk spirituality.*

with cattle raiding among the Turkana, as they do not consider the Turkana to be their neighbours. Clearly this practice, however people-oriented or community based, cannot be justified as good practice at a professional theological level. Maybe research-after-action could be an adequate alternative to research-through-action. While in research-through-action the action and research are undertaken simultaneously, research-after-action first commits available resources to action and only later to scientific recording and publication. "Research after action does not have that advantage of relevancy for the change process under review. It does, however, provide distance between the scientist and his activities allowing for more objective consideration".[91]

2.8 Conclusion

In this chapeter I tried to bridge this divide between commitment and criticism, between grassroots theology and ivory tower theology, by presenting the practical-theological spiral as a grounded theory approach to theology to promote understanding and collaboration between European academic or theory-oriented theologians and Third World applied or practice-oriented theologians. Of course, these labels are stereotypes and in reality these approaches and their advocates are more complex and differentiated. Moreover, the West and the Rest, European and Third World are not primarily regional categories but refer to various ways of conducting research. The methodology handbook by Mugenda and Mugenda[92] was developed at Kenyatta University in Nairobi, Kenya, but it reflects a largely Western approach; the methodology handbook by Verschuren and Doorewaard[93] was developed at the Radboud University Nijmegen, Netherlands, but it is open to methods other than the traditional ones.

---

[91] J. Kronenburg, *Empowerment of the poor*, Amsterdam and Nijmegen1986, 5-6.

[92] O. Mugenda and A. Mugenda, *Research methods*, Nairobi 2003.

[93] Verschuren and Doorewaard, *Designing a research project*.

The dichotomy between the two types of theology, academic and applied, is based on a false understanding of theory-oriented and practice-oriented research, as even a little reflection on the term 'practice' reveals. I showed some strengths and weaknesses of both forms of theology. In reaction to a narrow-minded, scientific type of theology I tried to show that the commitment advocated by Third World theologians is not necessarily an inadequate principle for gathering 'true' knowledge. This is a criticism of the dogma of scientific neutrality. On the other hand I showed that the detachment advocated by European theologians can make pastoral projects more objective. The danger is that theologians who are overly engaged in practice may no longer be capable of critical reflection; they tend to identify with the people and offer a justification of their practices.

Reflection on the four stages of the practical theological spiral may make it more relevant to both European and Third World theology. In the reflection on the preliminary stage there is shift from insertion to participant observation, and from participant observation to participatory objectification. Maybe this is the most important modification of the practical theological spiral, as it is foundational for all the other steps. Researchers become far more aware of their own contribution to the material. Insertion always occurs in a specific social position. The accent is not on experience as a first step but on the social conditions of this experience. Concerning the second step, there is a shift from, or a combination of, social and cultural analysis – a form of cultural analysis that looks at cultural symbolism not only from the perspective of its underlying grammar but also from the perspective of power relations that shape cultures, of culture as symbolic capital. In the third stage there is not only an evaluation of culture in the light of the gospel but also the other way round. Theological reflection offers a critical correlation, but I have learnt that it must be augmented by critical confrontation. In the fourth stage I moved from pastoral planning to action research, and from action research to research-after-action. In developing these steps I sought to strike a balance between commitment and criticism.

The real issue is not so much the use of methods as their underlying theory of science. In the 1970s and 1980s critical theory was accepted as scientific. Today this theory has largely disappeared from our universities, which equate science with positivism. Here I stand by Bourdieu's protest against the myths of our time, especially the myth of a disinterested science, and Schillebeeckx's view of theology as art of liberation. One question that still bothers me is whether or not academic standards are universal, irrespective of the context in which academic research is done. For the time being I maintain that in principle academic standards are universal, but in fact they are not. What our intercultural debate in theology can do is to make these standards more universal. This would mean that an academic standard created in a concrete context, by reason of historical significance and collegial cooperation, is embraced by other researchers in various contexts and finally achieves the status of universality, which is inclusive and accepted by all. But whether this will ever happen is questionable. It certainly has not happened in the recent past. So our struggle for symbolic capital in academia will continue, also in the field of theology.

2.9 Further readings on the method of mission studies

- D. Becker, *Mission verstehen. Themen und Thesen interkultureller Forschung*, Neuendettelsau 2012.
- A. Camps, Four key-notes of an empirical missiology, in: *Neue Zeitschrift für Missionswissenschaft* 29(1973) 135-142.
- E. Elliston, *Introduction to missiological research design*, Pasadena 2011.
- B. Lovett, *For the joy set before us. Methodology of adequate theological reflection on mission*, Oxford 2008.
- L. Rütti, Mission – Gegenstand der Praktischen Theologie oder Frage der Gesamttheologie?, in: F. Klostermann and R. Zerfass (eds.), *Praktische Theologie Heute*, München and Mainz 1974, 288-307.
- V. Søgaard, *Research in Church and Mission*, Pasadena 1996.

- C. Taber, *To understand the world, to save the world. The interface between missiology and the social sciences*, Harrisburg 2000.

2.10 Questions for better comprehension

1. According to the author, why is the first stage of the practical-theological spiral not 'pre-theological'?
2. What is a 'grounded theory approach'? And what is the difference between 'theory-testing' and 'theory-developing' research?
3. Explain the difference between 'participant observation' and 'participatory objectification'?
4. Explain the difference between confrontation and correlation in theological reflection.
5. Do you think that missiology is a theological discipline? Why do you think so?

Chapter 3 Dialogue and Syncretism in African Christianity

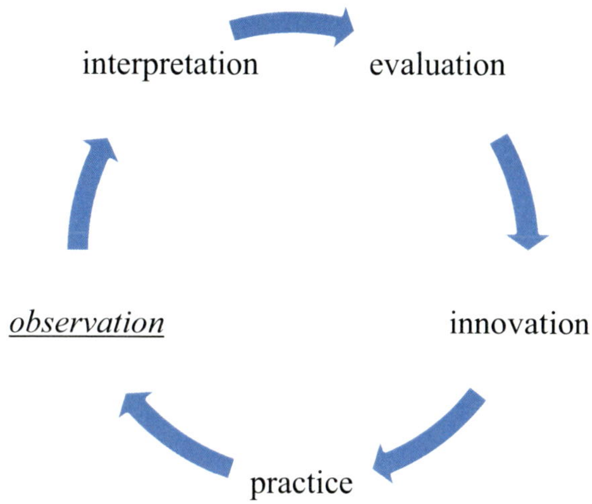

3.1 Introduction

In Africa there are three major religious traditions: the indigenous religion, Islam and Christianity.[1] It was estimated that in 1980 some 41.2% were Muslims, 44.2% were Christians, and 13.9% were indigenous believers.[2] Some countries are almost totally Islamic or totally Christian, other countries are religiously mixed. More and more Africans convert to one of the world religions. Islam in Africa is growing faster than Christianity. There are conflicts and confrontations in Africa, in which religious issues are instrumentalised for political gains. But in general, human solidarity and unity, hospitality and tolerance are

---

[1] By religion I mean any process of communication between a (group of) believer(s) and one or more meta-empirical agencies, whom they believe to exist and affect their lives.

[2] See D. Barrett (ed.), *World Christian Encyclopedia. A Comparative study of Churches and Religions in the Modern World*, Nairobi, Oxford and New York 1982, 782. Note that statistics in Africa are difficult to get and mostly coloured by politics.

great values in Africa.[3] In most families people of different faiths live together in harmony.

One aspect that fascinates scholars of religion in Africa is that converts of Christianity and Islam easily return to their indigenous religion, move from one religion to the other, belong to two or more religions at the same time, or create new religions, making use of elements from two or more religions. This religious dynamics is usually classified as 'syncretism'.[4]

The study of syncretism in Africa is not new. There have been studies of an anthropological and missiological point of view. In both disciplines the term syncretism had a negative connotation. Anthropologists were biased towards the study of 'pure', 'authentic', 'untouched' cultures; missiologists were concerned with 'true faith'.[5] Recently there have been tendencies to rehabilitate the term syncretism, both in anthropology and missiology.[6] As believers of different faiths nowadays frequently meet each other, be it for trade, science or entertainment,

---

[3] See A. Byaruhanga-Akiiki, African traditional values for human development, in: J. Agbasiere and B. Zabajungu (eds.), *Church Contribution to Integral Development*, Eldoret 1989, 50; S. Von Sicard, Christian-Muslim relations in Africa, in: J. Olupona and S. Nyang (eds.), *Religious Plurality in Africa. Essays in Honour of John S. Mbiti*, Berlin and New York 1993, 273-275.

[4] See J. Peel, Syncretism and Religious Change, in: *Comparative Studies in Society and History* 10(1967-1968)2, 121-141.

[5] An almost decisive factor determining the reaction of a religion to syncretism is the concept of truth. As defenders of the one 'true faith' missionaries often contributed to religious confrontation and conflict. In certain Christian denominations they still do.

[6] See A. Droogers, Syncretism. The problem of definition. The definition of the problem, in: J. Gort, H. Vroom, R. Fernhout and A. Wessels (eds.), *Dialogue and Syncretism. An Interdisciplinary Approach*, Grand Rapids 1989, 7-25; H. Siller, Synkretismus. Bestandsaufnahme und Problemanzeigungen, in: H. Siller (ed.), *Suchbewegungen. Synkretismus, kulturelle Identität und Kirchliches Bekentnis*, Darmstadt 1991, 1-17; C. Stewart and R. Shaw, Introduction. Problematizing syncretism, in: C. Stewart, R. Shaw (eds.), *Syncretism/Anti-syncretism. The Politics of Religious Synthesis*, London and New York 1994, 1-26.

scholars of religion recognise that they can learn from syncretism how religions can live together peacefully.[7]

In this chapter syncretism is investigated by way of a study of (evil) spirits in (East) Africa. Spirit beliefs are the most common part of religion in Africa. They touch the hearth of African religion: the concern for health and wealth in addressing meta-empirical agencies. Here the African pragmatic attitude of seeking help from all sides shows itself clearly. For this reason, Giles speaks of the *pepo* cult in terms of 'syncretic cult', 'dynamic interaction' and 'dynamic synthesis'.[8]

For African Christian studies spirits form an important theme. First, this is clear in pastoral practice. Every priest now and then is asked the question: "Father, I have (evil) spirits, would you bless me" (except if it is known that the priest would refer the sufferer to a hospital).[9] It is one of the merits of Evangelical and Pentecostal churches that they take seriously these beliefs. These churches force Protestant and Catholic missiologists to face this problem.[10] Secondly, interesting theological issues arise from this practice, such as the contextualisation of Christianity in African cultures and the dialogue between Christianity and the religions that are related to these cultures.[11]

Very often, though not always, religious confrontations are based on an exclusivistic understanding of truth. The question in this chapter is whether another understanding of truth promotes dialogue and if something can be learned in this respect from syncretism in African Christi-

---

[7] See U. Berner, Synkretismus und Inkulturation, in: Siller (ed.), *Suchbewegungen*, 134. Originally the term syncretism had a positive connotation. It meant 'brotherly love'. It signified the necessity of living together in compromise. See Stewart and Shaw, Introduction, 3.

[8] L. Giles, Possession Cults on the Swahili Coast. A re-examination of Theories of Marginality, in: *Africa* 57(1987)2, 234, 245, 237. *Pepo* is a Swahili term for spirit. The author says that her informants use *pepo* and *shetani* interchangeably (page 252 n. 22).

[9] Even lay missionaries get this request, as happened to me several times.

[10] See T. Kiogora, Angels, Demons and Spirits in African Christianity, in: A. Nasimiyu-Wasike and D. Waruta (eds.), *Mission in African Christianity*, Nairobi 1993, 52-66.

[11] Berner, Synkretismus und Inkulturation, 134.

anity.[12] This chapter will have three parts. First, the beliefs and practices concerning (evil) spirits are dealt with. I will consider the traditional beliefs and how they are effected by outside influences. Secondly, I will consider spirit beliefs and practices as a source of dialogue. Apparitions of Mary in Mwanza Town will serve as an example. Thirdly, I will investigate spirit beliefs as a source of conflict. The faith healing movement of Father Felician Nkwera and his followers (*wanamaombi*) will make this clear.

This chapter is based on three months (May - August 1995) of participant observation and ethnographic interviews in Mwanza Region.[13] It is anthropological in nature. More specifically, it is a treatise in missiological anthropology.[14] Missiological anthropology is not identical with missiology. It describes the context of mission and investigates conditions for the possibility of mission.

Mwanza Region is situated in Northwest Tanzania, South of Lake Victoria. Together with Shinyanga Region, Mwanza Region forms an area known as Sukumaland. The Sukuma people are the main ethnic group in this area. Most Sukuma are subsistence farmers, cultivating maize, rice, cassava, sweet potatoes and cotton (cash crop). Cows are a social and economic investment and serve in ancestor worship. About 85% of the Sukuma people adhere to the indigenous religion, 10% are Catholic, 3% are Protestant and 2% are Muslim.[15]

---

[12] By dialogue I mean a form of communication that is openended and mutual. The alternative form of communication is propagation. Dialogue aims at understanding, propagation aims at persuasion.

[13] I used the ethnographic semantics as developed by J. Spradley, *The Ethnographic Interview*, New York 1979; J. Spradley, *Participant Observation*, New York 1980.

[14] See L. Luzbetak, *The Church and Cultures. New Perspectives in Missiological Anthropology*, Maryknoll, New York 1989, 43.

[15] See F. Wijsen, *There is Only one God. A Social-scientific study of Popular Religion and Evangelization in Sukumaland, Northwest Tanzania*, Kampen 1993, 45-78.

3.2 Spirit beliefs and practices

To get a clear picture of beliefs in and practices concerning 'spirits' in contemporary Sukumaland is not an easy task. Maybe in the past spirit beliefs were clear; 'maybe', because several authors contradict each other on various points.[16] But in the present they are not, as they are affected by outside influences. Much the same could be said, of course, about Christian ideas in contemporary Europe.[17]

There is a great deal of literature on 'spirit beings' in Sukumaland. Several authors distinguish 'ancestor spirits' and other spirits, referred to as 'nature spirits' by Hans Cory and 'non-ancestral spirits' by Ralph Tanner,[18] to mention only some authoritative anthropologists that conducted fieldwork in Sukumaland. They are quoted frequently by various scholars of religion in Sukumaland,[19] however, without testing their ideas empirically.

Curiously, a word for 'spirits' does not exist in Sukuma language; in its book *Imani za Jadi za Kisukuma* the Sukuma Research Committee,

---

[16] This is not to ignore the fact that there were local differences between the Northern and Southern Sukuma, and even between the various kingdoms within these areas.

[17] For example, it is estimated that some 30% of the Christians in the Netherlands believe in reincarnation, although originally this was not a Christian idea.

[18] H. Cory, Religious beliefs and practices of the Sukuma / Nyamwezi tribal group, in: *Tanganyika Notes and Records,* 54(1960), 15; R. Tanner, An Introduction to the Spirit Beings of the Northern Basukuma, in: *Anthropological Quarterly* 29(1956)3, 69.

[19] See B. Millroth, *Lyuba. Traditional Religion of the Sukuma*. Doctoral Dissertation, Uppsala 1965; I. Pambe, *Symbols and Change in African Beliefs. Religious Symbols and the Leader-specialist among the Sukuma-Nyamwezi of Tanzania*. Doctoral Dissertation, Rome 1978; J. Healey and D. Sybertz, *I Pointed out to you the stars. An African narrative Theology of Inculturation*, Nairobi 1996; *Kamati ya Utafiti wa Utamaduni, Imani za jadi za kisukuma katika misemo, hadithi, methali na desturi za maisha*, Nantes 1988; Wijsen, *There is Only One God.*

Kamati ya Utafiti, uses the Swahili word *viroho*.[20] I asked several people to express: "I am possessed by (evil) spirits". They said: "*Nali na masamva*", "*nali na badugu*", "*nali na mahugi*", or "*nanding'wa masamva*", "*nanding'wa badugu*", "*nanding'wa mahugi*". The Sukuma words *masamva*, *badugu* and *mahugi* unambiguously refer to ancestors.

I was told that 'non-ancestral spirits' do not exist in Sukumaland. The Sukuma know only their ancestors. The so-called 'other spirits', mainly *majini* and *mashetani*, have been introduced from outside, by Islam and Christianity respectively.[21] They are collectively referred to as *mapepo mabaya* (evil spirits) and contrasted with 'ancestors', who are good only.[22] The activities of the 'other spirits' are quite different from those of the ancestors. Every Sukuma knows the difference, it was said.

Some scholars seem to suggest that there are other meta-empirical agencies. In the literature they are called lesser Gods or deities. Hans Cory speaks about demons, Ignatius Pambe about divinities.[23] Ralph Tanner writes that after death, mourners reply to the greetings of the bereaved by saying that the Spirit of Bad Luck has been here (*muliho nali welelo*) and that He has caused death to take the deceased (*liwelelo*

---

[20] Healey and Sybertz , *Kamati ya Utafiti*, 23. It is doubtful if this is proper Swahili. The first meaning of *roho* is soul, breath of life. The *vi*-prefix makes it a diminutive. *Viroho* is not understood by the ordinary people meaning spirits. Creative use of the vernacular at grassroots level can be illustrative for the process of religious transformation. However, here it remains a linguistic play of Sukuma intellectuals.

[21] As the first missionaries thought that the ancestors were demons, they used the Swahili word *mashetani* to refer to them. As the Christian attitudes towards ancestors changed, the word *mashetani* was used for other spirits, but its Christian connotation remained.

[22] In the literature not all *majini* are considered to be bad and not all ancestors to be good. R. Tanner even wrote: "There is no question of loving the ancestors, and they are feared rather than venerated". See R. Tanner, *Transition in African Beliefs. Traditional Religion and Christian Change. A Study in Sukumaland, Tanzania, East Africa*, Maryknoll, New York 1967, 21.

[23] Cory, Religious beliefs, 15; Pambe, *Symbols and Change*, 114. In Swahili the divinities are called *miungu*. Here again it is questionable if this is understood by the ordinary faithful.

likatwizilaga). When there is a serious illness in the family it is said that the Spirit of Bad luck is there (*liwelelo lylenili*).[24]

Healey and Sybertz quote a prayer of a magician, reported by Tomecko and Tomecko: "O Liwelelo. I beg you to give me the power of divination which has been offered to me by my ancestors. I implore you, O Spirit of Good Luck, so that I may have strong powers and be greater than other magicians".[25] The prefix *li* (often used before a name of grandeur) may be added to *Welelo*. But it is doubtful if it means 'Spirit of Good Luck'.

Here again I was assured that these are not separate entities, but attributes of God.[26] *Welelo* means 'world', 'universe'.[27] It is not correct to translate *welelo* by 'Spirit of Bad Luck'. There is nothing between God and men. As one informant put it: '*Mungu ni mmoja, majina ni mengi*', meaning: "There is only one God, but He has many names".[28]

I found, however, that there is a 'cultural contradiction' between the 'official image' that people seek to project of Sukuma religion and the 'insider's view' of what really goes on.[29] There are 'official' beliefs as

---

[24] See Tanner, An Introduction to the Spirit Beings, 71-72.

[25] See Healey and Sybertz, *I Pointed out to you the stars*, 292; D. Tomecko and J. Tomecko, in: *Sukuma*, n.p., n.d., 32.

[26] The Sukuma Research Committee (Healey and Sybertz, *Kamati ya Utafiti*, 23) introduced the Sukuma word *magele* for powers coming from God (*nguvu zinazotoka kwa Mungu*). It is doubtful if this is proper Sukuma. The committee members make it even more complicated as they see the Sukuma word *magele* as equivalent of the Swahili word *viroho* (see note 20).

[27] This seems congruous with the view in which God is associated with nature as a whole, rather than with a single personality. See Tomecko and Tomecko, 29.

[28] In his *Transition in African beliefs*, 5, Ralph Tanner mentions two concepts of God, the more popular one in which God is preeminent over a series of lesser spirits, and another one in which these spirits are aspects of God. If Tanner was right in his observation, it seems that the concept of God among the Sukuma is changing.

[29] For the concept 'cultural contradiction' see Spradley, *The Ethnographic Interview*, 200; Spradley, *Participant Observation*, 152.

taught by the important people (*watu wakubwa*).[30] And there are 'popular' beliefs as lived by the ordinary people (*watu wadogo*).[31] The educated and important people spoke about the 'pure', 'authentic', 'untouched' beliefs, how it used to be in the past or how it should be.[32] But the ordinary people are very much affected by outside influences. They do not live the 'pure' Sukuma beliefs, but seek help from all sides in their existential needs. As subsistence farmers they have a pragmatic attitude; they accept or reject religious beliefs and practices only in so far as they are functional.[33]

Despite the information gathered from some elders and healers, I found that many Sukuma, and especially the youth and town dwellers, do speak about other spirits. During previous periods of fieldwork in Sukumaland I seldom heard people speaking about *masamva* or *mizimu* (Sukuma and Swahili for ancestors). They did speak, however, about *mashetani* and *majini* quite a lot.

Even indigenous healers did so.[34] Most Sukuma are not 'untouched', as the elders would like them to be, but 'syncretic'. This is almost una-

---

[30] The level of education seems crucial. To know the difference between religious concepts one must know the linguistic and historical background. Hence, the purist view is the view of intellectuals or the elite view.

[31] It may be questioned if 'popular' and 'official' are correct terms, as there are no 'officials' in the Sukuma religion. Nevertheless, there are beliefs that represent the ideal, while the reality may be different. Droogers speaks of 'purists' and 'syncretists'. See A. Droogers, De minimale religiositeit van de meerderheid, in: R. Bakker, R. Fernhout, J. Gort and A. Wessels (eds.), *Religies in nieuw perspectief. Studies over interreligieuze dialoog en religiositeit op het grondvlak*, Kampen 1985, 93.

[32] The 'important' people, those who express 'official' beliefs, are not necessarily elders (*wazee*) or healers (*waganga*).

[33] 'Die Neigung zum Volksbrauchtum mit magischer Tendenz und Synkretismus nimmt mit abnehmenden Bildungsniveau und steigender Krisensituation zu'. See M. Kristin Arat, Die nichtamtliche Religiosität als dialogisches Element der Religionen am Beispiel von Christentum und Islam, in: *Zeitschrift für Missionswissenschaft und Religionswissenwissenschaft* 76(1992)2, 120.

[34] This shows a cultural dynamics. Indigenous healers easily accept concepts from Christianity and Islam, if they are functional. The 'purists' do not like

voidable in a world that is becoming a 'global village'. Again, this is not much different in Africa than in Europe.

I was told that speaking of *mashetani* and *majini* is just a new language (*lugha mpya tu*) or just modern language (*lugha ya kisasa tu*). It is a different way of saying the same (*usemi tu*). Several informants assured me that *masamva*, mashetani and majini is the same thing (*kitu kimoja tu*); there is no difference at all.[35] This is understandable, as there are no other spirits than ancestor spirits. So it seems that the malicious ancestor spirits merged with other (evil) spirits, for which the Sukuma adopted words with Islamic (*majini*) or Christian (*mashetani*) connotation.[36]

The question then arises as to why the contemporary Sukuma speak less about *mizimu* and *masamva* (ancestor spirits) and more about other spirits, *majini* and *mashetani*. In the past, each family had its own ancestors, still active in their lives and concerned with their well-being. Ancestors are something that only affects the family (*kitu cha ukoo tu*). Now the ancestors have become included in a more general pantheon of spirits who are not by definition related to particular individuals or families. To put it differently, in the past the ancestors were the only explanation of success or failure, now there are many.

Why is this so? In the past the ancestors were concerned with the well-being of the family. In the present, individuals move more frequently and to more distant areas. As such the present-day Sukuma are detached from the graves of their ancestors. Secondly, more Sukuma people marry exogamously and live in de-tribalised situations, such as towns. Here other spirits become more important. Thirdly, in the past

---

this. "They (indigenous healers) only seek money. They chase away *majini*, as the Arabs do, because this is what their clients want them to do. By doing so they destroy our culture", the latter complain.

[35] This was denied by other informants who said that the differences are clear. Here again, a cultural contradiction exists between the 'official' and 'popular' view.

[36] The word *shetani* (plural: *mashetani*) comes from *shaitan* and was introduced into Swahili via Arabic. As said before (see note 21), the word was used by the first missionaries to denote (ancestor) spirits.

the ancestors were the guardians of the fertility of land, cows and family. Now, more and more Sukuma have jobs and depend on cash. Thus, ancestor beliefs are no longer that functional in the present-day situation as they used to be in the past.

On the other hand, people do need an explanation for their misfortune and distress, and they do need guidance for behaviour. The more socially distant spirits have a similar moral supervision, but are not by definition related to particular individuals and families. Those spirits can pick on anyone and those who are concerned have to work hard to find out what is wrong.

This does not necessarily mean that ancestor beliefs will disappear, that ancestor beliefs are not popular anymore. It does mean, however, that they are no longer the only explanation for success and failure. As some informants said: there are now many denominations (*madhehebu mbalimbali*). Modernisation pluralises, and pluralisation relativises options that were absolute until now.[37] Again, this is not much different in Africa than in Europe.[38]

---

[37] See P. Berger, *The Heretical Imperative. Contemporary Possibilities of Religious Affirmation*, New York 1979.

[38] For example, in the Netherlands the faith healer Yomanda attracts thousands of people six times a week. In this society, which is considered to be one of the most secularised societies in the world, Yomanda seems to be functional.

3.3 Spirits as source of dialogue

For the sake of clarity I will take an example from the Catholic scene, the story of the Seer of Mwanza, Agnes Nyambuli.[39] Agnes was born in July 1975 and grew up in a normal way in Ghana Quarters, Mwanza.[40] The troubles started in January 1985.[41] Agnes slept for seven days continuously. Her parents consulted the local dispensary and an indigenous healer, but no disease was identified. Agnes was referred to the regional hospital (Bugando), but the specialists there could not find the cause of her suffering. Her mother then requested the Poor Clares (religious sisters) in Mwanza to pray for Agnes, which they did.

In June 1986 Agnes received Holy Communion. After that her situation became worse. Her legs and arms were paralysed as if she was attacked by polio. Her parents now consulted an Islamic teacher, who diagnosed that Agnes was possessed by evil spirits (the reports speak of *mashetani* and *mapepo*). The local parish priest was asked to give Agnes the anointment of the sick. After doing so Agnes went into a coma.

The godmother of Agnes now advised her parents to see Father Felician Nkwera, a faith healer who prays for the sick and casts out evil spirits.[42] So they went to Tabora, where Nkwera lived at that time (he now lives in Kibaha, near Dar es Salaam). This faith healer prayed for Agnes and performed the exorcism of evil spirits. He advised the parents of Agnes to arrange prayer meetings and to find her a statue of the Blessed Virgin.

---

[39] In religious studies the scientific study of the 'own' religion often serves as an eye-opener in the study of 'other' religions.

[40] This is a 'National Housing' area where lower middle class people are living. Agnes' parents are employees in governmental and para-statal offices.

[41] Although this happened more than ten years ago, the example is still relevant, as it caused the spread of a whole series of 'miraculous events' and a chain of prayer groups.

[42] A. Shorter describes his healing work. He uses the pseudonym Fr. Audax Mwaguzi. For every insider, however, it is clear that Fr. Felician Nkwera is meant. See A. Shorter, *Jesus and the Witchdoctor. An Approach to Healing and Wholeness*, London and Maryknoll, New York 1985, 190-195.

When they were back in Ghana Quarters, prayers were said in their house and her parents looked for prayer groups in order to pray for the cure of Agnes, following Nkwera's advice. A Catholic prayer group in Nyegezi joined the prayers, as did Evangelical-pentecostal Churches in Nyegezi and Igoma. On October 22nd, 1986, these prayer groups got the message that Agnes was cured. They were told that Agnes had been visited by the Blessed Virgin and that the Blessed Virgin and Agnes had prayed together successfully for the latter's recovery.[43]

This is in short the story of the Seer of Mwanza, Agnes Nyambuli. The following days the Blessed Virgin came back several times and more miracles occurred, thus the reports. The messages of the Blessed Virgin to Agnes Nyambuli were recorded, typed, duplicated and distributed, while her parent's house turned into a place of pilgrimage. Agnes was moved to a nearby sisters convent. There the apparitions continued. It is said that one of the sisters got apparitions as well, and that at one occasion hundreds of people saw the Blessed Virgin in Mabatini (a suburb of Mwanza Town), on the hills.

I investigated whether the apparitions were still going on and if the prayer groups were still active, more than ten years after the 'miraculous events' of Agnes Nyambuli. I found that there was not much going on at Agnes' place, but that there were prayer groups all over Sukumaland.[44] I visited several villages and suburbs of Mwanza (Nyakato, Nyegezi, Igoma, Kisesa) and found that the prayer groups were active and well. Some changes had taken place. The groups were more radical, better organised, and had links with Seers all over the world. New apparitions were being reported from Mwanza and other places.[45]

---

[43] This news was broadcasted by Radio Tanzania on 5 November 1986. See also All Africa Press Service, Virgin Mary visits Tanzania, in: *News and Features Bulletin*, July 13, 1987; P. Rweyemanu and G. Akilimali, *Si kiwete tena. Aonana na Bikira Maria*, Mshindi 1986, Teleo la 8, 1-3.

[44] At present, Agnes studies at a Secondary School in Moshi. Her parents hide her from the prayer groups.

[45] In Mwanza alone there are about fifteen Seers. The most popular ones live in Mabatini, Ghana Quarters and Bugando Milimani. In the village where I lived two women claimed to have *maono* (to hear the voice of the Blessed

In Bugando Milimani I had interviews with an elderly woman, Mama Mgomela, who claims to have apparitions of the Blessed Virgin. She participated in international meetings of Seers in Kenya and Uganda. She spread messages of Little Pebble, a Seer in Australia. Little Pebble's followers are called *wacharbeli*, as Saint Charbel Makhlouf (a hermit in Libanon) is the Patron of his prayer groups. According to Mama Mgomela the time is near that God will separate the sheep from the goats. An extreme cold wave will come over the earth, followed by three days of complete darkness. The members of the prayer groups, who wear scapulars and medals of the Holy Mother will be saved. However, they must hoard food and other necessities for these days to come.[46] But the members of the prayer groups will be saved.

Anthropologically speaking the question if these apparitions are true or not is not so interesting. Anthropologists cannot say anything about the meta-empirical agencies addressed in religion, neither in a positive way, nor in a negative way. Anthropologically speaking the questions are: Why do these prayer groups attract so many people? What do they mean to them? And how do they serve them in their daily needs? These questions can be answered from different perspectives.

From an economic point of view it can be said that people seek alternative ways of healing. Since the liberalisation policy was introduced in Tanzania people have to pay for health care and the gap between the rich and the poor is becoming wider.[47] Healing is certainly

---

Virgin), which the members of the prayer groups consider to be a preliminary stage of *matokeo* (apparitions).

[46] This is in short the contents of the 'Message of Our Lord Jesus Christ, our God, to Sister Guadalupe for the People of Guatemala and the World, 24 August 1987', which was spread among the members of the prayer groups in Usukuma by the Poor Clares (a copy of the full text is in my possession).

[47] As I have explained elsewhere in greater detail, evil spirits can be representations of socio-psychological problems caused by the introduction of the free market economy. See F. Wijsen, The Gold and The Spirits are Close. Popular Religion and Social Transformation in Sukumaland, North-west Tanzania, in: *Exchange. Journal of Missiological and Ecumenical Research* 24(1995)1, 47-48.

the big issue in the prayer groups. Moreover, there is a political element in them.[48] These prayer groups claim that the communist system collapsed because of their prayers and because of the prayers of so many groups in so many parts of the world. It is said that these groups are infiltrated by conservative organisations from Europe and the United States, that fight communism.[49]

Here I approach these groups from a religious point of view. From this perspective these groups are so popular because they very much parallel the indigenous Sukuma religiosity. In fact, it is indigenous Sukuma religiosity under a new cover.[50] This seems contradictory to what these groups themselves claim to be, as they very much attack the indigenous religiosity. They pray for the so-called ‘pagans’ that they may know the one and true God. Yet, in doing so they imitate the indigenous beliefs and practices. This imitation process has been observed in African Independent Churches as well.

It is said that the Blessed Virgin demands the faithful to wear rosaries, medals and scapulars against the *shetani*,[51] to mix drinking water with blessed water in order to avoid all kinds of diseases,[52] to put pictures of the Blessed Virgin and the Sacred Heart of Jesus on the walls of their houses to keep the *shetani* away. The parallels with the indigenous *hirizi* (protection of the body), *lukago* (protection of house) and

---

[48] I did my fieldwork just some months before the October 1995 elections. Prayers were said for Augustine Mrema, one of the presidential candidates. His wife is an active member, as is the wife and a daughter of former president Julius Nyerere.

[49] This was one of the conclusions of a research on Marian apparitions in Nairobi conducted by two staff-members of the Catholic University of Eastern Africa in Nairobi, Aylward Shorter and Joseph Kariuki.

[50] See also L. Stevens, Religious change in a Haya Village, Tanzania, in: *Journal of Religion in Africa* 21(1991)1, 20, who draws the same conclusion for the Haya people.

[51] An alternative is to anoint the body with blessed oil (*mafuta matakatifu*). It is said that blessed oil was stolen from several churches for this purpose.

[52] An alternative is to put a medal of the Holy Bernardus in the water. Note that during this period of fieldwork there was a sudden spread of the Ebola virus in Zaire that frightened people in Sukumaland very much.

buganga (medicine) are striking.[53] Everything is surrounded by secrecy, as the secret societies did.[54]

There is a parallel between these charismatic prayer groups and popular religion, as described earlier.[55] In both forms of religion 'spiritual healing' is the central phenomenon. Both reject 'scientific' medicine as being incomplete.[56] They do not confirm the European, modern, one-dimensional way of thinking and react against the deprivation of the world of its mysterious powers (*nguvu za ajabu*). In this sense these charismatic prayer groups are a Catholic counterpart of the Evangelical and Pentecostal religiosity.[57] Both are condemned by the church officials.[58] This shows a conflict between Africanisation 'from above' (inculturation) and Africanisation 'from below' (syncretism).[59]

---

[53] It may be objected that *hirizi* is not an indigenous but an Islamic concept. However, the Sukuma knew a similar protection of the body, *lupigi* (a small piece of wood worn round the wrist) and *mpembe* (a little horn with medicine). Moreover they created the Sukuma word *hirishi*. Several informants assured me that the Sukuma had *hirishi* for a long time (*toka zamani*). It seems that they prefer the word *hirishi* for protection of the body and *lukago* for protection of the house, although originally the word *lukago* (protective medicine) covered both. This is an example of religious dynamics and transformation.

[54] In Sukumaland the knowledge of indigenous medicine was not inherited from the parents but learned from indigenous healers, organised in secret societies.

[55] See Wijsen, *There is Only One God*, 37-99. By 'popular religion' I mean the religion of the ordinary faithful in contradiction to the religion of the church officials or 'official religion'. I distinguish 'dualistic' and 'syncretic' popular religion. See Wijsen, The Gold and the Spirits are Close, 55.

[56] In Africa medicine is never only physical. Even indigenous healers believe that the healing power comes from God and other meta-empirical agencies. See Shorter, *Jesus and the Witchdoctor*, 133.

[57] The link between popular religion and Pentecostal churches has been observed in Latin America as well. In the 'New Christian Movements' it is not always clear if an African Independent Church or a Pentecostal Church is dealt with.

[58] A theology taking seriously the Holy Spirit would be able to bridge the gap. However, this goes beyond the scope of this article.

[59] The tension between 'inculturation' and 'syncretism' reflects a struggle for the division of power within the church. See Wijsen, *There is only One God*,

One of the fascinating aspects of this story, and indeed of many stories of faith healing, is that there is cooperation, encounter and dialogue between people of different faiths, not only between members of different Christian denominations, but also between Christians and non-Christians. Boundaries between religions, created and reproduced by its officials, are not important and are transcended.

Christians, Muslims and believers of the indigenous religion are united. A pastor of the Evangelical-pentecostal Church, and a Roman Catholic priest, a local healer and a Muslim sheik, all pray for the little girl, suffering from evil spirits. The statue of the Blessed Virgin is said to be found by a Muslim woman and Muslims are said to be converted to Christianity.[60] Why is this so? Why are believers of different faiths united? There are explanations at different levels.

A first explanation may be seen in the fact that the story appeals to existential needs, common to all Sukuma, Muslims, Christians and indigenous believers alike.[61] For the Sukuma health and strength are major concerns and always threatened by severe living conditions in Sukumaland. The crippling of Agnes Nyambuli is a representation of the difficulties the Sukuma face and the struggle to overcome them. She is a symbol of the difficult life (*maisha magumu*). The sufferings (*mateso*) of this little girl speak to the imagination of all parents, and indeed of all Sukuma. It creates a feeling of solidarity. The situation of Agnes Nyambuli could have been their own situation.[62] Hence, the willingness to help is enormous.

293; G. Ter Haar, *Spirit of Africa. The Healing Ministry of Archbishop Milingo of Zambia*, London 1992, 234; B. Meyer, If you are a Devil, you are a Witch and, if you are a witch, you are a Devil, in: *Journal of Religion in Africa* 22(1992)2.

[60] Most Muslims have a great respect for Mary, due to revelations about her in the *Qur'an*. Because of the virgin birth she is a symbol of purity for many Muslim women.

[61] See Kristin Arat, Die nichtamtliche Religiosität als dialogisches Element, 128.

[62] The African saying that "I am because we are" is not mere linguistic embellishment peculiar to African languages but an authentic expression of mutual concern and personal involvement in the fate of others. See J. Nyasani, The

Secondly, this story appeals to what might be called a 'minimal religiosity', common to all people.[63] The existential needs (first level) give rise to problem solving by addressing spiritual agencies.[64] The ordinary believers are not so much interested in what these spirits are in and for themselves, but in what they do. They speak about *masamva*, *mashetani*, *majini* and *mapepo* interchangeably. They may have an initial idea about the differences between these concepts.[65] But these differences are put aside and commonness is stressed. 'Minimal religiosity' develops in situations of religious pluralism in which there is a need of a universal religious code, beside more specific expressions of religion (indigenous, Islamic, Christian). There may be a good deal of misunderstanding. But somehow this misunderstanding 'works'.[66]

The third explanation might be seen in the nature of rituals. The minimal religiosity (second level) does not express itself in intellectual formulations, but in symbolic actions, rituals. The main function of rituals is communication. When words fail to express the deeper feelings of people, rituals become an important medium. Ritual is a means of speaking about the 'unspeakable'. This is why rituals play an important role in religion, which is to be understood as communication with the 'unspeakable'. Even religions that are poor in ritual at official level, as

---

Ontological Significance of I and We in African Philosophy, in: *African Christian Studies* 7(1991)1, 54.

[63] See Droogers, De minimale religiositeit van de meerderheid, 105.

[64] I agree with Platvoet where he says that a modified version of Tylor's 'minimal definition of religion' as 'belief in spiritual beings' may be accepted because it is close to most 'folk' concepts of 'religion'. See J. Platvoet, *Comparing Religions. A Limitative Approach*, The Hague, Paris and New York 1982, 24.

[65] Kristin Arat, Die nichtamtliche Religiosität als dialogisches Element, 119, says: "Als Nichtfachmann sind ihm die Grenzen kaum bewusst".

[66] See Droogers, De minimale religiositeit van de meerderheid, 92, 93, 104. This is an example of what Tanner and I described as 'working misunderstanding'. See R. Tanner and F. Wijsen, Christianity in Usukuma. A Working Misunderstanding, in: *Neue Zeitschrift für Missionswissenschaft* 49(1993)3, 177-193. One and the same term can have various meanings for different people. For this reason Droogers, De minimale religiositeit van de meerderheid, 107, fears that there is no dialogue in 'minimal religiosity'.

is the case with Islam, develop a rich ritual in their popular religiosity. Religious rituals, however, are not only directed towards the 'unspeakable', but also towards the believers among each other. In this way, religious rituals are communion building.[67]

3.4 Spirits as source of confrontation

However, mentioning the work of Father Felician Nkwera brings us to the other side of the story.[68] The spirits are also a source of confrontation. Spirit possession and exorcism are certainly the central phenomena in Nkwera's healing Ministry. It is said that he often fails to heal blind and cripple people. With exorcism of evil spirits, however, he has a near 100% success.

Felician Nkwera was born on 28 April 1936 in Liftua village, Iringa Region, South Tanzania. He got his secondary education at the junior seminary in Songea and studied philosophy and theology at the major seminary in Peramiho. He was ordained a priest on October 11, 1968. After working as a country priest he studied at the University of Dar es Salaam, from 1970 till 1973, and attained a B.A. degree in education from there. Much later he obtained a M.A. degree in linguistics. He worked for the Tanzania Government in the Ministry of Education and wrote several books, among others on religious education.

According to his own testimony, seven months after his ordination he heard a voice telling him: "Felician, I am the Heavenly Mother. I have chosen you to help my children, whom I shall bring to you. You will pray for them and through your prayers God will heal them". His

---

[67] See Kristin Arat, Die nichtamtliche Religiosität als dialogisches Element, 128-130. Victor Turner says that 'communitas' is stressed in rituals. See V. Turner, *The Ritual Process. Structure and Anti-Structure*, London 1969, 131.

[68] See Tanzania's renegade priest - Felician Nkwera, in: *New African*, May 1992, 26; and S. Hanga, Kenyan Pilgrims Flock to Meet Tanzania's Priest of the Sick, in: *The East African*, Dec. 26, 1994 - Jan 1, 1995, 1-2. In the Sociology Department of the University of Dar es Salaam a research project on Nkwera's healing ministry is conducted by John Sivalon and Christopher Comoro.

actual healing ministry began in May 1969. A child that he was attending was cured from severe fever after being in a coma for a week. Since then he has helped more than 1,000 people. Father Nkwera says that it is not he who heals but God. He only prays for healing to take place. The only condition is that the client must have faith. He also says that his healing ministry is for all, as Christians, Muslims, Hindus, Buddhists and indigenous believers are all children of the One and Only God.[69]

When the Vatican announced a Marian year in 1987, Father Nkwera's followers quadrupled and new prayer groups sprang up all over Tanzania. He then started the Marian Faith Healing Ministry, whose followers are known as *wanamaombi*. Since the eighties the Tanzania Episcopal Conference tried to stop Nkwera from his healing ministry. Several discussions took place. In 1990 Nkwera was suspended from priestly work in his home diocese of Njombe. The same happened to him in the diocese of Dar es Salaam, where he resides. The problem is not so much the healing ministry as such, but the way he does it. The major accusations against him are the following.

First, his exercises do not fall within the official liturgical practices. The healing ministry should be carried out in a formal way, accepted by the church.

Secondly, Nkwera is accused of using witchcraft in his rituals and of satanism. It is said that he sees all evils, including illness and distress, as the work of Satan, the Evil One.

Thirdly, Nkwera is accused of syncretism and of mixing different concepts. What strikes many observers is that he uses the term *majini*, which is considerably more ambivalent and morally neutral than the *mashetani* of the Christian tradition.[70] However, the term *majini* refers

---

[69] Nkwera estimates that one-third of his followers are Muslims. He urges Muslims to be faithful to their own religion and to go to their mosques on Fridays.

[70] Remember that minimal religion provides a universal code that can be understood by different people in a situation of religious pluralism.

to an Islamic concept. "We Christians do not believe in them", thus the comments.[71]

Fourthly, by his repeated exorcisms he only strengthens the people's fears for evil spirits. Most of his clients suffer from psycho-sociological problems. "We better refer those people to a hospital", it is said.

Finally, Nkwera is accused of establishing a break-away church. The Marian Faith Healing Ministry is considered a separatist movement. What disturbs many parish priests is that the *wanamaombi* cause a polarisation in the parishes by their severe demands (receiving communion on the tongue, while kneeling on the floor).

In spite of (some interpreters say: because of) these accusations his movement expands. The more this priest is discredited, the more his popularity increases. There are Marian Faith Healing Groups all over Tanzania. In East Africa he is well known. Augustine Mrema (former 'minister of the poor') joined a fund-raising charity rally, despite the efforts made by Archbishop Polycarp Pengo of Dar es Salaam to change his mind. He was invited to celebrate the silver jubilee as priest of the famous faith healer Archbishop Emanuel Milingo in Rome (with whom he is in close contact) and in 1988 he met the Pope. Amazingly he attracts all kinds of people, rich and poor, Christian and non-Christian. It has been observed that Arabs and Indians joined his prayer services and brought their sick, some of whom converted to Christianity.

Here, again, the question arises: Why is this so? Why is Nkwera so popular? And why, exactly, is he condemned by the church? What goes on beyond the accusations against him? In the previous sections I stated that the people's motivation for joining charismatic prayer groups is the fear of evil spirits or witches, and the search for protection and healing. Nkwera somehow meets this need. The big attraction in Nkwera's healing ministry is that he takes seriously the existence of evil spirits and witches, while both church officials and modern theologians tend to

[71] Nkwera reacts: "It is not I who mixes these concepts, but the people do. If I want to help the faithful I have to take their language as starting point".

ignore their existence.[72] Priests use to say to possessed women: "Go to the hospital. We Christians do not believe in evil sprits".

The Sukuma, nowadays, might well accept the de-personalised concept of the Devil as an alternative to the Sukuma idea that all evils have a personal cause.[73] It would thus seem reasonable to bring the Devil into open religious consciousness again, as Nkwera does.[74] The fact that the Devil is currently unacceptable to Western theological thinking may not be an adequate reason for rejecting the pastoral usefulness of such an ambiguous and depersonalised concept.[75]

Nkwera's healing ministry is condemned as 'unscientific' and 'pagan' practice (*mambo ya upagani*). Being possessed by and to communicate with spirits are interpreted as symptoms of a mental disease. It does not fit into the Western, modern and scientific medical paradigm. Whereas church officials are expected to be on the spiritual side of reality, they favour Western 'scientific' medicine. It shows how much they are Westernised.

For Africans to hear voices and to get visions is not extra-ordinary, as this is one of the regular ways the ancestors communicated to their descendents. By saying that "we Christians do not believe in evil spirits" the church officials alienate the ordinary faithful from their spiritual heritage. The stress on spiritual healing, as we find it in Marian Faith

---

[72] See Meyer, If you are a Devil, you are a Witch, 102, 120; Beyond Syncretism. Translation and Diabolization in the Appropriation of Protestantism in Africa, in: C. Stewart and R. Shaw (eds.), *Syncretism/Anti-Syncretism, The Politics of Religious Synthesis*, London and New York 1994, 58.

[73] Kirwen, however, interprets the African idea of a personal cause of all evils positively. He sees a growing agreement between modern theological thinking and traditional African thinking in this respect. See M. Kirwen, *The Missionary and the Diviner. Contending Theologies of Christian and African Religions*, Maryknoll, New York 1987, 52.

[74] Of course, care has to be taken as too much emphasis on the work of the Devil may cause fear among ordinary faithful. This exactly is the criticism against Archbishop Milingo. See Shorter, *Jesus and the Witchdoctor*, 190.

[75] The advantage of this concept is that it is only vaguely described in the Bible and thus leaves room for various interpretations. See Meyer, If you are a Devil, you are a Witch, 106, 122.

Healing Groups, may be interpreted, on a deeper level, as an act of liberation in which African Christians free themselves from the pressure to conform to the Europeanisation of the world, dominated by the one-dimensional rationality of Western science and technology.[76]

Within the dominant Western medical paradigm spiritual healing is interpreted as being based on illusion and fantasy, or at best on the *placebo* effect, whereas scientific medicine is considered to be 'real' and 'true'. The conflict between Father Nkwera and the Catholic Church, then, reveals tensions between Europeanisation and Africanisation or between Africanisation 'from above' and Africanisation 'from below', between 'official' and 'popular' religion, 'inculturation' and 'syncretism', between dialogue as nothing more than propagation of the true faith and dialogue as joint searching for healing,[77] between 'elite' thinking and 'everyday' thinking, and ultimately between two model models of truth, one dualistic, the other holistic.

3.5 Epilogue

Contemporary ecumenical missiology understands itself as a hermeneutics of the missionary praxis.[78] For our discussion here this means that missiologists do not have a theory (theology) of religions that can be implemented into the praxis of interreligious dialogue. It is in the praxis of dialogue that a theory of religions emerges. For the missiologist the task remains to investigate if these theories are faithful to the Christian tradition. What then can the experiences of African Christians, in dialogue with their indigenous religions and Islam, teach us in our research into dialogue, truth and truthfulness? What can we learn from syncretism in African Christianity?

---

[76] See Ter Haar, *Spirit of Africa*, 234-235.

[77] Note that in Africa 'healing' is always understood in holistic terms including the integral liberation of the human being within a concrete society.

[78] See T. Sundermeier, Begegnung mit dem Fremden. Plädoyer für eine verstehende Missionswissenschaft, in: *Evangelische Theologie* 50(1990)5, 390-400.

1. For European partners in interreligious dialogue very often the main question is if religious beliefs are true,[79] if realities correspond to them, if thinking is in agreement with being. In my own field work, for example, I was eager to know if the Sukuma understand the spirits literally or symbolically.[80] For the Sukuma Christians the question if religious beliefs are true or not is irrelevant, as this question cannot be answered. For them the main question is not what the spirits are in essence, but what their function is.

Most Sukuma Christians, and indeed most ordinary faithful, do not seek dogmatic precision ('true faith') in their religion, but practical help in time of need.[81] As subsistence farmers they have an utilitarian and pragmatic approach to life. For them, solving every day problems is more important than seeking meaning in life. I doubt if this is different for ordinary faithful in Africa than in Europe.

If our main question in interreligious dialogue is whether religious beliefs are true or not, the danger exists that our view of religion remains too intellectual and that interreligious dialogue remains too much an elite affair.[82] For most ordinary faithful religion is a problem-solving strategy. I do not want to say that this is the best view of religion there is. I only want to say that if missiologists want to do something with the people for their own well-being, they should start from the people's

---

[79] Although most anthropologists claim to be 'methodical agnosticists', they do have certain presuppositions about the 'other world', in an affirmative or negative way, be it explicitly or implicitly. See Platvoet, *Comparing religions*, 8-11.

[80] I refer to the debate between the intellectualist and symbolist approach of religion, as represented in African studies by Robin Horton and Victor Turner. See E. Lawson and R. McCauley, *Rethinking religion. Connecting Cognition and Culture*, Cambridge 1990, 32-45.

[81] See also Droogers, De minimale religiositeit van de meerderheid, 105; Arat, Die nichtamtliche Religiosität als dialogisches Element, 119.

[82] There is interreligious dialogue in various forms and at different levels (popular, pastoral, professional). Here I have the dialogue between church officials and the ordinary believers of other faiths in mind.

everyday thinking.[83] If religion as problem-solving is not taken seriously interreligious dialogue, unless its meaning is limited to an intellectual debate between professionals, will remain irrelevant for the ordinary faithful, a misunderstanding governed by contrasting interests of knowing.[84]

2. In my fieldwork I asked several contrast questions, as is a fad in contemporary anthropology.[85] "Are there only ancestor spirits or are there also other spirits"? The people answered "yes". As I experienced that this was not the right way to ask the question, I separated the questions. "Are there only ancestors spirits"? The answer was "yes". "Are there spirits other than ancestors spirits"? The answer remained "yes". I then formulated my questions as statements and asked: "Which statement is true"? "There are only ancestors spirits". "True!" "There are also non-ancestral spirits". "True!" It drove me crazy sometimes.

In our European understanding of truth, truth is defined by exclusion. For Western people the statements that 'there is one God' and that 'there are many Gods', or that 'there is a God' and 'there is no God', seem a contradiction. If one statement is true the other must be false. Truth is essentially a matter of either-or. When Christianity moved from the Jewish to the Gentile context it inherited a dualistic understanding of truth from the Greek philosophy.[86]

---

[83] See J. Kamstra, Een moeilijke keuze: de godsdienst van de gewone man, in: *Tijdschrift voor Theologie* 20(1980)269.

[84] See D. Sperber and D. Wilson, *Relevance. Communication and Cognition*, Cambridge 1986, 46.

[85] It is presupposed that the meaning of one symbol is its relation to other symbols in the symbolsystem. See Spradley, *The Ethnographic Interview*, 95-99; Spradley, *Participant Observation*, 125.

[86] This Greek-European understanding of truth is the major problem for African Christians, thus S. Kibicho, *The Kikuyu Conception of God, Its Continuity into the Christian Era and the Question it raises for the Christian Idea of Revelation*. Doctoral Dissertation, Nashville 1972, 351-352. See also P. Knitter, *No other name? A Critical Survey of Christian Attitudes Toward the World Religions*, Maryknoll, New York 1985, 31-32, 183, 217-219.

For Africans this is different, as it is for most non-Western peoples.[87] Africans define truth by interrelation, not by exclusion. For them truth is a matter of 'and-and'.[88] Their view of reality is that it is a dynamic union of opposites.[89] What seems a contradiction at one level is a unity at a higher level.[90] As one of my informants said: "Just as all people see the same sun they worship the same God". Basically it is their conviction that 'all peoples have their own religion' and 'all religions are good'.[91] African Christians can teach their European fellow believers a holistic view of truth that enables authentic, thus openended, dialogue.

3. Does this mean that the Sukuma Christians do not grade religions? Yes they do! However, their valuation is not rational, but empirical. This seems to me a very concrete basis for interreligious dialogue. It does not matter where help comes from. If the help works it is good. As a Sukuma proverb says: "I have all kinds of medicines. No one can harm me".

---

[87] The visit of Queen Beatrix of the Netherlands to Indonesia (August, 1995) to celebrate fifty years of independence of this republic was full of misunderstandings because of the different view of truth in Europe and Asia. For example, there were misunderstandings about the date for her to arrive and the place for her to spend her holidays. Whereas the Dutch officials involved in the organisation of the visit wanted unambiguous answers to their questions (yes or no), their Indonesian colleagues gave answers that were flexible (yes and no).

[88] In this sense, the 'new model of truth', which Knitter is looking for, is not so new, as it has existed already in Africa and Asia for a long time. See Knitter, *No other name?*, 217-223.

[89] For example, for Western scholars it remains difficult to understand that blessing and cursing go together and that the healer is to be respected and feared. See Wijsen, *There is Only One God*, 129-130.

[90] "Modern thought has only one level of logic at its disposal, whereas traditional societies are capable of developing an infinite number of them", thus S. Tcherkézoff, *Dual classification reconsidered. Nyamwezi sacred kingship and other examples*, Cambridge 1987, 121-122.

[91] See Healey and Sybertz, *Kamati ya Utafiti*, 307.

There are, of course, serious objections against a pure pragmatic understanding of truth.[92] I do not mean to say that empirical evidence can be the only criterion for truth claims. The African understanding of truth, however, means that there is no truth without empirical evidence.[93] This attitude is profoundly biblical. "By their fruits you will know them" (Matthew 7:16).

Happily, in this respect Christians will get the support of their Muslim neighbours. "To each among you have We prescribed a Law and a Way. If God had willed, He would have made you a single people, but (his plan is) to test you in what he has given you. So strive as in a race in all virtues. The goal of you all is to God; it is He that will show you the truth of the matters in which you dispute" (Sura 5:21).

Here is a task ahead for a pluralistic theology of religions to base its criteriology in the 'fruits of the spirit', as was suggested by Kibicho.[94] If the task of missiology is to make explicit the universal relevance of the Christian faith,[95] it must show evidence that there is life in Christ, moreover "life in all its fullness" (John 10:10).

3.6 Further readings on the anthropology of mission

- E. Nida, *Customs and cultures. Anthropology for Christian Missions*, New York 1954.

---

[92] See H. Küng, What is true religion? Toward an Ecumenical Criteriology, in: L. Swidler (ed.), *Toward a Universal Theology of Religion*, Maryknoll, New York 1987, 232.

[93] As E. Schillebeeckx says: It is not decisive that Christians confess "Jesus is the Lord" but that they show fruits of liberation and reconciliation. See E. Schillebeeckx, Theologie als bevrijdingskunde, in: *Tijdschrift voor Theologie* 24(1984)4, 401. See also Knitter, *No other name?*, 205-206: "to know the truth, one must do it".

[94] S. Kibicho, The Teaching of African Religion in our Schools and Colleges and the Christian Attitude towards this Religion, in: *Africa Theological Journal* 10(1981)3, 29-37.

[95] See G. Collet, Mission und Kommunikation, in: *Zeitschrift für Missionswissenschaft und Religionswissenschaft* 74(1990)1, 14.

- W. Schmidt, *The Origin and Growth of Religion. Facts and theories*, New York 1972.
- W. Smalley (ed.), *Readings in Missionary Anthropology*, Tarrytown 1967.
- D. Whiteman, *Missionaries, anthropologists, and cultural change*, Williamsburg 1983.
- K. Tanner, *Theories of Culture. A new agenda for theology*, Minneapolis 1997.
- W. Urban-Mead and J. Cinnamon (eds.), *Missionaries and Ethnography. Social Sciences and Missions Nr. 19*, Leiden 2006.
- G. Van 't Spijker, Anthropology: a tool for missionary studies. In: K. Bediako et al. (eds.), *A new day dawning*, Zoetermeer 2004, 52-65.

3.7 Questions for better comprehension

1. Explain the term 'missiological anthropology' in your own terms. According to you, should anthropology be practiced from a missiological perspective? Or should anthropology be practiced in its own terms?
2. Comment on the statement, "Anthropologists cannot say anything about the meta-empirical agencies addressed in religion".
3. Ethnographic semantics assumes "that the meaning of one symbol is its relation to other symbols in the symbol system". Can you give an example of how the author uses this principle in analyzing spirit beliefs?
4. Comment on the 'minimal definition of religion' as 'belief in spiritual beings'? Explain the difference between the 'essence' and the 'function' of spirit beliefs in your own words.
5. Why has the term 'syncretism' a negative connotation in missiology? What is the significance of this term for understanding contextualisation of Christianity? According to the author, what

is the difference between communication as ‘propagation’ (of faith) and communication as (interreligious) ‘dialogue'.

Chapter 4 The resurgence of religion in a trans-modern world

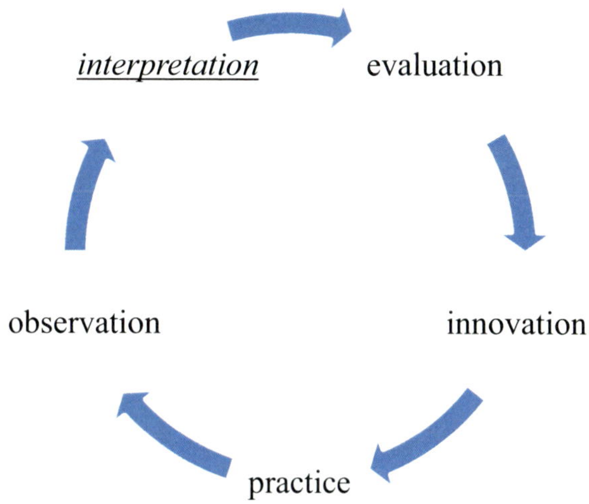

4.1 Introduction

In my book *Seeds of Conflict in a Haven of Peace* about interreligious relations in Africa[1] I made a content analysis of interviews that I conducted with religious leaders and university professors. Asking them about interreligious dialogue in Africa they said: "We Africans do not like dialogue, dialogue is something of the West". Dialogue was associated with relativism and pluralism. "Do not export your problems to Africa", it was said. "We accept the bible as it is". Reacting against relativism and indifferentism my informants said, "If everything is true, nothing is true".

Asking about Africa's tradition of peaceful co-existence, I was told: "People in the West promote peaceful co-existence". But, "There is no tradition of peaceful co-existence in Africa, at least not since the coming of Christ". Referring to Mathew 10:34, an interviewee reminded me of Jesus' words: "I have come to bring not peace but the sword". Ac-

[1] F. Wijsen, *Seeds of conflict in a haven of peace. From religious studies to interreligious studies in Africa*, Amsterdam and New York 2007.

cording to this interviewee, "To accept peaceful co-existence would be to destroy Christian uniqueness and universality, and to accept pluralism and syncretism". Thus "dialogue and Africa don't go together".

"We are uncompromising", I was told. "People in the West do not like our uncompromising views. People in the West say: I am okay, you are okay. But we are not okay. The strong opposition in Africa against the ordination of a homosexual bishop in the Anglican Church is just one example". By giving these quotes I do not want to suggest that they represent the dominant voice in Africa. But they do represent a strong voice.

What struck me in these interviews is the polarity between Africa and the West. "We Africans" are portrayed as "biblical" and "uncompromising", and pluralism and relativism are associated with "the West". To Westerners pluralism and relativism are consequences of modernity. Thus I came to understand that the interpretation of modernity is a stumbling block not only in the relation between Christians and non-Christians, but also in the relation between Western and non-Western Christians.

Some colleagues avoid terms such as 'non-Christian' or 'non-Western' because of their negative overtones. They prefer to speak about 'believers of other faiths' and 'world Christianity'. Although I see the point they want to make, I nevertheless keep the prefix 'non' to show the polemical character of the debate. In this chapter I aim to explore further the role of the 'values of modernity' and consequently the 'heritage of Enlightenment' in intra- and interreligious dialogue. The question that will be dealt with is how the interpretation of modernity influences the relation between Northern and Southern Christians, and between Christians and Muslims.

This chapter has seven sections. First we acquire insight into what modernity is, when it started and how it came about. Then we will explore how colonisation and Christianisation were connected with modernisation and Westernisation. Thereafter we will show how the decolonisation process went together with anti-Western and anti-Christian sentiments, and how these sentiments continue in the present-day spiritual decolonisation in Christianity and Islam. Next I will give a re-interpretation of modernity, and we will end by offering an alternative framework for analysis and interpretation.

4.2 Modernisation as Europeanisation

Let me first try to clarify what modernity is, when it started and how it came about. There are innumerable studies of what modernity is. Here I will limit myself to the reception of the modernisation debate in Africa. Probably the better question is not what is modernity, but how do we encounter it? I presume that most people who have lived in East Africa for some time can give many examples of how they encounter the *kijadi* and *kisasa* opposition in everyday conversations: The use of modern medicine instead of traditional herbs, the use of fertiliser and genetic manipulation instead of indigenous agriculture, the use of condoms instead of traditional contraceptives.

As is obvious in the given examples they imply the application of science and technology and an industrialised way of production. Indeed, "a modern or modernised society is a technically advanced industrial society", thus the Ghanaian philosopher Kwame Gykye.[2] In his book *Tradition and Modernity*, this philosopher gives a perfect analysis of the characteristics of modernity, and it is not necessary to repeat his analysis here in detail. It suffices to say that according to Gyekye, industrialisation led to concentration of job opportunities in specific centres and thus to urbanisation. Industrialisation and urbanisation in their turn destroyed the pre-modern communalism and generated individualism. The application of science and technology moreover led to an emphasis on instrumental rationality and materialism. And last but not least, instrumental rationality led to a marginalisation of the mysteries of faith and to a relegation of religion to the private sphere.[3]

---

[2] K. Gyekye, *Tradition and modernity. Philosophical reflections on African experience*, New York and Oxford 1997, 274.
[3] Gyekye, *Tradition and modernity*, 273-281.

In short, "Besides the advanced forms of science and technology developed by Western modernity, urbanism, individualism, the ascendancy of reason, the emergence of nation-state secularism and the relegation of religion to the private sphere of life – these, and others related to them, are among the central characteristics of Western modernity".[4]

More important than the material conditions are the specific worldview and lifestyle that are connected with modernity, in short, the shift from fate to choice.[5] In modern societies, nothing is simply taken for granted but everything is optional. Rather than a choice between being married or not being married, a modern person can choose between various forms of marriage. The modern person can choose to practice new religions instead of the older or traditional ones, or choose not to practice a religion at all. Modern people do not 'get' children but 'take' children. They are no longer born as a Christian or Muslim, but they may choose to become one.

In every-day language, a 'modern' person is a 'progressive' person in the sense that he or she beliefs in progress, the conviction that in principle all problems are solvable and all things are makable and changeable. One can even choose to change from male to female personality. As Gyekye says, "The cultivation of the innovative spirit or outlook is the most outstanding feature of the notion of modernity: it can be said to define modernity".[6] Used in this sense, a progressive person is contrasted with a conservative person, a person who is reluctant to great or sudden changes.

As to the questions when modernisation started and how it came about most scholars assume that the shift from medieval to modern society started with the shift from a predominantly agricultural to a predominantly industrialised society. When Gyekye says that the most outstanding feature of modernity is industrialisation, he assumes that

---

[4] Gyekye, *Tradition and modernity*, 275.

[5] P. Berger, *The heretical imperative. Contemporary possibilities of religious affirmation*, New York 1980, 15, 30.

[6] Gyekye, *Tradition and modernity*, 280.

modernisation started with the Industrial Revolution.[7] This revolution was made possible by the Scottish Enlightenment with its empirism.

In his *The Challenge of Modernity in Africa*, the French Missionary of Africa and psychology professor at the University of Dar es Salaam, Bernard Joinet mentions six characteristics of modernity, namely industry and technology, global free market, the scientific mind, secularism, democracy and individualisation, and – as a Frenchman – he relates these characteristics to the French Revolution and the French Enlightenment with its rationalism.[8]

Whatever the real root is, and it is safe to assume that there was not one root but that there were many roots, as also the Protestant Reformation is to be mentioned with its specific work ethos and stress on individuality as already Max Weber noted,[9] both enlightenments claimed the autonomy of the human person versus the authority of Gods Word.[10] This observation is crucial in my answer to the question how the interpretation of modernity influences the relation between Northern and Southern Christians, and between Christians and Muslims.

In his *Transforming Mission*, the South African missiologist David Bosch mentions seven characteristics of the Enlightenment and I shall mention them briefly.[11] First there is the belief that all people are gifted with reason and that reason is the starting point for proper knowledge. Secondly there is the separation of subject and object by which the animal, mineral and human world become objects of analysis and research. Third the introduction of direct causality comes and the elimination of purpose in science as a clue to understanding reality by which effects become predictable. As the fourth characteristic follows the belief in progress and the trust that people have the will and the ability to make the world better; consequently there is a desire to spread

---

[7] Gyekye, *Tradition and modernity*, 274.

[8] B. Joinet, *The challenge of modernity in Africa*, Nairobi 2000, 17.

[9] Berger, *The heretical imperative*, 52.

[10] D. Bosch, *Transforming mission. Paradigm shifts in theology of mission*, Maryknoll, New York 1991, 263.

[11] Bosch, *Transforming mission*, 264-267.

wealth to less advanced territories. The fifth characteristic is the contention that knowledge is true when it is based on facts; values are not based on knowledge but on opinion, belief. Sixth is the belief that in principle all problems are solvable and that the world, the human being and societies are makable. Lastly, the seventh characteristic is the trust in emancipated, rational and autonomous human beings; progress of humankind is assured by free competition of individuals.

In his book *The Invention of the Americas*, the Mexican philosopher Enrique Dussel says that modernity started in 1492 when Europe discovered the 'new' world and 'invented' the Others. This marked a shift of the centre of global power from the Muslim world to the Western world which marginalised the rest of the world to the periphery.[12] Dussel's work is not uncontested. Nevertheless I will borrow his concept of 'trans-modernity' later. For now it is important to add that the 'discovery' of the 'new' world was prepared by the changed world views and new navigation technologies in Europe in the later Middle Ages.[13]

From the previous considerations it is clear that "Modernity emerged and developed in Western European cultures and societies".[14] The meaning of the word 'modern' is therefore identical to the term 'Western'.[15] "Modernization, according to many scholars, means 'westernization' – taking on the values, ideas and institutions (political, economic, technological, etc.) of the West", says Gyekye.[16] Indeed, it is safe to assume that to most people, certainly in East Africa, *kisasa* and *kizungu* are identical. And this is another factor in my answer to the question how the interpretation of modernity influences the relation between Northern and Southern Christians, and between Christians and Muslims.

---

[12] E. Dussel, *The Invention of the Americas. Eclipse of 'Other' and the Myth of Modernity*, New York 1995, 12.
[13] Bosch, *Transforming mission*, 262.
[14] Gyekye, *Tradition and modernity*, 275.
[15] S. Hall, The West and the rest. Discourse and power, in: S. Hall and B. Gieben (eds.), *Formations of modernity*, Cambridge 1992, 277.
[16] Gyekye, *Tradition and modernity*, 274.

Bernard Joinet and Aylward Shorter, also a Missionary of Africa, tend to interpret (Christian) 'fundamentalist sects' and 'Islamic revivalism' as anti-modern and anti-Western.[17] By doing so these 'new religious movements' become part of the 'Clash of Civilisations' rethoric in which 'the rest' of the world is opposed 'the West'.[18] There is a remnant of the secularisation theory in this interpretation. As is well-known, secularisation theorists hold that the modern world will increasingly become a secular place. Thus, you are either a 'modern' person, thus a rational being; and consequently you are irreligious or you practice a form of religiosity that is highly secularised. Or you are a religious person, thus irrational, and consequently you are pre- or anti-modern. From this perspective, the 'global resurgence of religion' appears necessarily as anti-modern and anti-Western.[19] But as I hope to show, the resurgence of religion may be anti-Western, but not necessarily anti-modern.

4.3 Christianisation and modernisation

According to Hall and Dussel the notion of modernity is closely related to the European expansion in the world.[20] Enlightenment and modernisation brought a belief in progress and development, by means of science and technology, also for the new territories that had been discovered and explored since the 15th century onwards.[21]

However we interpret the history of colonisation, and undoubtedly conversations about colonisation and its present form of globalisation always lead to heated debates and mutual accusations between those

---

[17] Joinet, *The challenge of modernity*; A. Shorter, Secularism and emerging religious movements, in: J. Mugambi and M. Getui (eds.), *Religions in Eastern Africa under globalization*, Nairobi 2004.

[18] S. Huntington, *The clash of civilizations and the remaking of the world order*, New York 1996; P. Jenkins, *The next Christendom*, New York 2002.

[19] S. Thomas, *The global resurgence of religion and the transformation of international relations*, New York 2005.

[20] Hall, The West and the rest; Dussel, *The Invention of the Americas*.

[21] Bosch, *Transforming mission*, 265.

who see colonised people as only victims and those who see them also as agents,[22] apart from the interest in spices and raw materials that were needed for the expanding markets in Europe there was also an interest to bring a better quality of life to the less advanced territories in the world; and of course, 'better quality' was what West Europeans and North Americans considered to be 'normal': economic growth and modernisation through education and health care, science and technology. Thus in many cases colonisation meant modernisation, assimilation to European worldviews and lifestyles. In short, modernisation was Westernisation and Europeanisation.

If we look at 19th- and 20th-century mission history we clearly see that Christianisation and modernisation were equated. Even today, if we ask for 'the mission' in Africa (an anachronism, but still widely used) we are most likely to be shown first a school, a hospital and community hall and then a church. In many cases, conversion to Christianity meant embracing progress, economic growth, development and civilisation. And of course, civilisation was defined in terms of what was accepted as normal in Europe.

As such, 19th- and 20th-century mission differed largely from 15th- and 16th-century mission. To a large extent, the latter was an initiation into the mysteries of the Christian faith. What was brought to the non-Christian countries was the Church that the Spanish and Portuguese priests were accustomed to: a church of catechism and sacraments. In their understanding it was the salvation of the individual soul that mattered. The European and the African at that time had much in common. They shared a pre-modern, pre-Enlightenment world view.[23]

19th- and 20th-century mission was quite different. It was a mission after the great revolutions in Europe.[24] The Industrial Revolution

---

[22] M. Amaladoss (ed.), *Globalization and its victims as seen by its victims*, Delhi 1999; P. Kanyandago (ed.), *Marginalized Africa. An international perspective*, Nairobi 2002.

[23] A. Hastings, *The Church in Africa. 1450-1959*, Oxford 1994, 73-77.

[24] L. Malishi, *Introduction to the history of Christianity in Africa*, Tabora 1987, 104-105.

brought the belief in progress and development, and the French Revolution brought the ideals of freedom, equality and brotherhood. In this sense, 19th- and 20th-century mission was a mission of social works rather than of religious socialisation. Mission and modernisation was one and the same thing: bringing Christianity, civilisation and commerce.

4.4 Christianisation 'from below'

When the decolonisation process started it was to a large extent anti-Western and anti-Christian. And this process did not start only in the 1950s. Ever since the West started to penetrate in the rest of the World there have been anti-Western and anti-Christian sentiments. Already in 1938 the Dutch missiologist Hendrik Kraemer wrote in his *The Christian message in a non-Christian World*: "The Western penetration was in the nineteenth century an expression of the Western hegemony in the affairs of the world. During that period the East reacted to it either with sullenness or with eager enthusiasm ... Both attitudes were essentially reactions in the passive sense of the word … The great change that has come in the twentieth century is that the victims have become actors. Mainly passive impulsive reaction has become conscious action".[25] As far as we know, he was the first theologian to speak about a 'dialogue' between world cultures and world religions.[26]

Early examples of anti-Christian sentiments are the Ramakrishna mission in India, the Muhammadiya movement in Indonesia and the Muslim Brothers in Egypt. Most post-independence governments who took over from colonial rulers in Asia and Africa were based on secular-nationalist ideologies, such as Kwame Nkrumah's consciencism, Kenneth Kaunda's humanism, and Julius Nyrere's socialism, though not necessarily anti-religious.

---

[25] H. Kraemer, *The Christian message in a Non-Christian world*, London 1938, 20.

[26] H. Kraemer, *World cultures and world religions: The coming dialogue*, London 1960.

Ever since Christianity entered the non-Christian nations there was a Christianisation from below. The indigenous peoples of Southern and Central America accepted Christianity, but interpreted its message in their own terms. And so did the indigenous people of Africa and Asia.[27] The early African Instituted Churches were protests against the Europeanisation of Africa. Whereas the mission churches forced their converts to abandon African beliefs and practices, the African Instituted Churches did not. They claimed that one could be truly African and authentically Christian at the same time.

The experiment of African socialism in Tanzania was complex, but it claimed that it was based on African roots, *ujamaa* or familyhood. And one factor in the Marian Faith Healing Ministry in Tanzania is that it is a protest "against the dominant secularised explanations of mission Roman Catholicism".[28] In his *Transforming Mission*, David Bosch therefore spoke in his chapter on mission in the post-colonial era as 'post-modern' mission, a term which he replaced by 'ecumenical' in subsequent chapters.[29] Later I will argue that 'trans-modern' is a better term.

4.5 Ongoing spiritual de-colonisation

This process continues in the world today. After the political decolonisation comes the spiritual de-colonisation. A case in point is the ongoing debate about homosexuality in the Anglican Church that was referred to in the beginning of this chapter. In his book *The Next Christendom*, Philip Jenkins bluntly says: "Anti-gay rhetoric combines with anti-Western and anti-imperialist activism".[30]

---

[27] Jenkins, *The next Christendom*.

[28] C. Comoro and J. Sivalon, The Marian Faith Healing Ministry, in: T. Spear and I. Kimambo (eds.), *East African Expressions of Christianity*, Nairobi 1999, 277.

[29] Bosch, *Transforming mission*, 349.

[30] Jenkins, *The next Christendom*, 201.

It is well known that the centre of gravity of Christianity moved to the global south. In the beginning of the 20th century two-thirds of all Christians lived in Europe and North America. In the beginning of the 21st century two thirds of all Christians lived in the southern hemisphere. And this shift will continue. By the year 2050, 80% of all Christians will live in the global south. And again half of the remaining 20% of all Christians in the North are of non-Western descent, as can already be seen in the United States of America where 50% of the Roman Catholics are Latinos.

It goes without saying that the demographic shift goes together with a cultural shift. In the book *Global Christianity. Contested Claims* that I edited with Robert Schreiter,[31] Philip Jenkins writes that "we can reasonably say that many global South Christians are far more conservative in terms of both beliefs and moral teaching than are the mainstream churches of the global North, and this is especially true in Africa".[32] And he continues, "The churches that have made most dramatic progress in the global South have either been Roman Catholic of a traditional and fideistic kind, or radical Protestant sects, evangelical or Pentecostal".

"Global South Christians retain a very strong supernatural orientation, and are by and large far more interested in personal salvation than in radical politics", says Jenkins. And "These newer churches preach deep personal faith and communal orthodoxy, mysticism and puritanism, all founded in clear scriptural authority".[33] The contrast with the autonomy of the human person, which is seen as the hallmark of modernity as we showed before, is evident.

Thus we can clearly see that within World Christianity there is a struggle about what is called the 'heritage of Enlightenment' and the 'values of modernity' between Northern and Southern Christians.

---

[31] F. Wijsen and R. Schreiter (eds.), *Global Christianity. Contested claims*, Amsterdam and New York 2007.

[32] P. Jenkins, Christianity moves South, in: F. Wijsen and R. Schreiter (eds.), *Global Christianity. Contested claims*, Amsterdam and New York 2007, 18.

[33] Jenkins, Christianity moves South, 19.

While issues such as freedom of religion, acceptance of homosexuality, abortion and euthanasia, separation of church and state, equality of men and women, legalisation of soft drugs, single sex marriages and prostitution accepted as 'normal' by many of not most 'Northerners', for many 'Southerners' these issues are 'not normal'.

4.6 Muslim-Christian relations

We can see a close parallel between developments in Christianity and in Islam. If there is a resurgence of religion, as some scholars of religion state, this resurgence seems anti-Western and anti-modern, both in Christianity and Islam as Joinet and others suggest.[34]

The resurgence of religion and new religious movements is often interpreted as a critique on or alternative to neo-liberal and western-type modernisation processes. But the picture is more complex. In his book *Islam between globalisation and counter-terrorism*, Ali Mazrui distinguishes three schools of thought within Islam: Orthodox Islam, Modernist Islam and Liberal Islam.[35]

Orthodox Islam is literalist in its interpretation of the Qur'an and the Sunnah, ritualistic in its observations, traditionalist in gender relations, and is reluctant to accept other cultures and religions. Modernist Islam tries to bring Islam closer to science and technology. It puts less emphasis on Islamic rituals and more emphasis on Islamic rationalism. Traditional beliefs about *Iblis* and *jinns*, angels and Paradise are interpreted metaphorically rather than literally. Modernists stress that there is no compulsion in Islam and do not eschew collaboration with believers of other faiths. Liberal Islam is less concerned with updating Islam intellectually and more with updating Islam ethically. Islamic liberalism is anxious that Muslim women be treated as equals, that amputation of hands of thieves are relics of the past and that death penalty be

---

[34] Joinet, *The challenge of modernity*, 5; Thomas, *The global resurgence*, 10-11.

[35] A. Mazrui, *Islam between globalization and counter-terrorism*, Oxford 2006, 303-304.

either abolished completely or be limited to offences such as first degree murder.

Thus, just as there is not one Christianity, there is not one Islam. Christianity and Islam do not exist, at least they do not exist in the reified and essentialist way scholars of religion usually conceptualised them. This was already the message of Wilfred Cantwell Smith in his *The meaning and end of religion.*[36] What exists is a plurality of local and contextual interpretations of Christians and Muslims about the sources and teachings of their beliefs. In the same way we have to be very careful with container concepts such as 'Northerners' and 'Southerners', 'Westerners' and 'non-Westerners'. *The* Northerner and *the* Southerner simply do not exist, except between the ears of the analyst. This is the main critique on Samuel Huntington and – in his footsteps – Philip Jenkins.[37]

It is important to note that modernisation of Islam has existed for a long time. Mazrui refers to Ibn Khaldun in the fourteenth century, the Tunesian who is widely regarded as the founding father of modern social science. The macro-historian Arnold Toynbee considers Ibn Khaldun's book *al-Muqaddimah* as "the greatest work of its kind that has ever been created by any mind in any time or place".[38]

In the Golden Age of Islamic Civilisation there was no conflict between health science and traditional medicine in the Qur'an and Arabs were far ahead of Europeans as far as science and technology are concerned. Europeans copied the sciences from the Arabs. There are various Qur'anic verses that praise faithful seekers of knowledge. Thus, if it is suggested that Islam and secular rationality are incompatible, history clearly shows that this is a misconception.[39]

---

[36] W.C. Smith, *The meaning and end of religion. An approach to the religious traditions of mankind*, New York 1963.

[37] Huntington, *The clash of civilizations*; Jenkins, *The next Christendom.*

[38] Mazrui, *Islam between globalization and counter-terrorism*, 126-127.

[39] Z. Bagir, Islam, science and 'Islamic science', in: Z. Bagir (ed.), *Science and religion in a post-colonial World. Interfaith Perspectives*, Hindmarsh 2005, 37-61.

Also the suggestion that, better than Islam, Christianity succeeds in coping with modernity is a misconception. The homosexuality debate in the Anglican Church, the debate on contraceptives in the Roman Catholic Church and the debate on scriptural authority between Evangelicals and Ecumenicals in the Protestant Churches, clearly show that Christianity always has had an ambiguous relation with modernity till today.

In September 2007 it was exactly hundred years ago that Pope Pius X in his encyclical *Pascendi Dominici Grecis* of 8 September 1907 started his fight against modernism, especially against modern bible reading. And although the modern bible reading has been gradually accepted by the Roman Catholic Church, first by Pope Pius XII in his Encyclical *Divino Afflante Spiritus* of 30 September 1943 and later by the Second Vatican Council in its Constitution *Dei Verbum* of 18 November 1965, in his book *Jesus of Nazareth* the present pope Benedict XVI is critical about it, and with him millions of Charismatic, Evangelical and Pentecostal Christians who stick to the verbal inspiration and literal truth of the Bible.

I was reminded of the struggle against modernity by the magisterium of the Roman Catholic Church in Hamza Njozi's book on the *Mwembechai killings and the political future of Tanzania*. If Roman Catholics accuse Muslims of violating freedom of speech in Islam, Appendix 1 refers them to the investigations against "the most distinguished and intelligent theologians in the Church today".[40] Appendix 1 mentions explicitly Dr. Hans Küng and Fr. Edward Schillebeeckx, who is professor-emeritus of the university in which I hold a chair now. According to the Appendix, these investigations go back to the Holy Inquisition. And he calls the head of the Congregation for the Doctrine of Faith who was responsible for these investigations "the Church's modern day Grand Inquisitor".[41] Njozi's book is contested, among others by Lawrence

---

[40] H. Njozi, *Mwembechai killings and the political future of Tanzania*, Ottawa 2000, 192-193.

[41] Njozi, *Mwembechai killings*, 192.

Mbogoni,[42] but as far as the struggle against modernity and freedom of speech in the Roman Catholic Church are concerned, he has a point.

Going back to the Holy Scriptures would not help us either. Of course, one can find many verses in the Qur'an that can be interpreted as unfriendly against women, homosexuals or believers of other faiths. Apart from the fact that these texts are interpreted in a more humane way, even by Muslims who adhere to the more orthodox schools of thought, what about the polemics against the Jews in the New Testament? And what about the position of women and homosexuals in the Old Testament? This type of 'comparative religion', quite popular in certain Islamic and Christian circles, is not a way forward, as John Hick concluded in his essay *Comparing Religions*.[43]

In his book *Islam between globalisation and counter-terrorism*, Ali Mazrui argues that never before in world history Christians and Muslims have been so close.[44] When we look at global trends over the last hundred years there has been a convergence of mainstream Christianity and Islam.

Local Muslims may not always know where to draw the line between anti-Western and anti-Christian, henceforth there are tensions between Christians and Muslims in Egypt, Nigeria or Indonesia, says Mazrui.[45] But on a global level, Muslims and Christians are allies. They fight a struggle not against each other, but with each other against the 'evils of the West'. Thus, Muslim militants are neither anti-Christian nor anti-modern, but anti-Western. The 11 September 2001 attacks did not target a religious centre but the icons of economic and political power.

'The West' here stands for values such as secularism, materialism, individualism and liberalism.[46] Western societies are seen as a godless

---

[42] L. Mbogoni, *The cross versus the crescent. Religion and politics in Tanzania from the 1880s to the 1990s*, Dar es Salaam 2004.
[43] J. Hick, On grading religions, in: *Religious studies* 7(1981), 451-467.
[44] Mazrui, *Islam between globalization and counter-terrorism*, 224.
[45] Mazrui, *Islam between globalization and counter-terrorism*, 224.
[46] Mazrui, *Islam between globalization and counter-terrorism*, 236.

and lawless, filled with all kinds of degradation and evil: pornography, drug addiction, gambling, abortion, homosexuality, birth control, hiv/aids, divorce, single parent families, pre-marital sex, etc.[47] 'Orientalism' seems to have been replaced by 'Occidentalism',[48] but this debate goes far beyond the scope of this chapter.

4.7 Re-interpretation of modernity

The interpretation of modernity by Joinet and Shorter,[49] for whom 'consumer materialism' is an important if not the dominant factor in new religious movements, seems quite monolithic. Investigating the relation between religion and modernity, modernity is the independent variable and just as the secularisation theorists they investigate 'possibilities of religious affirmation' in the modern world.[50] Modernity is interpreted as an irreversible and worldwide process. So, modernity "is here to stay",[51] "we have to face it" and "to accept it as a fact".[52]

But, is there also a reverse? Is there an influence of religion on modernity? In his book *The Clash of Civilizations*, Samuel Huntington answers in the affirmative.[53] We can note that new religious movements that do well in terms of growth, at least in Africa, are those that are in some way critical of Western-type modernisation processes. In this respect one can agree with Scott Thomas in his book *The Global Resurgence of Religion and the Transformation of International Relations*.[54] But the picture is more complex. We must take into account that these new religious movements are not only reactions against modernity but

---

[47] Joinet, *The challenge of modernity*, 11.
[48] I. Burama and A. Margalit, *Occidentalism. The West in the eyes of its enemies*, New York 2004.
[49] Joinet, *The challenge of modernity*; Shorter, Secularism and emerging religious movements.
[50] Berger, *The heretical imperative*.
[51] Joinet, *The challenge of modernity*, 29.
[52] Joinet, *The challenge of modernity*, 49.
[53] Huntington, *The clash of civilizations*.
[54] Thomas, *The global resurgence of religion*.

also products and manifestations of modernity or different ways of being modern. The new religious movements, "even those commonly known as fundamentalist", are modern not only in their methods, e.g., the use of information and communication technologies, but also in the way they set their goals, says Grace Davie.[55] According to Davie, the notion of 'multiple modernities' might be helpful to grasp the complex realities in our present-day world.

Of course we must not exaggerate. But if "The cultivation of the *innovative spirit* or outlook is the most outstanding feature of the notion of modernity" and even "can be said to define modernity", as Gyekye says, we can see this spirit in the new religious movements, both in Christianity and Islam.[56] Whether something is seen as innovative and progressive or conservative and traditional depends on ones standpoint in history. Those who stick to nationalist secularism are seen as conservatists by 'born again' Christians. They see 'liberals' and 'secularists' as people who long back to 'the good old 1960s', which are often associated with dictatorial and corrupt regimes by colonised and oppressed peoples. There is a hankering for spiritual and social renewal in some of the new religious movements. Being 'born again' is a metaphor for being liberated from suffering and liberated to a radical new and better quality of life.

The link between modernisation and Westernisation is conceptual not empirical, says Gyekye.[57] Some of the so called 'Asian tigers' are modernised societies in the sense of industrialised and urbanised without becoming Westernised in the sense of secular, liberal and individualistic. Thus modernisation cannot simply be equated with Westernisation. Possibly in the same way South African *Ubuntu* management could be interpreted as a form of modernisation based on Africa's community spirit.[58]

---

[55] G. Davie, *Europe: The Exceptional Case. Parameters of Faith in the Modern World*, London 2002, 158-159.
[56] Gyekye, *Tradition and modernity*, 280.
[57] Gyekye, *Tradition and modernity*, 274.
[58] L. Mbigi, *Ubuntu. The African dream in management*, Randburg 1997.

Also in the Western world there are philosophers who advocate a restoration of communal values and who say that reason and religion are not incompatible. Science and technology are no longer only seen as obstacles to religion but also as sources of a new spirituality. In post-modern and post-secular holism it is accepted that the more we know about the natural and social worlds, the less we understand them. Matter and mind are no longer separated and the source of life force is no longer seen as only meta-physical but also as physical.[59]

4.8 An alternative analytic framework

Analysing and interpreting Christianity and Islam in the present-day world we need a different frame of reference than the modernisation and secularisation models offer. New religious or spiritual movements in Islam and Christianity may be interpreted as anti-Western, but not necessarily anti-modern. If there is a clash of civilisations is not a clash between tradition and modernity, but between different forms of modernity, both in Islam and Christianity.

We can link the struggle about the 'values of modernity' with a pre-modern, a modern, a post-modern and a trans-modern model for analysis and interpretation. I use the term model here in harmony with Clifford Geertz as model of and model for.[60] The way forward as I see it is not a nostalgic return to pre-modern values of those embrace traditional or indigenous cultures uncritically; not a naïve continuation of the claim of universal validity of the values of modernity; not a post-modern relativism in which it is no longer possible to determine which values are good or bad.

---

[59] C. Du Toit, Secular spirituality versus secular dualism, in: C. du Toit and F. Mayson (eds.), *Secular spirituality as a contextual critique of religion*, Pretoria 2006, 58-61.

[60] C. Geertz, *The interpretation of cultures*, London 1993.

The way forward as I see it is a trans-modern search for a new or concrete universalism.[61] Concrete universalism refers to a value or practice created in or by a specific culture that by reason of historical significance, interaction and cooperation, is embraced by other peoples and cultures and finally is accepted by all.[62] That this search is not an easy one is shown by the debate on the Universal Declaration of Human Rights, and the alternatives to it, e.g., the African Charter on Human and Peoples' Rights and the Universal Declaration of Human Rights in Islam.

Trans-modernism is a shift from the universalism of modernism over the fragmentation of post-modernism to a new order of society. Its main theorist, Enrique Dussel, is a philosopher 'from the periphery'. Thus, trans-modernism is not indifferent, but anti-imperialist in the sense that it has a preference for peripheral voices of marginalised social groups or ethnic minorities.

Trans-modernism is best understood in contrast to post-modernism. Post-modernism is the ultimate consequence of modernity and as such a radical opposition to tradition. Trans-modernity is a transformation of modernity using the resources of tradition. Trans-modernists are fed up with 'old' interpretations of modernity that did not bring the peace and prosperity that they promised to the colonised peoples. They use their respective traditions to build up a better quality of life, to move beyond narrow-minded interpretations of modernity to new societies where solidarity and consensus rule over European understandings of development and democracy, where the dignity of the human persons have priority over their liberty.[63]

Therefore, in the research on Muslim-Christian relations in East Africa that my co-workers and I are presently doing we ask how Muslim

---

[61] A. Krieger, *The new universalism. Foundations for a global theology*, Maryknoll, New York 1991.

[62] A. Tarimo, *Human rights, cultural differences and the church in Africa*, Morogoro 2004, 28-29.

[63] Z. Sardar, *Postmodernism and the Other. The new imperialism of Western culture*, London 1997.

voices are suppressed by the dominant nationalist-secular ideologies of national unity; and how some Muslim and Christian groups reclaim their religious identity: their religion may be interpreted as their way of being modern.

4.9 Conclusion

In this chapter we aimed to explore the issue of modernity in intra- and interreligious interaction and we asked how the interpretation of modernity influences the relation between Northern and Southern Christians, and between Christians and Muslims. We showed that there is an intra- and interreligious struggle over the so called 'heritage of Enlightenment', and that this struggle is worthwhile, necessary and inevitable. We can overcome the 'clash of civilisations' or 'the West and the rest' rhetoric that goes together with this struggle if the 'resurgence of religion' in Christianity *and* Islam is interpreted from the framework of 'trans-modernity'. Then new religious movements, and even some forms of fundamentalism, are not necessarily seen as pre- or anti-modern, but as different ways of being modern, hankering to overcome the limitations and false promises of free-market economy and multi-party politics that is imposed on the 'two-thirds world' by European modernity.

4.10 Further readings on the history of mission

- S. Bevans, *A century of Catholic mission*, Oxford 2013.
- W. Bühlmann, *The coming of the third church. An analysis of the present and the future of the church*, Maryknoll, New York 1978.
- D. Robert, *Christian mission. How Christianity became a world religion*, Malden 2009.
- L. Sanneh, *Disciples of all nations. Pillars of world Christianity*, Oxford 2008.

- A. Van Leeuwen, *Christianity in world history. The meeting of the faiths of East and West*, London 1960.

4.11 Questions for better comprehension

1. Give a definition of modernisation in your own words. According to you, what are the most important characteristics of modernisation?
2. What is the relation between modernisation and Europeanisation? What do we mean by the notion of ‘multiple modernities’?
3. In your opinion, have Christianisation and Europeanisation been equated in mission history?
4. Can you explain why the present religious revival and even extremism can be interpreted as a spiritual de-colonisation process?
5. According to you, is modernisation a European process? What does the author mean by mean by trans-modernity?

Chapter 5 African Christianity, syncretism or inculturation?

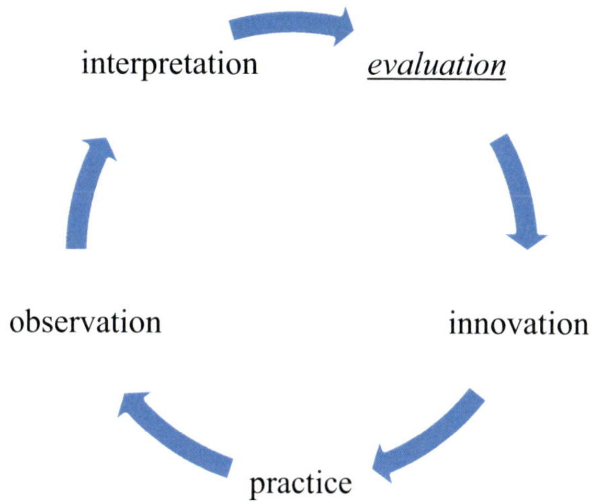

5.1 Introduction

Before the Second Vatican Council the Catholic Church in East Africa was ahead in issues as developing a participative liturgy, an adapted catechesis, democratic models of church and new forms of lay apostolate.[1] According to several observers the spirit of renewal in East Africa got stuck shortly after the council. The Catholic Church in East Africa "has almost no programme for change or advance. Its bishops are cautiously anxious to displease neiter local politicians nor the Roman Curia", thus Hastings.[2] In this chapter I wish to describe an exper-

---

[1] The 'African Ecclesiastical Review', edited from the seminary of Katigondo (Uganda), the 'Pastoral Istitute of Eastern Africa' at Gaba (Uganda) and the 'Social Training Centre' at Nyegezi (Tanzania) may serve as examples.

[2] A. Hastings, *African Catholicism. Essays in Discovery*, London 1989, 136; see also E. Hillman, *Many paths. A Catholic approach to religious pluralism*, Maryknoll, New York 1989; R. Mosha, The prophetic role of the Church in Tanzania today, in: L. Magesa (ed.), *The prophetic role of the Church in Tanzania today. Spearhead 115*, Eldoret 1991, 13-32; L. Magesa, The Church in

iment in inculturation in Usukuma,[3] to analyse and evaluate the obstacles this experiment encountered in pastoral and theological circles, and to show what can be learned from this in building-up a new church for the third millennium.

5.2 An experiment in inculturation

Inspired by Joseph Blomjous, one-time Bishop of the (Catholic) Diocese of Mwanza and initiator of the Africanisation of Christianity in East Africa,[4] and with the help of the St. Cecilia Group, David Clément, a White Father and the parish priest of Bujora Parish, started to 'adapt' the Catholic Liturgy to the culture of the Sukuma people in Bujora, 18 kilometers East of Mwanza, in 1954.[5] In the beginning the aim was to translate the existing Catholic hymns and chants into the local language using local melodies and rhythms. Soon new songs were being composed. Later this led to the composition of biblical plays in the African manner.

From the performance of these plays it became apparent that music is not the only medium that can be used in the Africanisation of Christianity. In 1961 some members of the St. Cecilia Group, under the guidance of Father Clément and his religious superior Father Jan Hen-

Eastern Africa, in: A. Radoli (ed.), *How local is the local Church? Spearhead 126-128*, Eldoret 1993, 3-35.

[3] I worked as a missionary in Usukuma (Sukumaland) between 1984 and 1985 and again between 1986 and 1987. Since then I conducted various long periods of fieldwork in Usukuma up to the pesent. Usukuma is situated in North-west Tanzania, South of Lake Victoria.

[4] J. Blomjous, Development in Mission Thinking and Practice, 1959-1980. Inculturation and Interculturation, in: *African Ecclesial Review* 22(1980)6, 293-298.

[5] The Sukuma people inhabit the area referred to as Usukuma. They number about six million and mainly live from small-scale agriculture. Most Sukuma people adhere to the indigenous religion (85%). Some 10% of the population are Catholic, some 3% are Protestant and some 2% are Muslim.

driks, formed the 'Sukuma Research Committee'.[6] Its members started to collect information about herbs and healing methods used in local medicine. Later they began collecting articles used by chiefs and local healers. What had started from a pure religious interest developed into an exercise that embraced all aspects of the Sukuma culture. This is how the 'Sukuma Museum' started, which is according to Hudson one of the 'Museums of influence' in the world.[7] "The primary aim of the centre has been, and still is, first to adapt Christian liturgy to the culture and traditions of Tanzanians; second, to help to develop people's own natural resources for human developent".[8] As time went on, the view of the Africanisation of Christianity evolved from 'adaptation' to 'inculturation'.

At present, the members of the Sukuma Research Committee assume a positive outlook on Sukuma culture, including its religion. In their book *Imani za jadi za kisukuma* they remind the reader of Abraham who recognised that his king Melchizedek was not a pagan but that he believed in the one God who is creator of everything. "This is the aim of this book", the authors write, "let us look at the Sukuma Traditional Religion as Abraham himself would do today".[9] Starting

---

[6] D. Clément, The Research Committee at Bujora, in: B. Flou, B. Knudsen, G. Pedersen and D. Clement, *Folk Research in Mwanza Region*, in: *Tanzania Notes and Records* (1977)81 and 82, 75-78.

[7] K. Hudson, *Museums of Influence*, Cambridge 1987, 192-194. At present the 'Sukuma Museum' is called the 'Sukuma Cultural Centre'. See All Africa Press Service, Religious Plays Promote Inculturation of Gospel in Tanzania, in: *News and Features Bulletin*, July 20, 1987, 1-2; Bujora Village leads in blending culture and faith, in: *News and Features Bulletin*, January 29, 1990, 1-2; J. Lupande, *The Sukuma of Tanzania. Bujora cultural centre*, Denmark 1994; A. Bessire and M. Bessire, *Sukuma*, New York 1997; F. Wijsen, 'All people see the same sun'. Liturgy in Africa between inculturation and syncretism, in: *Studies in Liturgy* 77(1996)1-2, 77-95.

[8] Lupande, *The Sukuma of Tanzania*, 15.

[9] Kamati ya Utafiti wa Utamaduni, *Imani za jadi za kisukuma katika misemo, hadithi, methali na desturi za maisha*, Nantes 1988, 21.

from a "theology of inculturation" they want to build bridges between Sukuma Culture and Christian tradition.[10]

Father David Clément died in 1986. He is praised by the members of the Sukuma Research Committee for being the first missionary with a positive view of the Sukuma culture. According to the members of the committee, David Clément accurately foresaw the future course of the church in Usukuma. However, many pastoral workers in Usukuma do not like the activities and the views of Father Clément and 'his' Sukuma Research Committee. In fact, missionaries such as Father Hendriks and Father Clément are said to have caused confusion (*udanganyifu*) among the Sukuma about what is Christian and what is not by their 'thoughtless' adaptations.[11]

Father Hendriks, who was the theorist of the two (Father Clément being more concerned with practical implementations), thought that there were many similarities between Sukuma traditional sacrifice (*kitambo*) and Holy Mass; amulets from the traditional healer (*mhigi)* and medals or crucifixes blessed by the priest; personal belongings of the ancestors (*shitongelejo*) and relics of the true cross or the saints; the cults of the ancestors (*masamva*) and the cult of the Saints; traditional rituals to obtain protection from the power of sorcerers (*kukagwa na nkagi*) and the blessings of persons or homes; the traditional rainmaking ceremonies (*kugema mbula*) and the blessings of seeds and crops; the consultations of traditional healers (*kuj'ulagulwa*) and Christian pilgrimages; traditional dances (*mbina*) and Christian processions; initiation ceremonies and the sacraments of baptism or marriage; the penances done for a traditional healer and the Christian penance; the sign of the cross made by the traditional healer and the Christian sign of the cross.[12]

---

[10] Kamati ya Utafiti, 193-196.

[11] For example, when Father Clément started to build a round church in Bujora in 1956, as one of the first in Africa, it was said that it would remind the Sukuma of their *nyumba za masamva* (houses of the ancestors).

[12] J. Hendriks, Adaptation [Paper presented at the Pastoral Formation Centre], Kipalapala 1962. (mimeographed), 4-5.

Father Hendriks and the members of the Sukuma Research Committee thought that the Sukuma beliefs and practices mentioned above could be replaced by their Christian equivalents. However, their opponents commented that this was too simplistic, as the people interpreted these Christian equivalents "in their pagan ways".[13] Father Hendriks and Father Clément "have destroyed a lot of things", "they try to explain away what is wrong", "they have contributed a lot to the confusion of the people", to mention the remarks of only a few opponents, both expatriate and Tanzanian. In short, the pioneers of the Sukuma Research Committee are said to have promoted religious syncretism (*mchanganyiko wa dini*) instead of the inculturation of the gospel (*kuutamadunisha injili*).

This assessment raises many questions. What is the difference between syncretism and inculturation? Why are certain fruits of localisation called 'syncretism' and other fruits 'inculturation'? What criteria do the participants in this debate use to distinguish both forms of the Africanisation of Christianity? And for whom is 'syncretism' a problem?

It has been noticed that the dialectic of inculturation has shifted. It is no longer between missionary Christianity and African religion; it is fundamentally between popular inculturation and official inculturation.[14] This is an important contribution to the inculturation debate. Yet, there is still another dimension to this problem, as not all church officials hold the official teachings of the church. There is also a dialectic

---

[13] Indeed, this was an unintended consequence of the Christian replacement of indigenous symbols. This shows the ambiguity of the outworkings of mission methods. As symbols are polysemy, the interpretation of the Christian message by the receiver may oppose the interpretation that was intended by the sender. It shows also that the receivers are not passive but active in the conversion process (B. Meyer, Beyond syncretism. Translation and diabolization in the appropriation of Protestantism in Africa, in: C. Stewart and R. Shaw (eds.), *Syncretism/Anti-Syncretism. The politics of religious synthesis*, London and New York 1994, 60-63).

[14] L. Magesa, The present and the future of inculturation in East Africa, in: P. Turkson and F. Wijsen (eds.), *Inculturation. Abide by the Otherness of Africa and the Africans*, Kampen 1994, 70.

between different attitudes towards Africanisation among the church officials.

5.3 Culture contact and change

However different syncretism and inculturation may be, both have to do with the interaction of Christian tradition and African cultures, including their religions. Generally speaking it can be said that most Sukuma knew only their indigenous religion till 1850, except for some Sukuma people who were carriers of goods in the Arab caravans to and from the coast and were known to be porters of some of their ideas and practices, including new forms of spirit possession.[15]

The first culture contact came from the Arabs who reached the Lake Shore (Kageye) probably around 1825. They penetrated Usukuma for trading purposes mainly. They settled down in the resting places along the caravan routes from Kageye to the Coast via Tabora, and to Uganda via Karagwe. However, these Muslim traders looked across the Ocean to Arabia and India, from where they came. Moreover they did not aim to convert others to Islam and they were mainly town-centred. As they intermarried with Sukuma women, some Islamic influence in and around Kageye cannot be excluded. In general, however, the influence of Islam remained too little to be of much effect on the Sukuma culture in this first period of culture contact.

The first Christian missionaries who entered Usukuma were the missionaries of the (Anglican) 'Church Missionary Society'. They reached Kageye in 1877, followed one year later by missionaries of the (Catholic) 'Society of Missionaries of Africa' (better known as 'White Fathers'). Both societies were on their way to Uganda. But they founded missions in Usukuma. The Church Missionary Society started in Buzalima in 1882 (in 1887 this mission was removed to Usambiro, the present village of Kabiga) and at Nassa in 1888. The missionaries of the Society of Missionaries of Africa started in Bukumbi in 1883, fol-

[15] T. Ranger, Movement of ideas, in: I. Kimambo and A. Temu (eds.), *A history of Tanzania*, Nairobi 1969, 167-168.

lowed by Ushirombo in 1891, Kagunguli in 1895, on Kome Island in 1900, Mwanza in 1907, Murutungulu in 1909, Nyegezi in 1911 and Buhingo in 1923.

After these first missionaries the missionaries of the Africa Inland Mission came at the beginning of this century, followed by the Seventh Day Adventist Church. In 1946 the (Catholic) Foreign Mission Society of America (better known as 'Maryknoll Missionaries') took over from the White Fathers in the then erected Vicariate of Musoma-Maswa, the present-day dioceses of Shinyanga and Musoma.

It is important to know how the ordinary people reacted and continue to react to culture contact. Dr. Ignatius Pambe, a Roman Catholic priest from Usukuma, distinguishes four attitudes. Some people keep a foot each in African Religion and in Christianity, taking the advantages of spiritual and material help from both sides. This attitude is found among the well-to-do Christians.[16] Others reject completely either African Religion or the Christian view. Traditional healers and diviners on the one hand and members of Evangelical and Pentecostal Churches on the other tend to react in this way. Some people reject both African Religion and Christianity. This reaction may be found among the intellectuals who favour African socialism or humanism. However, a large number creates an intermediate set of beliefs and practices which offers a synthesis between African religion and Christian message.[17]

This 'large number' is striking if it is considered that only about 13% of the Sukuma people are Christian. But it is noteworthy that Pambe gives also examples of adherents of the indigenous religion who find it quite normal to carry a rosary or to consult a priest.[18] It shows that the interaction is mutual, that there is not only a movement from

---

[16] The well-to-do Christians and the priests occupy common places on a ladder of social evaluation and approach each other as equals. Hence, it is an interest of well-to-do Christians to remain on speaking terms with the priests and not to show deviant behaviour.

[17] I. Pambe, Christianity and meaning, in: *Pastoral Orientation Service* (1982)4-6, 22.

[18] I. Pambe, Religious symbols, inter culture communication and change in Africa, in: *Pastoral Orientation Service* (1980)5-6, 38.

Christianity towards the indigenous religion, but also the other way round. For example, it has been observed that the indigenous religion is more theocentric than it was before its contact with Christianity and Islam; that there is less emphasis on ancestor spirits and more on other spirits.[19] These changes are not only caused by the influence of world religions as such. They are also consequences of the enlargement of the Sukuma world in general, through its opening to the world market by cotton production and gold mining.

When the synthesis of African religion and Christian message is institutionalised in 'African Independent Churches' it attracts much attention. The first Independent Church to be present in Usukuma was the *Dini ya Mininga* (Religion of Mininga). It was founded in 1924 at Nassa. It reacted against the take-over of the mission stations of the Anglican Church Missionary Society by the (Baptist) African Inland Mission. Another example is the 'Last Church of God'. This church was founded in 1925 by Jordan Msumbwa, a Malawian who had travelled to South Africa and on his return brought some men who were suspended from Jehovah's Witnesses for polygamy.[20] More recent examples are the 'Church of Witnesses of Christ' and the 'Immanuel Church of Africa'. The 'Witnesses of Christ' were founded by Samwel Bugal, previously a member of the Seventh Day Adventist Church, at Kasamwa in 1974. The 'Immanuel Church' was founded by Thomas Shella, a devoted Catholic who got in trouble with his parish priest, at Geita in 1987. The priority of the first church is the acceptance of indigenous, thus holistic, healing; the priority of the second church is the acceptance of indigenous, thus polygynous, marriage.

When the synthesis is made on an individual level, however, it remains largely unnoticed. Yet this is the Christianity of the majority in Africa. This is what we mean by 'popular Christianity' or the Christianity of the ordinary faithful that contrasts with 'official Christianity' or

---

[19] F. Wijsen, *There is only one God. A social-scientific and theological study of popular religion and evangelization in Sukumaland, Northwest Tanzania*, Kampen 1993, 64-67.

[20] T. Ranger, *The African Churches of Tanzania*, Nairobi 1974, 22-25.

the Christianity of the church officials.[21] Two forms of popular Christianity may be distinguished, a dualistic and an integrative form.[22] In the first form the believers do not mix both systems, but leave them as they are, using them according to their needs. They are Christian on Sunday and adherents of the indigenous religion on the other days of the week. The second form consists of an existential mix of African religion and Christianity. In this form Christian symbols get an indigenous meaning or indigenous symbols get a Christian meaning. For example, *hirizi* (amulets) are interpreted as *rosari za kinyeji* (local rosaries), or priests are referred to as *waganga* (healers).

5.4 From 'abolition' to 'adaptation'

The first missionaries came to Usukuma in order to bring to the so called 'pagans' the light of Christ and his message of salvation in order to save them from eternal damnation. According to them the pagans lived in the shadow of the dead. Fully in line with the then prevailing theology they were convinced that outside the church there was no salvation. 'Abolition' was the key word in their understanding of mission.

Consequently, the first missionaries saw it as their task to preach the 'Good News' and to convert the Sukuma from 'paganism'. This attitude can easily be recognised in the "Letters from Africa" that White Father Jan Hendriks wrote between 1929 and 1938 about his missionary work among the Sukuma people.[23] Closing his letter from Sayu Sa-

---

[21] By 'official' Christianity I mean the Christianity as it is expressed in the teachings of the Supreme Pontiff, the Episcopal College, the Bishop's Conferences and each individual bishop, as stipulated in canons 752 and 753 of the Code of Canon Law.

[22] In this chapter the adjective 'popular' does not refer to a specific socio-economic group, although very often the term coincides with such a group, as the supporters of 'official' Christianity are mostly members of the upper classes. However, here we approach popular Christianity primarily as a religious issue, not primarily as a social issue.

[23] J. Hendriks, *Brieven uit Afrika, Witte Paters*, n.p. n.d. [Boxtel: Prokuur der Witte Paters, 1948].

yu on 13 April 1932 he says: "Maybe you are not interested in the ideas of these primitive tribesmen. But if you followed them carefully you understand how foolish and superstitious a pagan is. A real pagan is blinder than a mole. It makes his conversion difficult".[24]

In his preface to an unpublished manuscript called "Struggle and Hope",[25] written between 1947 and 1949 in Sumve, Hendriks writes: "There is struggle in pagan-land. The church attacks; paganism is being attacked. The fighters are the missionaries, the indigenous helpers, the just converted ones, but also the friends at home. And there is hope, hope of conversions, of many conversions, of a complete victory".

But already before the Second World War a new approach grew. The aim of mission remained more or less the same. But the way to achieve this aim became different, more communicative. Still the missionaries wanted the 'pagans' to enter the church. But the church from her side could meet the 'pagans' by adapting some of its externals, like language, vestments and certain rituals. Their key word became 'adaptation'.

This new approach is clearly demonstrated in two publications that the same Father Hendriks, but now some twenty to thirty years later, wrote under the titles *Ha Kikome* and *Liwelelo*.[26] In his pamphlet on "Adaptation" Father Hendriks, who was the regional superior of the White Fathers from 1954 till 1961, wrote in the introduction: "Caution: It may be that some of the ideas or proposals expressed therein run contrary to, or at least are not completely in accordance with, directives given by the local Ordinary. In this case consider such ideas or proposals as the personal opinions of the writer and in practice follow the directives of the higher authority".[27]

---

[24] Hendriks, *Brieven uit Afrika*, 115.
[25] J. Hendriks, *Strijd en Hoop*, n.p. n.d. [Sumve 1947-1949; Nyegezi: Regional's House, White Fathers]. (type-written manuscript)
[26] J. Hendriks, *Ha Kikome*, St. Justin 1959; *Liwelelo*, Tabora 1960.
[27] Hendriks, Adaptation. Note that Hendriks was superior of the White Fathers when Blomjous, who was also a White Father, was bishop of Mwanza. Probably Hendriks had not his own bishop in mind.

This shows how controversial this positive outlook on local cultures at that time still was. In the same year 1962, on 24 June, a diarist in Sengerema Parish wrote the following observations about the *Corpus Christi* celebrations: “The church was full for high mass. People from Nyantakubwa were present and from our own stations as well as from Nyanchinji belonging to Nyantakubwa but nearer to us. There were hundreds of pagans as primitive as they were 1000 years ago, the only difference being they wear medals and rosaries as decorations. The outdoor altar was at the brothers. The processionists were asked to walk four abreast but they mostly walked single file. The pagans talked during the whole Benediction and then went to their own obscene dances accompanied often by Christians”.

5.5 From ‘inculturation’ to ‘liberation’

Whereas the ‘adaptation’ approach was still very strong in the sixties some missionaries and local priests worked out a new understanding of mission, already before the Second Vatican Council. The aim of mission, they said, is not the transplantion of Christianity to Africa. Mission is concerned with the ‘incarnation’ of Christ in Africa. ‘Incarnation’ was the key word of this approach. Later it changed into ‘inculturation’.[28]

Although most native and expatriate bishops from Africa spoke in terms of ‘adaptation’ during the Second Vatican Council, this council was working out a new vision of mission and non Christian religions. The classic conciliar texts are *Ad Gentes* and *Nostra Aetate*. *Ad Gentes* (No. 10) said that “the Church must become an integral part of all these groupings, just as Christ himself, by his incarnation”.

---

[28] The term ‘inculturation’ is preferred since the late seventies. Jesuits in Rome, however, used this term already in the early sixties. On the official level the term ‘inculturation’ was used by Pope John Paul II for the first time in a speech for the Pontifical Bible Commission, and appeared for the first time in his Apostolic Exhortation *Catechesi tradendae*, No. 53.

In line with the spirit of the Second Vatican Council, Pope Paul VI closed the first meeting of the Symposium of Episcopal Conferences in Africa and Madagascar in 1969 saying: "An adaptation of the Christian life in the fields of pastoral, ritual, didactic and spiritual activities is not only possible, it is even favoured by the church. The liturgical renewal is a living example of this. And in this sense you may, and you must, have an African Christianity".[29]

After the 1974 Synod on 'Evangelization in the Modern World' the bishops of Africa and Madagascar declared: "Following this idea of mission, the bishops of Africa and Madagascar consider as being completely out of date, the so called theology of adaptation. In its stead, they adopt the theology of incarnation".[30]

The influence of the Second Vatican Council was also felt in Usukuma. In 1971 three students of Kipalapala Major Seminary wrote a booklet on the communication between Christianity and Sukuma Religion: Aloys Balina (presently bishop of Geita and Shinyanga), Justin Mabula (who taught at Nyegezi and Makoko Seminaries) and Anthony Mayala (presently Archbishop of Mwanza).[31] Their ideas reflect an open attitude towards the Sukuma culture based on Karl Rahner's theology of universal salvation. "For this reason, the Sukuma traditional prayers to God should be considered as lawful and valid for the salvation of anyone who firmly adheres to it [Sukuma religion]".[32]

The debate between the representatives of the adaptation and inculturation models is still going on. But a new horizon of the debate on

---

[29] The value of African cultures was already recognised by Pope Paul VI in his Apostolic Exhortation *Africae terrarum*, No. 17, published in *African Ecclesial Review* 10(1968)71-84, 86.

[30] Statement of the bishops of Africa, in: *African Ecclesial Review* 17(1975)1, 58.

[31] Archbishop Mayala was a member of the preparatory committee of the Special Assembly for Africa of the Synod of Bishops in which 'inculturation' was the central theme. In the preface to the book *Imani za jadi* (*Kamati ya Utafiti*) he encouraged the Sukuma Research Committee to continue its work.

[32] A. Balina, A. Mayala and J. Mabula, *Sukuma expression of traditional religion in life*, Kipalapala 1971. (mimeographed), 56.

mission arises. There is a small but growing group of pastoral workers that holds that the discussion mentioned above remains at the surface of the problem facing the church in East Africa. Will not the church, as usual, by locating its vital issues in this sphere, once again miss the boat, they ask? These pastoral workers are convinced that it does! They say that the real problem facing the church in East Africa is the material and ideological dependency of its people.

The proponents of this model of mission bring a new perspective into the debate, namely the context of Africanisation. They say that there will be no real Africanisation if Africa remains dependent. They urge an economic, political, cultural and religious liberation. In short, what East Africa needs is not inculturation, but liberation! As Cyprian Tirumanywa, a priest from the Archdiocese of Mwanza, says: "Instead of being an instrument of liberation and joy, official theology is an instrument of oppression and fear".[33] Later he adds: "Human liberation implies exploding the so called truths (i.e., 'mysteries of faith and dogmas') implanted in a people's consciousness by the colonial indoctrination".[34]

There is a fifth model. In reaction to those who wish to abolish indigenous religion in Africa the adherents of this model want to abolish Christianity in Africa. They hold that there is more salvation in African religion than there is in Christianity and hold the world religions responsible for religious intolerance in Africa.[35]

5.6 Rejection and reluctance

Maybe the impression has been given that the attitudes mentioned above follow each other in time. But this is not the case. All of these

---

[33] C. Tirumanywa, *Christian religion on trial. The Good News is justice and peace for all on Earth*, Dar es Salaam 1991, 68.

[34] Tirumanywa, *Christian religion on trial*, 100.

[35] This was the tendency of an open letter that a priest of Rulenge Diocese (Privatus Karugendo, Bujora, 15.5.1995) wrote to his bishop, preparing the first centenary celebration of his diocese (this letter is in possession of the present author).

attitudes exist up to the present time. In the following two sections we shall describe attitudes towards popular Christianity, understood as the existential mix between African religion and Christian tradition. This description is based on fieldwork in the Catholic Diocese of Geita.[36] The methods of data collection were observation by participating in pastoral activities and interviews with pastoral workers. The main informants were the bishop, the priests, sisters, seminarians, catechists and lay missionaries in the diocese.

Some pastoral workers say "no" to popular Christianity. As one of the older expatriate priests stated: "From the bible it is clear that Christianity asks a real break with all the traditional stuff. Christ brings something new. To gloss over all local customs, as some of us do nowadays, I cannot accept". These informants perceive a great deal of similarity between Sukuma culture and the Old Testament. One catechist argued: "We know many beliefs and practices that are mentioned in the Old Testament in our culture. But the Gospel brings something new. The Old Testa-ment has been abolished by the New Testament. The same holds true for Sukuma religion and *ukristu wa vijijini* (village Christianity)".

The informants who reject popular Christianity stress the radicalism of the gospel values. As one young Tanzanian priest argued: "Our Christianity is a *mchanganyiko* (mixture) of traditional religion and Christianity. Our Christians go to the *waganga wa kinyeji* (native doctors), they hold to the *ndoa ya kinyeji* (native marriage) and their children wear *chapa za badugu* (marks of the ancestors). But this is not Christianity. Jesus said: Anyone who starts to plough and then keeps looking back is of no use to the Kingdom of God (Luke 9:62)".

A middle aged expatriate priest complained: "We are *nusu nusu tu*" (only half way).[37] Referring to Saint Paul's Letter to the Galatians (5:19-21) he said that many Christians follow the *mambo ya shetani* (things of the devil), like *uzinzi* (adultery) and *ulevi* (drunkenness). But it is impossible to be *nusu mkristo, nusu mpagani* (half Christian, half

[36] Wijsen, *There is only one God.*
[37] Meaning "we are only half-way on the way of conversion".

pagan), as Bishop Mwoleka says in his book.[38] One has to follow Jesus completely, or not at all. Jesus said: "None of you can be my disciple unless he gives up everything he has" (Luke 14:33).

These informants are of the opinion that the Christians in *Usukuma wanakaa hivi hivi tu* (lead a life without principles). They speak with respect to popular Christianity in terms of conversion, *kubadili dini* (literally: to change religion) or *kugeuza dini* (literally: to alter religion). They still form a minority within the Catholic Church in Usukuma. However, the conversion model is growing, not only in the Pentecostal Churches, but also within the Catholic Church, as for example the influence of 'Evangelization 2000' shows.[39]

Most pastoral workers say "yes" and "no" to popular Christianity. One of the younger expatriate priests made a distinction between 'religion' and 'faith'. Popular Christianity, he uttered, is an expression of religion. Basically it is God's Spirit working in man. But as a human reality it is affected by sin. Therefore it needs salvation. Jesus Christ came to redeem 'religion'. Thus the basic question is: How faithful is popular Christianity to the message of Christ?

Just as those who reject popular religion, the informants who are reluctant to accept it perceive also a great deal of similarity between the Sukuma culture and the Old Testament. But the latter judge this similarity positively. They argue that the Sukuma culture is a "preparation for the gospel". Thus the church can meet the converts somewhere by *kurekebisha ukristu* (adapting Christianity) to the Sukuma culture.

But care has to be taken, these informants warn. According to several catechists and priests, both expatriate and Tanzanian, "we have to follow the *sheria ya kanisa* (rules of the church) otherwise we are no-

---

[38] Referring to C. Mwoleka, *Do this. The Church of the Third Millennium*, Ndanda and Peramiho 1988. This bishop (of Rulenge Diocese) propagated 'integrated' communities as the new model for the church of the third millennium.

[39] This organisation sponsored Worldwide Retreats for Priests in Rome (in which one priest of Geita Diocese participated) and initiated a decade of worldwide evangelisation. Its aim is "to give Jesus Christ a more Christian world as the best 2000th birthday gift possible".

where". As one of the younger Tanzanian priests argued: "We cannot help the people, the rule is the rule". Baptism and marriage regulations were given as examples. And an older expatriate priest reasoned: "We cannot be too easy, otherwise they cheat us". Once he was asked to baptise an old man he exemplified. He was told that the man had followed two years of religious instructions. Hence he baptised him. Next day he found the man wearing amulets.

One catechist was of the opinion that "The rules of the church are implementations of the ten commandments. They are universal traffic rules. Imagine if some people keep left and others right. It becomes a mess". One of the younger Tanzanian priests argued: "We have to be strict, otherwise our Christians will walk away to the Protestant sects, which are even more strict. The people want to be challenged. They need security, that is why they like the rules".

The informants who have this view stress the universal aspect of the church. One catechist stated: "We cannot allow Sukuma values to take root in the church, otherwise we lose the unity in the church". Another catechist reasoned: "Inculturation cannot go too far. Imagine if we introduced the Sukuma language in the church. Large crowds of people would not understand us". This catechist preferred Latin as the official language in the church, as "this language is universally understood".

Some informants stated that also in the Pope's view the time is not yet ripe for inculturation in Africa. According to one of the Tanzanian priests Pope John Paul II spoke very carefully and reservedly about inculturation during the Eucharistic Congress in Nairobi in 1985, for example at the occasion of the official opening of the Catholic University of Eastern Africa. The Pope stressed that inculturation may not endanger the universality of the church and should occur under the leadership of the bishops.

One expatriate priest argued that popular beliefs and practices are irrational, "they have no scientific foundation at all". Another expatriate priest added "that popular religion is just a lower stage in the development of evolution. It is based on a primitive mentality". And he continued: "Did we not have the same mentality in Europe thirty years ago?

There is an evolution from a mythological, pre-scientific to a scientific and rational world view". This priest concluded: "Magical understandings of the sacraments are no problem. In the long run they will disappear".

5.7 Sympathy and acceptance

Other informants say "yes" to the existential mix of African religion and Christian message. However, they immediately add a "but". The Christianity of the masses is an authentic Christianity, but it is incomplete, imperfect, and it is the task of the church to make it perfect, to bring it to completion (kukamilisha). The Sukuma religion, however, does contain the "seeds of the Gospel".

One expatriate priest quoted the words of Jesus talking about the law of Moses and the teachings of the prophets: "I have not come to do away with them but to make their teachings come true" (Matthew 5:17). "The same holds true for Sukuma religion", he argued. "We must inculturate the gospel" (*kuutamadunisha injili*). Another expatriate priest reasoned that Jesus himself had an open attitude towards other cultures. He pointed at the stories of the Canaanite woman (Matthew 15:21-28), the Roman centurion (Matthew 8:5-13) and the Good Samaritan (Luke 10:30-37). "What Jesus admired in them was their faith", this priest said.

Others hold that the history of the church is a history of continuous inculturations. As one Tanzanian priest stated: "When Christianity moved to new areas in the past it always changed. Why could it not change coming to Africa?" According to him the history of the church is one of the strongest arguments in support of the inculturation of the gospel in Africa.

Another expatriate priest argued: "What would Christmas be without the Christmas tree and candle lights? What would Easter be without the Easter fire and Easter rabbit? It should be recognised that these 'Christian' customs (except the rabbit, which was not Christianised) are derived from pagan practices. In the same way we could inculturate

Sukuma practices". And he continued: "For me Father Gregory Mwageni, the prior of the African Benedictines Monastery of Hanga, formulates the meaning of inculturation most clearly: to develop the good which is already there, to install the good which is missing, to eliminate the bad thing by the good thing".[40]

Other informants hold that the teachings of the church are more and more taking the religion of the people seriously. One expatriate priest stated that the documents of the Second Vatican Council, such as Ad Gentes and Nostra Aetate, show this clearly. A Tanzanian priest quoted the words which Pope Paul VI spoke at the closing of the first SECAM meeting in 1969 at Kampala: "You may and you must have an African Christianity".[41] The same view is expressed in his Apostolic Exhortation Africae Terrarum and his Apostolic Exhortation Evangelii Nuntiandi. His teaching has been confirmed by Pope John Paul II, this informant uttered, especially in his address in 1983 to the bishops of Zaire where he said that Catholic doctrine is unfolded through the pluralism of cultural expressions. And he showed his intention to build an African Church by opening the procedure for an African Synod.

An expatriate priest claimed that it has always been the policy of the church that the riches of the sensus fidelium must be given a chance to come to full flowering, that the church always was against sects which want to reserve salvation for only a few, and that the 'people's theology' contains important starting-points for a real African theology.

Some informants say "yes" to popular religion. This attitude is still very vague, not as consistent as the previous ones, and adhered to by only a few informants now and then. They feel that this is the consequence of the inculturation approach. They stress the freedom (*uhuru*) of the people and they want to liberate (*kuweka huru*) them from everything that oppresses them: economic oppression, political oppression, cultural oppression, even oppression in the field of religion.

---

[40] Referring to G. Mwageni, The Church in the African society, in: *Pastoral Orientation Service* (1980)1, 36-46.

[41] Pope Paul VI, Address at the closing of the all African Bishop's symposium, in: *African Ecclesial Review* 11(1969)4, 402-405.

One expatriate priest reasoned that according to Matthew 25:31-46 the criteria for the final judgement are neither membership in the church nor belief in Christ. The only criterion is what people have done for their neighbours in need, especially the poor and oppressed. According to this priest the most important Christian values are that attention should be paid first to the beam in one's own eye (Matthew 7:1-6), that others should be forgiven not seven times, but seventy times seven (Matthew 18:21-22) and that it is not our task to separate the weeds from the wheat (Matthew 13:24-30). He was furious against those who stress the rules of the church. "The Sabbath was made for the good of man; man was not made for the Sabbath" (Marc 2:27). "It was our task to bring the people the Good News and liberate them", he reasoned, "but we made them afraid and enslaved them".

One Tanzanian priest was looking for criteria to judge concrete phenomena such as going to a traditional healer. He quoted Jesus' words: "whoever is not against you is for you" (Luke 9:49-50). Another Tanzanian priest stated: "the only question is whether it makes them happy and does not harm others". He stressed the "freedom of religion" expressed by the universal declaration of human rights and recognised by the Second Vatican Council. For him "Christian liberation" included freeing people from the fears that were imposed on them by the rules of the church.

It is important to add that all views speak of conversion. But conversion is understood increasingly in a deeper way. It is not to win individuals for Christ, in order to save their souls from eternal damnation; it is not to bring them to the church, in which God's saving grace is visible. Conversion is to make people do the will of God, thus bring nearer his Kingdom.

5.8 The theological debate

The different missionary approaches are connected with various theological views of the relationship between the Christian message and the African cultures. Moreover, they reflect the opinions of the major policy-making bodies of the various denominations in East Africa. In order to discover the restraint against accepting African cultures, including their religions, to exist in their own right, we will investigate different interpretations of the relationship between 'Christ and culture' and give one example of each.[42]

The conversion model is connected with an exclusivistic view of the relationship between Christ and culture. According to the exclusivistic theologians there is no revelation and no salvation in African religion. The African religion and the Christian tradition are absolutely discontinuous; they have no 'common ground' or 'meeting point'. Thus 'building bridges' between the two religions is not possible. It is only possible to witness that Jesus is the way, the truth and the life and that no one goes to the Father except by Him (John 14:6).

An example from East Africa is Tokunboh Adeyemo who is general secretary of the Association of Evangelicals in Africa and Madagascar, based in Nairobi. He addresses himself to five mistakes in the salvation debate: pluralism, universalism, second chancism, syncretism and humanisation. Against these five attitudes he formulates an Evangelical response. "As Evangelicals we must guard against these pitfalls. We must tenaciously hold to the primacy of God's Word. God's eternal unchanging Word must remain supreme in matters of faith and practice. It is not a product of the literary activity of the Church. Rather the Church bows before the authority of the Word. *Sola Scriptura* must ring loud and clear in our day", thus Adeyemo.[43]

If the view of the exclusivistic theologians that Christianity and African religion are "absolutely discontinuous" is supported, it will be admitted that popular Christianity is a false understanding of God. This leads to a practice concerning popular Christianity in terms of dis-

---

[42] In the theological debate the labels 'exclusivistic', 'dialectic', 'inclusivistic' and 'pluralistic' are used to describe different interpretations of the relationship between Christ and culture. Although it has been accepted that these labels represent simplifications of rather complex relationships, they are used here as heuristic models.

[43] T. Adeyemo, The Salvation Debate and Evangelical Response, in: *East Africa Journal of Evangelical Theology* 2(1984)2, 19.

placement and abolishing of this religion. Generally speaking, the exclusivistic view is held by members of the Association of Evangelicals in Africa and Madagascar. It is also called the Evangelical model.

The 'adaptation' approach is connected with a dialectical view of the relationship between Christ and culture. The dialectical theologians hold that there is revelation in African religion, because all people are created in the image of God. But there is no salvation in African religion, because salvation is to be found through 'Christ alone'. In all the world there is no one else who God has given who can save (Acts 4:12).

An example from East Africa is John Mbiti, an Anglican theologian from Kenya, at present teaching at Bern University. Mbiti admits that the African religion is a *praeparatio evangelica*. Africans have a true knowledge of God.[44] There is also salvation in African religions. However, this is salvation from calamities here and now. Though African religion has saved man from adversities, man has not been saved from death. Only through Christ death is conquered and eternal life is possible. For Africans this is "the most significant consequence of accepting the Christian message of salvation".[45]

If the view of the dialectical theologians that there is salvation in 'Christ only' is held, it will be said that popular Christianity is just a partial understanding of God. This will lead to an attitude towards popular Christianity in terms of fulfilment and completion. Generally speaking this is the view of the All Africa Conference of Churches. The dialectical view is based on the 'Protestant principle'. Therefore this model is called the Protestant model.[46]

---

[44] The recognition of revelation in African religion forms a common ground with Christianity. It is a merit of Mbiti that he laid, among others, the foundation for a real African theology.

[45] Mbiti, Our Saviour as an African experience, 412. In 1980 Mbiti states that he no longer uses the word "only" with respect to revelation in the scriptures. He then uses the word "also". However, he does not speak about salvation.

[46] The labels 'Evangelical', 'Potestant' and 'Catholic' do not refer to Christian denominations here, but to theological models. It may be that a Catholic (in

The 'inculturation' approach is connected with an inclusivistic view of the relationship between Christ and culture. The inclusivistic theologians say that there is revelation and salvation in African religion. But the 'highest revelation' and 'fullest salvation' is in Christianity. Thus the task of missionaries is not to do away with the African beliefs, but to make their teachings come true (Matthew 5:17).

An example from East Africa is Patrick Kalilombe, former bishop of Lilongwe, Malawi, who taught at the Selly Oak Colleges in Birmingham until recently. He says that the evangeliser does not offer something that is completely new to his fellow men, because God is already present among men through his Spirit. The evangeliser will observe man's sinful resistance to God. As such evangelisation is a break with man's sin. But he must also discover the 'seeds of the word', for his role is to offer himself humbly to the Spirit as his instrument to promote and to bring these seeds to full maturity.[47]

If the view of the inclusivistic theologians that the "highest revelation" and the "fullest salvation" is in (official) Christianity is supported, it will be held that popular Christianity is an imperfect religion. This leads to a practice concerning popular Christianity in terms of purification and perfection. Generally speaking this is the view of the Symposium of Episcopal Conferences in Africa and Madagascar. As the inclusivistic view is typically Catholic, this is called also the Catholic model.

The 'liberation' approach is connected with a pluralistic view of the relationship between Christ and culture. Like the inclusivistic theologi-

---

the sense of a denomination) theologian holds to the 'Protestant' principle, as is the case with Charles Nyamiti, as will be shown later.

[47] P. Kalilombe, Evangelisation and the Holy Spirit, in: *African Ecclesial Review* 18(1976)1, 8-18. In an essay recently published the salvific value of African spirituality remains an open question: P. Kalilombe, Spirituality in the African perspective, in: R. Gibellini (ed.), *Paths of African Theology*, London 1994, 134-135. Earlier, however, Kalilombe said that African Religions "are to be respected as the normal divinely-given means of salvation": P. Kalilombe, The salvific value of African religions, in: *African Ecclesial Review* 21(1979)3, 156.

ans, the pluralistic theologians say that there is revelation and salvation in African religion. However, they do not add "but it is incomplete". All religions are unique and relative ways to salvation. Whether one religion is better than the other can be judged only from what is done for the least important of our brothers and sisters (Matthew 25:40).

An example in East Africa is Samuel Kibicho, a Presbyterian minister from Kenya who is teaching at Nairobi University. In his view the previous attitudes towards African religion are in error. There is no reason to look upon African religion as a kind of inferior or incomplete understanding of God. Rather there is good reason to see it as full and fully salvatory revelation, as the "fruits of the Spirit" are already present in African religion. This is not to say that African religion is perfect. It too has its share in sinfulness and ignorance, just as Christianity has its share in human weaknesses.

However, if the 'fruits of the spirit' are already present in Africa, what is mission good for? Mission is good for the mutual correction and uplift of the religions. "Each religion must evangelize as if it is the only carrier of the only fully-saving revelation", says Kibicho.[48] "However, in its continuing dialogue and cooperation with other religions, every religion must acknowledge and accept the claim of uniqueness and ultimacy of finality in every other genuine religion".

If the view of the Pluralistic theologians that there is a 'radical continuity' between African religion and the Christian faith is supported, it will be held that popular Christianity is a full and fully saving religion. This leads to a practice concerning popular Christianity in terms of mutual enrichment and critical interrogation. This view is shared by some members of the Organization of African Instituted Churches, although

---

[48] S. Kibicho, The mission of the church of Jesus Christ today from the perspective of the younger churches, in: A. Ngindu Mushete, *The mission of the Church today. Reports of the Yaoundé meeting (4-11 April, 1984). Special Issue of the Bulletin of African Theology* 7(1985)13-14, 24-25.

it must be recognised that – paradoxically – there are also Independent Churches which share the view of the Evangelical churches.[49]

Recently a new approach developed under the heading of 'reconstruction'. According to its representatives the dilemma between 'inculturation' and 'liberation' is based on the Western dualism of body and soul, material and spiritual development, secular and religious values, and has to be conquered. For this a theology is needed that orients itself not towards the exodus from Egypt, but towards the entry into the Promised Land and the necessity to build it up.[50]

5.9 Charles Nyamiti and Laurenti Magesa

In order to put this debate back to the context of our fieldwork, we shall present two theologians from Tanzania, Charles Nyamiti and Laurenti Magesa. Nyamiti is a priest from Tabora Archdiocese, Magesa from Musoma Diocese. Nyamiti holds a doctorate in dogmatic theology from Louvain, Magesa holds a doctorate in moral theology from Ottawa. Both lectured at Saint Paul Major Seminary in Kipalapala (Tanzania) and at the Faculty of Theology of the Catholic University of Eastern Africa in Nairobi (Kenya); Nyamiti still does.[51]

Charles Nyamiti is convinced that African theologians can use African concepts for explaining Christian doctrines. But this use may not go too far. The result would be a "syncretistic theology characterized

[49] Among the members of the 'Ecumenical Association of African Theologians' all views can be found, even the first one. This shows that categories used mainly by European and American theologians are not always adequate nad that we need to move beyond these stereotypes. See also T. Sundermeier, Begegnung mit dem Fremden. Plädoyer für eine verstehende Missionswissenschaft, in: *Evangelische Theologie* 50(1990)5, 390-400.

[50] J. Mugambi, *From liberation to reconstruction. African Christian theology after the Cold War*, Nairobi 1995.

[51] Magesa was side-lined academically by his superiors in 1992, mainly because of his ideas on the ethics of homosexuality and 'aids' prevention in Africa. Presently he is working as a parish priest in his home diocese, but lecturing at the 'Maryknoll School of Theology' and the 'Institute of African Studies' (Nairobi) regularly.

by an unlawful mixture of Christian teachings and African traditional beliefs and practices".[52] The use of African tradition in Christian theology needs a 'radical criticism', as African concepts are full of superstitions. A 'radical criticism' is a "powerful weapon against syncretism".[53] Nyamiti, in other words, is concerned with the authenticity of the Christian message in Africa.

Nyamiti prefers to speak of 'confrontation' rather than of 'correlation'. He frequently calls his approach 'dialectical' rather than 'dialogical'.[54] This shows a curious mixture of a typically 'Protestant' and a typically 'Catholic' way of speaking. Thus, Nyamiti is a living example of the transition from 'adaptation' to 'inculturation'.[55]

Magesa wrote less about inculturation, more about liberation. In his view, inculturation is an interest of utmost importance for African theology. However, one should not understand culture in a reductionist sense. Culture is a system of how a society organises itself in its major dimensions of life: socially, economically and religiously. All these have a political content.[56]

Magesa is suspicious of inculturation theologians who do not take into account the economic and political structures in which inculturation takes place. In short, Magesa is concerned with the relevance of the Christian message in Africa. Whereas Nyamiti speaks about the interaction between Christian tradition and African culture in terms of confrontation, Magesa tries "to correlate the values of the people of a locality and the Christian vision of, and hope for, life".[57]

---

[52] C. Nyamiti, A critical assessment on some issues in today's African theology, in: *African Christian Studies* 5(1989)1, 7.
[53] Nyamiti, A critical assessment, 15.
[54] Nyamiti, A critical assessment, 12, 16.
[55] C. Nyamiti, My approach to African theology, in: *African Christian Studies* 7(1991)4, 35-53.
[56] L. Magesa, Politics and theology in Africa, in: *African Ecclesial Review* 31(1989)3, 147-148.
[57] L. Magesa, Assessing pastoral ministry in a parish situation, in: *African Ecclesial Review* 33(1991)5, 280.

Magesa does not extend the principles of his theology of liberation to his theology of inculturation. He does not go so far that Africans must free themselves from everything that oppresses them, even if Christianity is concerned. He does not accept the idea that there is revelation and salvation in the African religion independently of the Christ event, as for example Kibicho does.[58] Thus Magesa is an example of the transition from inculturation to pluralistic theology.

5.10 Syncretism or inculturation?

In the beginning of this chapter I introduced two contrasting views of popular Christianity, the view of those who accept popular Christianity as a form of inculturation, be it an unoffical one, and the view of those who reject popular Christianity as a form of syncretism, as an 'unlawful mixture' of African religion and Christian tradition. Thereafter I investigated briefly the history of Africanisation and contemporary attitudes towards popular Christianity, both at the level of the pastoral workers in Usukuma and at the level of professional theologians in East Africa.

Among the pastoral workers in Usukuma I discovered four attitudes which we labeled "no", "yes and no", "yes but" and "yes". Their key words were conversion, adaptation, inculturation and liberation. Generally speaking these four pastoral attitudes correspond with four models in professional theology, reflecting on the relationship between Christ and culture, namely the Evangelical, the Protestant, the Catholic and the Pluralist model. Their key words are exclusivism, dialectics, inclusivism and independence.

As I have shown in the first section, a 'large number' of Sukuma reacted to the culture contact in an unofficial way. Popular Christianity is a spontaneous form of Africanisation. The main task of the professional theologian in this respect is "to find out what is in harmony or not with

---

[58] In his book *African Religion*, however, he does accept salvific revelation in African religion.

the Christian faith", thus Nyamiti.[59] The problem can be summarised in one question: How do we prevent Africanisation from leading to heresy? In other words, what is authentic Christianity, and what is not? According to some theologians the spontaneous Africanisation of popular Christianity goes too far. They speak of the dangers of 'syncretism' (Evangelicals) and 'relativism' (Protestants). Others say that official Christianity does not go far enough. They are afraid that Christianity is irrelevant (Catholics) or even alienating (Pluralists).

The underlying problem seems that of discontinuity or continuity, replacement or fulfillment of African religion by the Christian faith. For some theologians there is no common ground or meeting point between these traditions.[60] For others a radical continuity is the foundational basis of African theology,[61] to mention only the extremes.

For the future of Christianity in Usukuma it is important to investigate the tension between Africanisation 'from below' and 'from above',[62] or 'popular' and 'official' inculturation.[63] It is, however, equally important to investigate why there is a tension among the church offficals themselves. Why are some forms of Africanisation rejected as 'syncretism' and others accepted as 'inculturation'? From an outsiders perspective, anthropologists would label many instances of inculturation as 'syncretism' in so far as they involve mixing of different traditions. Moreover, syncretism is not always considered unauthentic. Syncretism thus refers to the politics of religious synthesis.[64]

What criteria then do insiders in this debate use to distinguish both forms of Africanisation? Inculturation is seen as the encounter of African religion and Christian faith guided by the bishops and their priests, syncretism as the encounter of both traditions as done by ordinary faith-

[59] Nyamiti, A critical assessment, 9.
[60] Adeyemo, The Salvation Debate.
[61] Kibicho, The mission of the church.
[62] B. Meyer, If you are a Devil, you are Witch and, if you are a Witch, you are a Devil, in: *Journal of Religion in Africa* 22(1992)2, 122.
[63] Magesa, The present and the future, 70.
[64] C. Stewart and R. Shaw (eds.), *Syncretism/Anti-Syncretism. The politics of religious synthesis*, London and New York 1994, 11.

ful. Inculturation has to be an intellectually justified endeavour; syncretism is a spontaneous and intuitive process. Inculturation is official policy, syncretism is judged to be just popular practice. It seems then that what makes Africanisation to be syncretism is that it is contested as 'unlawful' by some church officials.

Thus the tension between the interpretation of popular Christianity as inculturation or syncretism reflects a struggle for the definition of 'true' faith within the church. It then has to be asked: Who has the power to decide on what grounds what is authen-tically Christian and what is not? What is the criterion for true faith, the *magisterium*[65] or the *sensus fidelium*?[66] Of course, there need not be a conflict between these two. In a mature Christian situation the *sensus fidelium* is a source of vitality for the development of doctrine within the church. The problem of Christianity in Usukuma is the growing gap between the two. How to bridge this gap?

5.11 Towards a theology 'from below'

It has been suggested that those who reject popular Christianity as 'unlawful mixture' do so because they do not want to lose power, that the struggle for the definition of true faith reflects a social struggle. This may be the case, as 'symbolic capital' leads to 'economic capital', and vice versa.[67] Becoming a leader within the church provides an avenue to a higher status and authority. Church leaders in East Africa have been blamed for their bourgeois mentality, associating themselves mainly with *watu wakubwa*, wealthy and powerful people.[68]

With the increase of African leaders in the church after independence, the hope had been there that things would change. But change has been very little. On the contrary, there is a general depression in the

---

[65] Nyamiti, My approach to African theology.
[66] L. Magesa, Some critical theological and pastoral issues facing the Church in East Africa today, in: *African Christian Studies* 4(1988)4, 43-60.
[67] P. Bourdieu, *Outline of a Theory of Practice*, London 1977.
[68] Mosha, The prophetic role of the Church, 28-29.

Africanisation movement. African churches have almost no programme for renewal. Why is this so? African church officials have stepped into the shoes of early European missionaries. This makes them privileged, but also dependent. The cost of dependence is that they are not able to reflect the religiosity of the majority of the faithful in Africa.[69]

This is not a merely ecclesiastical development. It relates to the economic crisis in Africa as a whole.[70] As people and thus also churches in Africa are becoming poorer, they depend more on financial assistence from abroad. In this situation the church leaders feel strongly the value of the support of the ecclesiastical headquarters. To lessen the link with Rome would be unwise indeed. Thus too much Africanisation by arguing for a popular Christianity is seen as undesirable.

But, economic gain cannot explain all cases. If the struggle for true faith is considered only as a social struggle, what about the faithful and humble Evangelical, Pentecostal and Charismatic (Protestant and Catholic) pastors, who do not seek material benifits for themselves, yet do not accept popular Christianity? Undoubtedly, unjustice would be done to them. Beneath the social struggle, which may be there in many cases, there is a methodical struggle.[71]

Those who reject popular Christinity as a form of syncretism do so because they do not see salvation 'outside the church' or 'without Christ'. If they had followed a more contextual approach they would have known that judged from the 'fruits of the spirit' there is not more salvation within official Christianity then there is in popular Christianity. This raises the issue of method in theology. If the magisterium (or the sola scriptura principle, its equivalent in protestant theology) pre-

---

[69] Magesa, The Church in Eastern Africa, 10-16.

[70] Hastings, *African Catholicism*, 133-134.

[71] Given the dialectic between the socio-economic position of theologians and their theological concepts, the social struggle and the methodical struggle are often interrelated. There is a deep theological significance in the socio-political context within which we do our theologising, says Kibicho: *The Kikuyu conception of God, Its continuity into the Christian era and the question it raises for the Christian idea of Revelation*. Ph.D. Dissertation. Nashville: Vanderbilt University, 1972, 315, 338.

vail, Christian beliefs serve as a filter which permits pastoral workers to see what they want to see.

What is needed for the future is not primarily new theological concepts, but new theological methods, which involve social sciences as an integral part of theological reflection.[72] Even if practical theology is lectured it is basically applied theology, a top-down approach. I would like African theology to be developed as empirical theology, using cultural anthropology and science of religion not in a two-phase model but in an intra-disciplinary approach.[73]

5.12 Epilogue

It may seem that I am forcing an open door here by pouring old wine in new skins. Are not theologians like Nyamiti and Mbiti trained anthropologists and writing about anthropological issues? Yes they are! But the point is that it does not seem to influence them as theologians very much.[74] At best they follow a two-phase model, observing and analysing the facts as anthropologists, and evaluating them in the light of the gospel as theologians. If training programmes are considered, mainly in major seminaries and higher institutes in Eastern Africa, courses in cultural anthropology and science of religion are still very rare. Mostly they are not in the regular programme, but offered as optional subjects. What is needed for a new church in the third millennium is to develop education programmes for reflective ministry, in which pasto-

---

[72] A challenging new start is given in the pastoral circle, as introduced in Eastern Africa by Rodrigo Mejía.It includes participant observation and social analysis as research instruments. See R. Mejía, The new understanding of pastoral theology, in: C. McGarry, R. Mejía and V. Shirima (eds.), A new light on our path, Nairobi 1993, 27-37; and. R. Mejía, Pastoral Theology and the Pastoral Circle: The Methodology and Dynamics of the Pastoral Circle, in P. Ryan (ed.), *New Strategies for a New Evangelization in Africa,*Nairobi 2002, 111-128.

[73] J. Van der Ven, *Practical theology. An empirical approach*, Kampen 1998.

[74] It is my impression that people as Kibicho are not taken very seriously as theologians, as their works are classified as ‘religious studies’ mainly.

ral-theological reflections are based on profound social-scientific research.[75]

5.13 Further readings on the theology of mission

- S. Bevans and R. Schroeder, *Constants in context. A theology of mission for today*. Maryknoll, New York 2004.
- A. Bünker and L. Weckel (eds.), *"ihr werdet mein Zeige sein .." Rückfragen au seiner störrischen theologischen Disziplin*, Freiburg, Basel and Wien 2005.
- A. Camps, *Partners in dialogue. Christianity and other world religions*, Maryknoll, New York 1983.
- A. Kirk, *What is mission? Theological explorations*, London 1999.
- K. Müller, *Mission theology. An introduction*. Nettetal 1987.
- H. Niebuhr, *Christ and culture*. New York 1951.
- H. Wrogemann (ed.), *Missionstheologien der Gegenwart. Globale Entwicklungen, kontextuelle Profile und ökumenische Herausforderungen*, Gütersloh 2013.

5.14 Questions for better comprehension

1. What are the differences between the mission models of abolition, adaptation, inculturation and liberation?
2. Can you relate each of these models to the theologies of revelation and salvation? Which model do you prefer? Why is that so?
3. What does 'continuity' and 'discontinuity' between Christ and culture mean? Explain the significance of the notions of 'common ground' or 'meeting point' between general specific revelation in your own words.

---

[75] J. Van der Ven, *Education for reflective ministry*, Louvain 1998. A more practical elaboration can be found in my contribution to the East-Asian Pastoral Review 1997 no. 4, titled: The Pastoral Circle in the Training of Church Ministers.

4. What is the difference between syncretism and inculturation? Formulate your answer in relation to the definition of Christian truth.
5. What does the author mean by a 'theology from below'? What does the notion 'sensus fidelium' mean? What is its significance for a theology from below?

Chapter 6 Mission, from inculturation to interculturation

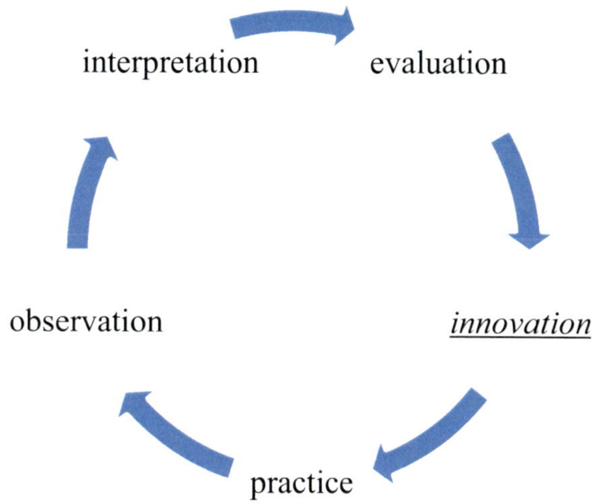

6.1 Introduction

Long before colonial administrators, Christian missionaries accepted that their presence in Africa was temporary. Inspired by the then economic crisis, they nevertheless promoted a local church guided by the principle of being self-governing, self-supporting and self-propagating. During the later part of the 20th century, but especially after the Second World War, the main mission aim was to localise Christianity in Africa. Since the late 1970s official Vatican documents use the word 'inculturation' for this practice. But, in the light of our present-day global and multicultural world, the question is: is inculturation going to help Africa in the 21st century?

It is my contention that inculturation helped Africans to re-gain confidence in themselves after independence. But in the present-day global and multicultural world, a further step is needed, namely interculturation, both contextually (locally) and inter-contextually (globally). I borrow the term interculturation from the Dutch White Father, Joseph Blomjous, one time bishop of Mwanza Diocese (1955-1966), in

Northwest Tanzania.[1] In this chapter I first look at developments in the 20th century that led to shift from the translation model to the inculturation model of mission. Secondly I look at a new understanding of culture in anthropology. Then I explain the need to shift form inculturation to interculturation. Next I deepen my argument from the perspective of the re-tribalisation of the world. Thereafter I look for a theological foundation for interculturation, a theology of interculturation, or inter-cultural theology. And I close with a plea for mission as intercultural mediation.

6.2 From translation to inculturation

After the Christianisation of Europe in medieval times, there was little missionary activity in Western Christianity. New impetus to missionary activity came from the so called 'discoveries' in the 15th and 16th century. Europeans saw Europe as the cradle of Christianity and civilisation as opposed to the non-Western world which was perceived as uncivilised and unsaved. Thus the dominant understanding of mission was to bring the so called 'pagans' the light of Christ and to save them from eternal damnation.

In Roman Catholic mission this meant to win the pagans for the Church as the missionaries believed that outside the church there was no salvation (in Protestant mission it read: without Christ no salvation). But already before the Second World War it became evident that this mission method was not very effective. In consequence another approach developed. The aim remained more or less the same, but the method changed. Still the missionaries wanted non-Christians to enter the church. But the church from her side could meet the pagans halfway, by an 'adaptation' of Christianity in its externals, language, vestments and rituals.

---

[1] Bishop Blomjous accurately foresaw the future course of the Church in Africa. After the Second Vatican Council, in which he participated actively, he resigned as a bishop, at the age of 58, to hand over to an African successor.

Whereas the 'adaptation' approach was still very strong in the 1960s, and has become stronger again in the 1990s, among others, due to the rise of the Pentecostal and Charismatic movements, some missionaries and local priests worked out a new understanding of mission. It was recognised that Christ was already present in the non-Christian cultures. The missionary's task was only to help the non-Christians to discover the active presence of Christ in their lives. This 'deeper adaptation' or 'incarnation' approach was justified by the Second Vatican Council.

I will not go into details as this history has been described again and again.[2] In this chapter I am more interested in the social, political and religious changes that lead to these shifts. Sociology of knowledge teaches that paradigm shifts in mission do not start with theology, but with societal developments. I argue that present-day societal developments make a new shift in mission thinking necessary.

The First and even more so the Second World War caused doubt about the simplistic dichotomy between civilised and uncivilised, saved and unsaved people, on which European mission was built. It became evident that there were many uncivilised people in Europe. The Holocaust, among others, had shown this clearly. The collapse of the colonial system soon after the Second World War lead to formation of independent states in Africa, and also the Churches there became local, beginning with the African independent churches.

Together with the political de-colonisation process there was a loss of triumphant feelings of superiority in Europe on the one hand, leading to cultural relativism and secularisation, and the revival of neo-traditional movements in Africa on the other, such as African authenticity in Zaire, African socialism in Tanzania African humanism in Zambia.

Then there are the demographic changes. In the early 1970s it was widely acknowledged that the center of gravity of Christianity would shift to the southern hemisphere, and that this shift would continue in

---

[2] Cf. F. Oborji, *Concepts of Mission in the evolution of contemporary missiology*, Rome and Lagos 2005.

the next decades.[3] The Second Vatican Council may be considered as the first manifestation of the World Church.

Last but not least there are theological changes. The Second Vatican Council recognised that mission is primarily a responsibility of the local church. Thus after the council localisation, indigenisation, contextualisation or inculturation became imperative. The term 'inculturation' was used by the Jesuits in Rome in the early 1960s and it was introduced in official Vatican documents in the late 1970s.[4] I consider 'inculturation' to be the dominant mission model in the late 20th century.

6.3 Cultural consequences of globalisation

But the question is: inculturation in what culture? Because of the rapid expansion of information- and communication technologies, and the internationalisation of economic activities and political institutions, contacts between people of various cultural backgrounds increase. On the one hand there is a process of blending cultures and religions ('creolisation'). On the other hand people and groups define narrow-minded identities ('retribilasation') and fight a 'jihad' against other 'tribes'.[5]

As far as we know, Africa has always been multicultural. And there has always been contact between cultures. This fact is demonstrated, among others, by the Indonesian presence in Madagascar and the Indian Ocean trading complex which has linked East Africa with the Arab world, India and China for more than two thousand years. Swahili language and Taarab music is a cultural mix of African, Arab and Indian cultural influences.

What is new is not that there are various cultures and that various cultures meet, but the speed and extent of culture contact. Most socie-

---

[3] Cf. F. Wijsen and R. Schreiter (eds.), *Global Christianity. Contested claims*, Amsterdam and New York 2007.

[4] Cf. J.-M. Waliggo et al., *Inculturation. Its meaning and urgency*, Nairobi 1986; A. Shorter, *Toward a theology of inculturation*, Maryknoll, New York 1988.

[5] Cf. B. Barber, *Jihad vs. McWorld*, New York 1995.

ties in the world are multicultural, not in the sense of a patchwork or a mosaic of separate pieces with hard, well-defined edges, but in the sense of a salad bowl or a fruit cocktail.[6]

Cities such as Paris and London, but also Accra or Nairobi, create cultures that are a mix of Hindu, Sikh, African and Muslim traditions, combined with secular-political and ethnic ideals, bound together by reggae or rap music. The situation is not much different in the rural hamlets where trans-national culture reaches through returning migrants, who bring North America or Europe to the African villages, or development workers and native expatriates who come to the rural areas from the capital cities to implement governmental development policies.

The village where I used to live in Northwest Tanzania has become 'glocal',[7] with a United Nations High Commission for Refugees office in Mwanza with its 'missions' to the troubled territories in Central Lake Region and Northern Uganda, South African gold mines in Geita and Kahama, the Lake Fisheries fishing for Nile Perch in Lake Victoria for European markets, and the Sukuma Dance Group in Bujora selling ethnicity as commodity and making their traditional harvest festival a performance for tourists.[8]

Multiculturality has always been part and parcel of local communities. The popular image of Africa as a content of more or less closed and homogeneous communities may be nothing but a Lost Paradise ideology, based on romantic notions of *Heimat* and *Gemeinschaft*, not so much destroyed by globality but rather produced by it.[9] Poly-

---

[6] Cf. U. Hannerz, *Cultural complexity. Studies in the social organization of meaning*, New York 1992.

[7] The film *Darwin's Nightmare* by film-maker Hubert Sauper shows all the evils of 'glocalisation', without showing the benefits for the local people and the creativity by which they make use of them.

[8] W. Van Binsbergen, *Intercultural encounters. African and anthropological lessons towards a philosophy of interculturality*, Münster 2003.

[9] Cf. R. Robertson, Glocalization. Time – space and homogeniety – heterogeneity, in: M. Featherstone, S. Lash and R. Robertson (eds.), *Global modernities*, London 1995, 25-44.

ethnicity and war were normal states of affair. This is as true for Africa as it is for Europe.

What anthropologists acknowledge now more than before is that there is a plurality of overlapping cultural orientations, associated with language, gender, ethnicity, nationality, education, profession and social background. In *public life* people are situated at the intersection of ever changing cultural orientations with little systematic connection between them. Even in their *private lives* people have diverse cultural orientations that cannot simply be integrated.

6.4 Beyond inculturation

For our understanding of mission as inculturation this new understanding of culture has enormous consequences. The process of inculturation is not simply the interaction between two or three cultures, the culture of the bible, the culture of the missionary and the culture of those who receive the bible, as scholars such as Eugene Nida and David Hesselgrave suggest.[10]

To begin with, 'cultures do not exist', at least not in the way modern anthropologists thought they existed.[11] What exists is a multiplicity of overlapping cultural orientations, none of which coincides with a particular society or territory. Anthropologists now would not write about *the* Nuer or *the* Ndembu as Evans Pritchard and Victor Turner did. Of course, also these anthropologists were aware of the cultural contradictions, but these contradictions were unified in what was thought to be shared meaning-systems. Now anthropologists stress culture as organisation of diversity.[12]

Moreover, scholars of religion and theologians have become aware that the Bible and Christianity are multicultural phenomena. Speaking about Christianity in general, the Tanzanian theologian Laurenti Mage-

---

[10] Cf. D. Hesselgrave, *Communication Christ cross-culturally. An introduction to Missionary Communication*, Grand Rapids 1978.
[11] Cf. Van Binsbergen, *Cultural encounters*, 459-522.
[12] Cf. Hannerz, *Cultural complexity*, 217-267.

sa says: "there is no 'pure' Christianity. Neither now nor at any other time, anywhere in the world, has there ever been a form of Christianity free from cultural influences. What we have had, and what we have got, are simply 'christianities', local theologies and spiritualities".[13]

And last but not least, the missionaries are not mono-cultural either.[14] At best, Christianity is a cultural orientation alongside other cultural orientations. He or she may have strong nationalist sentiments, political opinions or economic convictions. When a missionary is visited by a women who says that she is possessed by evil spirits, it is more likely that the missionary tells her to go to the hospital and see a medical doctor than that he or she gives her a blessing. Much of what missionaries do is based on a dominant secular – scientific world rather than the Christian belief.[15]

More than twenty-five years ago the Dutch White Father bishop Joseph Blomjous coined the term interculturation "in order to express that the process of inculturation must be lived in partnership and mutuality".[16] According to Blomjous (1980: 398) this term indicates "that we are at the take-off point of a new age in Mission development." The term 'interculturation' did not find its way into the missiological debate, but I find it most appropriate for today's discussion on mission in a new key.

---

[13] L. Magesa, Being honest about inculturation on Africa, in: *Service* (2006)5, 38.

[14] At present psychologists speak about multiple identities or polyphonic selves. Cf. H. Hermans and H. Kempen, *The dialogical self. Meaning as movement*, San Diego 1993.

[15] This is one reason for the rapid growth of spirit movements in Africa. Cf. C. Comoro and J. Sivalon, The Marian Faith Healing Ministry. An African expression of popular Catholicism in Tanzania, in: T. Spear and I. Kimambo (eds.), *East African expressions of Christianity*, Oxford and Nairobi 1999, 275-295.

[16] J. Blomjous, Development in mission thinking and practice. 1959-1980. Inculturation and Interculturation, in: *African Ecclesial Review* 22(1980)6, 293.

6.5 Re-tribalisation of the world

There is another reason to go beyond inculturation. The globalisation process gives rise to an opposite trend, that of a revival of ethnocentrism, referred to above as a 're-tribalisation' of the world,[17] not seldom through inventions of traditions.[18] The situation in Central Africa, but also in Northern Uganda, Western Sudan and the Horn of Africa, may serve as examples.

At present 18 out of 54 member states of the African Union have civil wars raging on their territory. Four of the five largest refugee populations in the world are African. Of course, ethnicity is not the only factor in these wars. There are African states that have many ethnic groups on their territory and that are relatively stable. There are also African states that have only one ethnic group but where things went terribly wrong. In most cases there is a multiplicity of factors involved: ecological, political, economic, religious *and* ethnic.

The Kenyan scholar of religion and theologian, Jesse Mugambi notes, "corporate identity is essential in African thought". And "Kinship relation is the basis of this corporate identity". According to him, "it is this fact that makes 'tribalism' a great problem in modern Africa".[19] Therefore, Mugambi urges, "At the beginning of the third millennium, it is important to strongly affirm that African identity transcends race and religion … We need as broad a frame of reference as that which the Pan-Africanists promoted at the end of the nineteenth century".[20]

---

[17] Cf. M. McLuhan, *The Gutenberg galaxy*, Toronto 1962.

[18] Cf. T. Ranger, The invention of tradition in colonial Africa, in: E. Hobsbawm and T. Ranger (eds.), *The invention of tradition*, Cambridge 1983, 216-254.

[19] J. Mugambi, *African heritage and contemporary Christianity*, Nairobi 1989, 136.

[20] J. Mugambi, *Christian theology and social reconstruction*, Nairobi 2003, 112-113. I would like to add: At the beginning of the 21st century, Africans need a frame of reference much broader than Pan-Africanism. Africans need

Missionary approaches towards ethnicity have been ambiguous. Sometimes the ethnic identity of a people was abolished as being possessed by the devil and consequently replaced by Christianity. In other cases the missionaries preserved and even promoted ethnic identity as resources of local theology and church development.

Undoubtedly, by safeguarding local traditions, attempts at inculturation gave Africans a psychological boost for self-discovery and self-realisation.[21] But if this is too strong, churches can become channels for ethnocentric and nationalist sentiments, as was the case with some missionaries' support for Tutsi political aspirations in Rwanda.[22]

If inculturation means the immersion of the church in the divisions of multicultural societies, if it re-enforces ethnic identities rather than criticising them, be they Hutu-Tutsi, Kikuyu-Luo, Ibo-Yoruba, this is certainly not going to help social cohesion in Africa. The church must challenge the givenness of cultural boundaries. This requires a critical theory of culture and a critical theology of acculturation.[23]

6.6 Theology of interculturation

When mission at the Second Vatican Council was defined in terms of a 'deeper adaptation' and 'incarnation' this was a break-through in the understanding of mission. It meant a recognition of other cultures in their own right. Yet, it is my contention that this breakthrough does not go far enough.

---

to become 'global' Africans, or even better 'glocal': think globally, act locally.

[21] Cf. S. Eboh, *African communalism. The way to social harmony and peaceful co-existence*, Frankfurt am Main and London 2004, 4.

[22] If inculturation affirmed culture rather than criticising it may compromise the gospel as happened with the German *Volkskirche* under the Nazi regime, and the identification of the Orthodox Church with Serbian identity in Bosnia Herzegovina.

[23] Cf. I. Linden, The Churches and genocide. Lessons from the Rwandan tragedy, in: *The Month*, July 1995, 256-263.

If we contrast the major mission models and their respective theologies we can say that translation was based on exclusivist theology, adaptation on dialectical theology and inculturation on inclusivist theology. But in my view, inclusivist theology does not facilitate dialogue. The incarnation theology is based on cultural imperialism, presupposing that other religions are already included in the own religion.[24]

For being really dialogical another model is needed, one that acknowledges pluralistic revelation. For solving this problem I take inspiration from the Kenyan scholar of religion and theologian, Samuel Kibicho, who holds that there is full and fully saving revelation in African cultures and religions *independently* of Christ.[25]

The idea that there is salvation in African cultures *independently* of Christ seems far removed from a genuine Roman Catholic understanding of inculturation. The official teaching of the Roman Catholic Church since the Second Vatican Council is that there can be salvation in other religions through God's action in the Spirit. But this Spirit is the Spirit of Christ and does not work independently of Him.[26]

How to go about this problem? Within the New Testament – and within early Christianity – there are at least two ways of speaking about the Spirit in relationship to Christ: Christ is the carrier of the spirit, and He is the sender of the Spirit.[27] Later on the second idea started to predominate in theology. For our purpose, however, it is important to keep the two ideas together.

---

[24] Cf. S. Kibicho, *God and revelation in an African contexts*, Nairobi 2006, 176.

[25] Cf. Kibicho, *God and revelation*, 171-172.

[26] Cf. Pope John Paul II, Encyclical Letter 'Redemptoris Missio', nos. 21 and 29; International Theological Commission, Christianity and the religions, Nos. 81 and 94; Congregation for the Doctrine of the Faith, Declaration 'Dominus Jesus'. Vatican City 2000, No. 12.

[27] Cf. W. Kasper, Geest – Christus – Kerk, in: J. Lescrauwaet et al. (eds.), *Leven uit de Geest. Theologische Peilingen aangeboden aan E. Schillebeeckx*, Hilversum 1974, 46-64; P. Schoonenberg, *De geest, het Woord en de Zoon*, Averbode 1991.

In the Greek Orthodox Church the first line of thinking predominates. It never accepted the idea that the Holy Spirit is the spirit of the Father and the Son (*filioque*). It holds that the Spirit originates directly from God and that the Spirit is not subordinated to Christ. In its dialogue with the Greek Orthodox church, the Roman Catholic Church tends to interpret the relationship between Christ and the Spirit 'in full harmony' with the Greek Orthodox view. It says that there is a 'legitimate complementariness' between the theologies of both traditions and that the Father is the only source of both the Son and the Spirit.[28]

This ecumenical dialogue can pave the way for missionary dialogue, as happened more often in church history.[29] The theology of the 'two hands of the Father' allows for a theology of interculturation that makes room for unity-in-diversity.[30] Already Karl Rahner spoke about a twofold mission of God. God sends the Word into the history as a human being, and He sends the Spirit into the history as an empowering gift. The sending of the Son results in Christian particularity, the sending of the Spirit results in the universality of God's grace. Both 'missions' are distinct, but not separated, since they are extensions of the persons within the Trinity.[31]

---

[28] Cf. Pontifical Council for promoting Christian Unity, Traditions regarding the procession of the Holy Spirit, in: *Eastern Churches Journal* 2(1995)3, 35-46; *Catechism of the Catholic Church*, Dublin 1994, No. 248.

[29] I do not want to suggest that in its practice the Geek-orthodox Church is more open to African culture than the Roman Catholic Church, but in theory it is.

[30] It was Archbishop Makarios of the African Orthodox Church (Greek Orthodox Patriarchate of Alexandria and All Africa) in Kenya, and the dean of the African Orthodox Seminary "Makarios III" in Nairobi, Innocentius Byakotonda, who made me aware of this. In my interview with them (27.02.04) they said, "You [Westerners] corrupted the faith by adding *filioque* to the Apostolic Creed. The Apostolic Creed was accepted by a Ecumenical Council. And it can only be changed by a Ecumenical Council".

[31] Cf. K. Rahner, Einzigkeit and Dreifaltigkeit Gottes, in: A. Bsteh (ed.), *Der Gott des Christentums and des Islam*, Mödling 1978, 133.

6.7 Mission as intercultural mediation

In the beginning of the 21st century, missionaries as cross-cultural ministers will almost always operate alongside indigenous pastoral workers. Their special vocation is not to do what local pastors do or should do, but to add a specific inter-cultural orientation to pastoral ministry. The inter-cultural orientation starts from the assumption that 'we' and the 'others' (e.g., Europeans and Africans) are not basically the same (identity model) nor radically different (alterity model) but that there are cultural overlaps between us and them (analogy model).[32]

That is why there is neither total translatability nor radical un-translatability of religious concepts. Understanding is always partial understanding. Necessarily there is a misunderstanding understanding or understanding misunderstanding between people of various cultural (religious) backgrounds.[33] Thus, intercultural communication is a source of social cohesion, but also of conflict.[34]

Intercultural mediation tries to make people aware of the cultural dimension in conflicts.[35] On the one hand, it starts from the assumption that cultural orientations do not determine human behavior, as cultural orientations are not shared by people of the same society to the same

---

[32] Cf. R. Mall, *Intercultural philosophy*, Lanham 2000.

[33] Earlier I wrote about Christianity in Northwest Tanzania as a "working misunderstanding". Cf. R. Tanner and F. Wijsen, Christianity in Usukuma: A working misunderstanding, in: *Neue Zeitschrift für Missionswissenschaft* 49(1993)3, 177-193.

[34] The German missiologist Theo Sundermeier speaks about the 'trader' model. The other is a resource to serve one's interests. That is why intercultural encounter is always ambiguous: today's companion can be tomorrow's competitor. See T. Sundermeier, Aspects of interreligious hermeneutics, in: M. Frederiks, M. Dijkstra and A. Houtepen (eds.), *Towards an intercultural theology*, Zoetermeer 2003, 71.

[35] Cf. D. Busch, *Interkulturelle Mediation. Eine theoretische Grundleging triadischer Konfliktbearbeitung in interkulturell bedingten Kontexten*, Frankfurt am Main 2005; D. Busch and H. Schröder (eds.), *Perspektiven interkultureller Mediation. Grundlagentexte zur kommunikationswissenschaftlichen Analyse triadichen Verständigung*, Frankfurt am Main 2005; C.-H. Mayer, *Intercultural Mediation and Conflict Resolution*, Stuttgart 2005.

extent. Many conflicts that are called inter-cultural are nothing but inter-personal. On the other hand, it makes people conscious if the fact that cultural orientations can play a role in inter-personal misunderstanding.

Missionaries as intercultural mediators may also protest when cultural traditions are misused, e.g., to oppress women or to exclude youngsters from decision-making. Traditional rituals in South Africa, Rwanda and now in Northern Uganda have been used for peace and reconciliation processes, where people cry for justice to be done.[36]

6.8 Conclusion

Whereas inculturation was the main mission model of the second half of the 20th century, interculturation will be the main mission model of the first half of 21st century, both contextually (locally) and inter-contextually (globally). Undoubtedly, inculturation will continue. Cultural imperialism still exists, thus mental de-colonisation must go on. But at the same time, a further step is needed. In our 21st century Africans cannot be satisfied with narrow-minded ethnic identities. They must go for concrete universality, without losing their particularities. This is what interculturation is all about.

6.9 Further readings on the pedagogy of mission

- A. Bellagamba, *Mission and ministry in the global Church*, Maryknoll, New York 1992.
- S. Bevans and R. Schroeder, *Prophetic dialogue. Reflections on Christian Mission today*, Maryknoll, New York 2011.
- A. Gittins, *Mission at the margins. Strategy and spirituality for mission*, Maryknoll, New York 2002.

---

[36] Cf. T. Allen, *Trial justice. The International Criminal Court and the Lord's Resistance Army*, London and New York 2006, 128-186.

- I. Illich, *Mission and midwifery. Essays on missionary formation*, Gwelo 1974.
- K. Jørgensen, *Equipping for service. Christian leadership in Church and society*, Oxford 2012.
- C. Ott and J. Payne (eds.), *Missionary methods. Research, reflections and realities*, Passadena 2013.
- F. Scheuerer, *Interculturality. A challenge for the mission of the Church*. Bangalore 2001.
- J. Woodberry, C. Van Engen and E. Elliston (eds.), *Missiological education for the 21st century. The Book, the circle and the sandals*, Maryknoll, New York 1997.

6.10 Questions for better comprehension

1. In your opinion, has there been a convergence or divergence of cultures in the process globalisation and culture contact?
2. According to you, have non-Western peoples been active participants or passive victims in the history of mission?
3. What is the difference between inculturation and interculturation? According to the author, why is interculturation the mission model for the 21st century?
4. What is the relation between Christ and the Spirit in God's salvation history? How can there be salvation in African cultures independently of Christ?
5. Why is there neither total translatability nor radical untranslatability of religious concepts? What does the author mean by 'understanding misunderstanding', or 'misunderstanding understanding'?

Conclusion Communication between Europeans and Africans

The debate on multiculturalism has been raging in the Netherlands for some ten years.[1] By and large it centres on the question whether ours is, or ought to be, a multicultural society and whether new migrants must adapt to our lifestyle, or whether they can and may retain their distinctive character. The discussions we are hearing currently in the course of election campaigns clearly demonstrate how unprepared the Netherlands is for a multicultural society. Whether it is a matter of head scarves, female circumcision, arranged marriages, Islamic primary education, acceptance of homosexuality or separation of church and state: on the whole the Dutch are completely at a loss what to do about it or, even worse, believe they know best.

The thesis I want to defend in this conclusion is that missionaries and missionary institutions have considerable expertise in dealing with cultural differences. Often they have worked for many years in non-Western societies abroad and nowadays they are increasingly working in multicultural communities in the Netherlands. As an empirical study and theological reflection on missionary practice,[2] missiology can not

---

[1] The term multiculturalism was first used in the United States in the early 20th century in contradistinction to the idea of multicultural society as a crucible. In the Netherlands the social debate got under way in 1994 when the then leader of the National Party for Freedom and Democracy, Frits Bolkestein, put the subject of integration without forfeiting identity up for discussion. Within universities the debate has been nourished partly by the brochure 'Multicultural and Pluriform Society in the Netherlands' of the Netherlands Organisation for Scientific Research (The Hague 1997).

[2] It is not possible to go into the whole debate on the definition of missiology. You are referred to L. Ramambason, *Missiology: its subject-matter and method. A study of mission-doers in Madagascar,* Frankfurt am Main 1999; F. Verstraelen (ed.), *Oecumenische inleiding in de missiologie,* Kampen 1988, 17-23; D. Bosch, *Transforming mission,* Maryknoll, New York 1991, 8-11; S. Karotemprel (ed.), *Following Christ in mission,* Nairobi 1995, 21-36; and S. Karotemprel et al., *Promoting mission studies*, Shillong 2000.

only contribute to a theory of intercultural (religious) communication but also help to reduce conflict in a multicultural society.

Between 1800 and 1940 some 7,500 Dutch missionaries left for overseas countries. Round 1950 one out of every 550 Dutch Catholics was working as a missionary in a remote part of the world and one out every nine missionaries operating in the world was Dutch! In 1963 another 1,029 Dutch missionaries left for foreign parts. This made the Netherlands the country with the largest number of missionaries in the world.

Today there are still some 1,800 Dutch missionaries operative in the world, not counting development workers in missionary related organisations. Although this is a much smaller number than the 10,000 Dutch missionaries who were working abroad in 1968 admittedly a disproportionately high figure it is still a respectable number, certainly compared with the 1,600 parish pastors ministering in the Netherlands.[3]

And even though the membership of missionary institutions in the Netherlands is declining, they are still part of global networks who perpetuate the missionary experience, for instance in new provinces or congregations overseas and local lay movements or missionary organisations. The Catholic co-funding organisation Cordaid alone employs 285 people and the Central Mission Commissariat, the umbrella organisation of the missionary institutions of religious orders, another fifty people. These people maintain close daily contact with partners in the southern hemisphere and non-Westerners in our own society. They strive for equal relations and reciprocity.

But is it really true that missionaries and missiologists have special expertise in dealing with, and reflecting on, cultural differences? And if

---

[3] Cf. A. Van den Eerenbeemt, *De missie-actie in Nederland. 1600 - 1940,* Nijmegen 1945; A. Freitag (ed.), *Emigranten voor God: wereldbetekenis van het Nederlandse missiewerk.* Parts 1 and 2, SteijlTegelen 1949. The number of missionaries abroad is taken from the review, 'Mensen met een missie' of the 'Centraal Missie Commissariaat', 1 August 2000. The number of parish pastors, excluding pastors working in care institutions, is taken from J. Massaar and L. Spruit, 'Kerncijfers uit de kerkelijke statistiek 2000 van het R.K. Kerkgenootschap in Nederland', KASKI memorandum no. 321, October 2001.

so, what is the nature of this expertise? In answering this question I confine myself to communication between Europeans and Africans, firstly in Africa (more particularly East Africa) but also, because of the growing influx of African migrants, increasingly in Europe as well. I also confine myself to the intercultural communication of religious meanings that has occurred in the missionary movement since the 19th century.

7.1 The 'African Myth'

Let me say at once that there are some grounds for claiming the exact opposite, namely that missionaries, as propagandists of the one true faith and collaborators of colonial administrative officialdom, have destroyed local cultures and contributed to 'anthropological poverty' in Africa and the 'cultural death' of Africans, as some African theologians maintain.[4]

After the conversion of Constantine the church inherited the imperialist perception of the Roman empire, which regarded its own culture as the only civilised one and everything else as 'barbaric', but assimilable. In the eastern Roman empire at any rate, the church was subordinate to the state. In the West the church became the guardian of classical culture for many centuries. 'Secular' authorities had only nominal power over Christian subjects. Mission was imperial mission. At an imperial level other forms of religion were not to be tolerated. This is in fact the difference between Christianising and conversion. Christianising entails making the public arena 'Christian'. Conversion is aimed at personal access to faith.

The doctrine of 'no salvation outside the church' also represented a revolutionary development in Western history: recognition of individuals' personal responsibility for their salvation. This required the sacra-

---

[4] Cf. E. Mveng, *L'Afrique dans l'église,* Paris 1985, 199; L. Magesa, Overview of 100 Years of Catholicism in Kenya, in: *African Ecclesial Review* 32(1990)1, 42-50. See also A. Ngindu Mushete, *Les thèmes majeurs de la théologie Africaine,* Paris 1989, 102-105.

ments, which were available only in the church. To put it in present-day terms: conversion was 'above' culture; Christianising meant public submission to 'Christian' culture. As a result conversion was a monastic preserve for many centuries. In addition the missionaries that were sent to Africa in the 19th and 20th centuries knew next to nothing about mission in earlier centuries. The doctrine of 'no salvation outside the church' legitimised an expansionist mission practice.[5]

In his study of Dutch missionaries' conceptions of Africans a former colleague, Albert de Jong, said "that the average missionary, up to the Second Vatican Council, had a negative and destructive approach to African culture".[6] The 'average missionary' regarded Africans as primitive, irreligious, stupid and lazy. In his recently published memoirs a Dutch missionary who worked for many years in Sukumaland in northwestern Tanzania, a region where I myself lived and worked for some time, writes that round about 1950 elderly people often said, "We are living in darkness", echoing the eulogy of Zacheus in Luke's gospel which they had learnt from an earlier generation of missionaries

This missionary added, however, that even at that time, twelve years before the start of Vatican II, he felt that "the distance [between Christianity and African culture] is being maintained artificially" and that "Africans have a worthwhile culture of their own".[7] As early as 1946 the Flemish missionary Placide Tempels indicated in his *Bantu philosophy* that Africans are by no means primitive but are perfectly capable of logical thought, thus laying the foundation for 'adaptation' theology.

---

[5] Cf. D. Bosch, *Transforming mission,* 214-238; A. Bredero, *De ontkerstening der Middeleeuwen,* Baarn 2000; T. Schäfer, P. Schallenberg and U. Zzelinka (eds.), *Zur Mission herausgefordert,* Paderborn 1999.

[6] Cf. A. De Jong, Africans viewed in the missionary mirror, in: *Exchange. Journal of Missiological and Ecumenical Research* 30(2001)1, 49-77. Also see J. Heijke et al., *In elkaars spiegel. Westers Christendom in Afrika,* Baarn 1993.

[7] Cf. N. de Bekker, *Hand in hand met Afrika,* Tilburg 2000, 35. Similar views can be found in the memoirs of another Dutch missionary who worked in Sukumaland earlier. Cf. J. Hendriks, *Brieven uit Afrika* [Boxtel 1948], 53, in which he describes mission as (our translation) "getting the heathen to cross from darkness into Light".

In his *Bantu philosophy* Tempels demolished some previously accepted anthropological theories.[8]

The cultural destruction wrought by missionaries is often exaggerated and missionaries' influence on Africans is overestimated. Nowadays this is acknowledged by historians and anthropologists.[9] Besides, practice often differed from theory, and in the field there was often a great deal more construction (schools, hospitals) and dialogue than is evident in the accounts of missionaries, something which Theo Salemink does not allow for sufficiently in his *Afrikaanse Mythe.*[10]

7.2 'Christianity' and 'cultures'

Thus practice was more advanced than theory. But gradually the theory improved: missiologists like John Taylor (former missionary in Uganda), Adrian Hastings (former missionary in Uganda and Tanzania) and Aylward Shorter (former missionary in Tanzania, currently working in Kenya) no longer thought in terms of 'adaptation' but of 'incarnation'. Local culture does not have to disappear, because Christ was already present in that culture. Christ was there before the missionaries arrived. The missionaries' task was not to bring Christ to Africa but to

---

[8] Cf. P. Tempels, *Bantoe-filosofie,* Antwerp 1946. For arguments for and against Tempels see M. Nkufu Nkemnkia, *African vitalogy: a step forward in African thinking*, Nairobi 1999, 38-106; H. Kimmerle, *Mazungumzo. Dialogen tussen Afrikaanse en Westerse filosofieën,* Amsterdam 1995; T. Sundermeier, *Nur gemeinsam können wir leben. Das Menschenbild schwarzafrikanischer Religionen,* Gütersloh 1988.

[9] Writing on 15th- and 16th-century Portuguese mission in Congo A. Hastings claims that missionaries and Africans communicated on an equal footing. A. Hastings, *The church in Africa. 1450 - 1950,* Oxford 1994, 73-75; D. Petersen and J. Aallman (eds.), Africans meeting missionaries: rethinking colonial encounters, in: *Journal of Religious History,* 23(1999)1. U. Bitterli, *Die 'Wilden' und die 'Zivilisierten',* München 1976, 106-130, who is highly critical of Western expansionism, is very mild in his judgment of missionaries.

[10] Cf. T. Salemink, *De Afrikaanse mythe,* Kampen 1997. In his scientific appendix (218-226) the author does not ask whether the missionaries' stories correspond with the historical facts of mission in Africa, nor what aims the editors of the missionary journals he studied had in mind.

discover and identify Christ in Africa. This was a reversion to the old missionary ideal of 'pilgrimage to God'. In 1963 John Taylor wrote in his *The primal vision*:

> It is the lordship of Christ which is in question. Either he is the Lord of all possible worlds and of all human cultures, or he is the Lord of one world and one culture only. Either we must think of the Christian Mission in terms of bringing the Muslim, the Hindu, the Animist into Christendom, or we must go with Christ as he stands in the midst of Islam, of Hinduism, of the primal world-view, and watch with him, fearfully and wonderingly, as he becomes dare we say it? Muslim or Hindu or Animist.[11]

After Pope Paul VI's solemn declaration at the end of the first gathering of the Symposium of Episcopal Conferences of Africa and Madagascar at Kampala in 1969 that Africans are entitled to an African Christianity, the bishops of Africa and Madagascar stated, in their preparation for the Synod on Evangelisation in the modern World in 1974, that they regarded the 'theology of adaptation' as completely outdated. In its place they embraced the 'theology of incarnation'.[12]

But this theory, too, obstructed justice to Africa culture, since truth and goodness in African cultures were related to Christ. As a result a theory was developed which posited that African religions contained truth and goodness independently of Christ. This notion was substanti-

---

[11] J. Taylor, *The primal vision. Christian presence amid African religion,* London 1963, 113. Also see A. Hastings, *Church and mission in modern Africa,* London 1967, 15-32; A. Shorter, *Priest in the village: experiences of African community,* London 1979, 3; V. Donavan, *Christianity rediscovered,* Notre Dame 1978; J. Healey, *A fifth Gospel. The experience of black Christian values,* Maryknoll, New York 1981, 4-5.

[12] Cf. Pope Paul VI, Address at the closing of the all African Bishop's symposium, in: *African Ecclesial Review* 11(1969)4, 402-405; Statement of the bishops of Africa, in: *African Ecclesial Review* 17(1975)1, 56-59.

ated in Christian terms on the basis of the work of the Holy Spirit as an independent line running throughout salvation history.[13]

Some missiologists also maintain that the abolition of Africa's indigenous cultures, as practised by the first missionaries to the continent, should now be followed by the abolition of Christianity in Africa and a reversion to 'the ways of the ancestors'. In my view this theory is inadequate and cannot be justified theologically. Still, missiological theory is increasingly accommodating and valuing African cultures and the missionary movement, itself an age-old catalyst of universality and uniformity, is coming to appreciate the particularity of Africa and Africans. This transition occurred at a time when anthropologists were still speaking about Africans in semi-evolutionist terms. Okot p'Bitek recalls:

> I first met a number of Western scholars at Oxford University in 1960. During the very first lecture in the Institute of Social Anthropology, the teacher kept referring to Africans or non-Western peoples as barbarians, savages, primitives, tribes, etc. I protested; but to no avail. All the professors and lecturers in the institute, and those who came from outside to read papers, spoke the same insulting language.[14]

In this respect Dutch people can learn a lot from missionaries and missiologists. For in everyday speech 'non-Western' and 'African' often still connote 'barbarian' or 'primitive', as witness the horror stories that keep cropping up. Recently it was suggested that the 'young girl of Nulde' might have been the victim of ritual murder, which, according

---

[13] Cf. J. Taylor, *The go-between God: The Holy Spirit and Christian mission,* London 1972, 25-41; S. Kibicho, *The Kikuyu conception of God,* Nashville 1972, 309-324.

[14] O. p'Bitek, *African religions in Western scholarship,* Nairobi 1970, vii. Also see D. Westerlund, The study of African religions in retrospect from 'Westernization' to 'Africanization', in: J. Olupona and S. Nnyang (eds.), *Religious plurality in Africa,* Berlin and New York 1993, 43-66.

to a police spokesperson, is 'quite customary in Africa'. This actually led to the dispatch of a research team to Africa.[15]

7.3 From inculturation to interculturation

In missiological terms we are dealing with the problem of inculturation, a term derived from the anthropological concept of acculturation which takes us to the border area between missiology and anthropology. Missiological literature on inculturation distinguishes between two aspects: the indigenisation of Christianity, and the insertion of the missionary in the local culture, which may be rendered more aptly by the anthropological concept of enculturation.[16]

Many missionaries have experienced in the flesh what it means to live in another culture; most have had to learn wisdom the hard way; some were trained for it in missionary induction centres for the study of languages and culture. Missionaries have also contributed greatly to the study and preservation of cultures and languages, a point made by Lamin Sanneh when he described mission as a translation movement.[17]

---

[15] The 'young girl of Nulde' was the name given to a young girl whose torso was found on Nulde beach. She was a victim of crime. Similar stories did the rounds about mummified children's bodies found in the Netherlands, which are said to relate to Nigerian voodoo practices; similarly single minor asylum seekers from Nigeria who end up as prostitutes are attributed to voodoo practices.

[16] By now there is a vast literature on inculturation. You are referred to A. Roest Crollius and T. Nnkeramihigo, *What is so new about inculturation?* Rome 1984; A. Shorter, *Toward a theology of inculturation*, Maryknoll, New York 1988; J.-M. Waliggo et al., *Inculturation. Its meaning and urgency*, Nairobi 1986; A. Gittins (ed.), *Life and death matters: the practice of inculturation in Africa,* Nettetal 2000.

[17] See A. De Jong, *De missionaire opleiding van Nederlandse missionarissen,* Kampen 1995, 96-99. B. Joinet, I am a stranger in my father's house: the insertion of the missionary into a local community, in: *Pastoral Orientation Service* No. 8-9, 1972, 17-28 remains a gem. Also noteworthy is the paper 'Adaptation' (1962) that father Jan Hendriks uses in his course at the Pastoral Formation Centre at Kipalapala, Tanzania. For mission as a translation

It is not surprising, then, that missionaries who have returned to the Netherlands are often to be found in places where large numbers of foreigners and refugees congregate, that they exert themselves on behalf of asylum seekers who have been turned down or migrant women who have been commodified.

Missiology abounds in theories on the question whether, and if so, how and in how far, missionaries can and should adapt to local cultures.[18] Missionary anthropology in particular dwells on such issues, encouraged by such agencies as Missionaries of the divine Word and the Anthropos Institute.[19] The American journal *Missiology* still carries the subtitle, 'continuing practical anthropology' and the renowned German *Zeitschrift für Missions- und Religionswissenschaft* retains this title to this day, even though elsewhere missiology and religious studies have long been separated.

Gradually missiologists have come to realise that in the missionary enterprise there are no senders and recipients of messages, only participants in a process, hence that inculturation is an interactive affair. This led Joseph Blomjous, former bishop of Mwanza in Sukumaland, to

---

movement see L. Sanneh, *Translating the message. Missionary impact on culture,* Maryknoll, New York 1989.

[18] Cf. E. Nida, *Customs, culture and Christianity*, London 1954; L. Reed, *Preparing missionaries for intercultural communication*, Pasadena 1985; W. Smalley (ed.), *Readings in missionary anthropology*, New York 1967; A. Shorter, *African culture and the Christian Church*, London 1973, and the totally revised edition: *African culture. An overview*, Nairobi 1998; C. Kraft, *Anthropology for Christian Witness*, Maryknoll, New York 1996; L. Luzbetak, *The Church and cultures. New Perspectives in Missiological Anthropology*, Maryknoll, New York 1989.

[19] Well-known names are Wilhelm Schmidt, founder and eventually director of the Anthropos Institute, Louis Luzbetak, author of the previously cited book *The church and cultures,* the anthropological journal *Anthropos* and the missiological journal *Verbum SVD*. See J. Piepke (ed.), *Anthropology and mission,* Nettetal 1988; H. Bettscheider (ed.), *Reflecting mission, practising mission,* Nettetal 2001.

speak of 'interculturation' rather than inculturation, a term which, alas, has not (yet) found its way into missiological discussions.[20]

While the principle of reciprocity may be commonly accepted in the theory of intercultural communication, that has certainly not happened in practice in multicultural society in the Netherlands. In fact, the prime grievance of African migrants against European societies is that the 'integration' required of them actually amounts to 'adaption'.[21] Missionaries who have learnt from the errors of the past are increasingly emphasising that communication between Africans and Europeans is a two-way traffic, not propaganda but dialogue.

The paradigm of 'mutual missionary assistance' is rapidly making way for the paradigm of 'reverse mission', though we should guard against simply putting up a one-way traffic sign the other way round. As far back as 1974 Richard Friedli (former missionary in Ruanda) said in his reflection on the phenomenon of cultural circulation that the evangelisation of non-Christians by Christians should be amplified by evangelisation of Christians by non-Christians.[22]

---

[20] Cf. J. Blomjous, Development in mission thinking and practice 1959-1980: inculturation and interculturation, in: *African Ecclesial Review* 22(1980)6, 293-298. Also see Bosch, *Transforming mission,* 455-457; Waliggo, *Inculturation,* 12; Shorter, *Toward a theology of inculturation,* 13-14.

[21] Cf. G. Ter Haar, *Halfway to Paradise. African Christians in Europe*, Cardiff 1998; G. Ter Haar (ed.), *Strangers and sojourners. Religious Communities in the Diaspora*, Leuven 1998; I. Van Kessel and N. Tellegen (ed.), *Afrikanen in Nederland*, Leiden and Amsterdam 2000; R. Gerloff (ed.), Open Space. The African Diaspora in Europe and the Quest for a Human Community, in: *International Review of Mission* (2000)354.

[22] Cf. R. Friedli, *Fremdheit als Heimat: auf dem Suche nach einem Kriterium für den Dialog zwischen den Religionen,* Zürich 1974, 26, 203. With his inversion of the traditional concept of misson Friedli relates closely to the Dutch missiologist J. Hoekendijk, *De kerk binnenste buiten,* Amsterdam 1964. See the warning of G. Collet, Mission und Kommunikation, in: *Zeitschrift für Missions- und Religionswissenschaft* 74(1990)1, 1-18.

7.4 All religion is inculturated

Missionaries are often amazed at the ease with which people in the Netherlands speak about interreligious dialogue when they have seldom if ever met a person of another faith in the flesh. Missionaries who have lived and worked in countries like Nigeria and the Sudan for lengthy periods know that the encounter between cultures and religions is complex and that in practice it is often more a matter of confrontation than of dialogue or cooperation.

In the first place we rarely deal directly with people of other faiths. Interreligious dialogue, in the Netherlands and elsewhere – apart from the discussions of religious specialists – is conducted with unskilled farm workers, Berbers, peasant farmers, migrants, refugees. We sometimes act as if people are believers first and foremost, but in most cases this does not apply. To most people religion is not something they do but something they are. That is why folk religion – which in the case of, for instance, Islam is based on local custom rather than on the sharia – is so important and why apparently 'religious' conflicts often have little to do with religion.

Missiologists have discovered that religion is always inculturated or, as anthropologists put it, that religion is a cultural system. Although the chair I now occupy carries the specific rider of 'theology of interreligious dialogue', I prefer to speak of intercultural religious dialogue.[23] It should also be noted that 'religion' is a Western concept, based on a division between the secular and sacred domains. To most people in Africa, and in the world for that matter, this is not the case. To them the material and the spiritual are one, something which 'modern' Europe-

---

[23] This is also the name of the interdisciplinary workgroup in our faculty in which we research the construction of religious identity through intercultural interaction. See W. Valkenberg and F. Wijsen (eds.), *The polemical dialogue: research into dialogue, truth and truthfulness,* Saarbrücken 1997.

ans manifestly find hard to grasp, considering the debate on secularisation.[24]

It is an illusion to think that if one strips away all the cultural overlays, one will be left with pure religion and that this will enable one to compile a list of key concepts of religion that can then be operationalised and measured by means of questionnaire research. This is not to deny – on the contrary, it is roundly accepted – that religions and cultures have certain essential characteristics. But these are always spatiotemporally determined, or they become so generalised as to be practically meaningless. This is in fact the problem with the *Projekt Welthethos* and the human rights debate.[25]

There is another reason why the conjunction of the teaching tasks of missiology and the theology of interreligious dialogue needs clarification. In certain settings it is better not to use the word 'mission'. Certainly the qualification, 'more particularly dialogue between Christianity and Islam', which appeared in the advertisement for the vacancy for a professor of missiology, is extremely loaded. While some Muslims are still prepared to consider dialogue, mission is of the devil.

Does that mean that we should forget the word 'mission' and replace it with something else – development, liberation, dialogue, presence – as did sometimes happen in the past? Personally I see no need for this. If businesses, universities, NGOs and governments can refer to their 'mission', why can churches not do the same? Besides, over time every alternative comes up against the same objections.

I also think that Catholic doctrine on dialogue is often misconstrued. Mission and dialogue are different things, as Pope John Paul II and Francis, Cardinal Arinze, prefect of the Pontifical Council for Interreli-

---

[24] Cf. B. Bujo, *Foundations of an African ethic: beyond the universal claims of Western morality,* New York 2001, 95-102. For holistic thought in Africa see L. Magesa, *African religion: the moral traditions of abundant life*, Maryknoll, New York 1997, 35-76; G. Ter Haar, *The spirit of Africa,* London 1992; A. Shorter, *Jesus and the witchdoctor,* London 1985.

[25] Cf. H. Küng, *Projekt Weltethos,* München and Zürich 1990; B. Bujo, *The ethical dimension of community: the African model and the dialogue between North and South,* Nairobi 1998, 143-156.

gious Dialogue, repeatedly insisted. Mission is preeminently witness, accounting for the hope that is in you (1 Pet. 3:15). Dialogue is aimed at understanding and cooperating with others.[26] The distinctive quality of mission is in fact that it maintains the tension between full commitment to one's own faith and complete openness to the faith of others. Kibicho says:

> In the present day pluralistic society, each religion must evangelize as if it is the only carrier of the only fully saving revelation, as indeed it is for those predestined (through the peculiar circumstances of their birth, history and idiosyncrasy) to be saved through that way. However, in its continuing dialogue and cooperation with other religions, every religion must acknowledge and accept the claim of uniqueness and ultimacy or finality in every other genuine religion.[27]

7.5 No dialogue without liberation

The reference to interreligious dialogue needs one further clarification. Since the attacks on the World Trade Centre in New York on 11 September 2001 calls for interreligious encounter in the Netherlands have increased. After being marginalised as socially irrelevant in earlier social democratic and liberal cabinets, religion is suddenly the centre of political interest. 'No integration without religion' and 'religion as cement' have become slogans overnight. The prime minister and mayors

---

[26] In his encyclical *Redemptoris Missio* Pope John Paul II acknowledges that God's Spirit is also active in other cultures and religions (No. 28). For tis reason alone interreligious dialogue is necessary, which can enrich both parties and which is aimed at mutual growth (No. 56). Also see F. Arinze, *Meeting other believers,* Nairobi 1997; Pontifical Council for Interreligious Dialogue, Dialogue and Proclamation, in: *Bulletin of the Pontifical Council for Interreligious Dialogue* 26(1991)2, 210-250; Secretariat for non-Christian religions, attitudes of the church toward the followers of other religions, in: *Bulletin of the Secretariat for Non-Christian Religions* 19(1984)2,126-241.

[27] S. Kibicho, The mission of the church of Jesus Christ today from the perspective of the younger churches, in: A. Ngindu Mushete (ed.), *The mission of the church today: reports of the Yaoundé meeting*, Kinshasa 1984, 24-25.

visit mosques and the minister of metropolitan and integration policy is organising interreligious conferences. While these initiatives are estimable, they should not be overrated.

In the 1960s many people thought, on the lines of critical theory and the Frankfurt school, that all problems were economic and political, hence that the solution lay in economic and political progress. That was a reduction. But now many people seem to have gone to the other extreme, maintaining that all problems are cultural and religious.[28] What has emerged from most of the wars and conflicts in Africa is that they are not caused by religious and ethnic differences, as is commonly believed, but by a struggle for fertile land, clean water and control over natural resources such as oil, gas, diamonds, gold and tropical hardwood.[29]

What the events of 11 September 2001 and subsequent developments have made clear is that there is widespread protest against Western expansionism in the world. This was pointed out long ago by Max Warren, former missionary in Nigeria, in his introduction to John Taylor's *The primal vision*,[30] but it is obviously hard for Westerners to understand. The 'global coalition against terror' certainly does not mean that the world has suddenly embraced the Western notions of human beings and society. Anybody who engages in intercultural and interreligious dialogue knows that in this regard 'the West' is often diametrically opposed to 'the Rest'. Africans like to remind their European

---

[28] Cf. S. Huntington, *The clash of civilizations and the remaking of the world order,* New York 1996. He modifies his theory in S. Huntington and L. Harrison (eds.), *Culture matters: how values shape human progress,* New York 2001.

[29] Cf. I. Elbadawi and N. Sambanis, Why are there so many civil wars in Africa? Understanding and preventing violent conflict, in: *Journal of African Economies* 9(2000)3, 224-269; M. Klare, *Resource wars. The new landscape of global conflict,* New York 2001.

[30] "What we are called upon to recognize is that in the world of our time there is a widespread revolt against any form of domination by the West," writes M. Warren, General introduction, in: Taylor, *The primal vision*, 6. For an even earlier view see H. Kraemer, *The Christian message in a non-Christian world,* London 1938, 1-30.

dialogue partners of the history of slavery, imperialism and colonialism. "You brought the Bible but you took our country". Intercultural religious communication alone cannot resolve the conflicts.[31]

Mission, then, cannot confine itself to the problem of pluralism, but must always consider the problem of poverty as well. This implies, furthermore, that a theology of interreligious dialogue cannot exist without a theology of integral liberation. That is what African theologians mean when they advocate a theology of reconstruction which does away with the Western distinction between inculturation and liberation.[32] In terms of such a 'comprehensive approach' (a concept from Anglo-Saxon mission of the 1920s) it is extremely unwise to banish liberation theology from the curricula of theological faculties as 'no longer applicable' and replace it with intercultural and interreligious theology.

7.6 From technique to hermeneutics?

It has been the experience of many missionaries that the longer you live in another culture and the more you learn about it, the less you understand it. Unlike tourists and business people, who often conclude, from a very superficial knowledge of the other culture, that it is much the same as their own culture, missionaries know that it is very different. Hence at the moment missiological reflection on the experience of missionaries is contributing greatly to an intercultural hermeneutics.

Anthropologists generally accept these days that human potential is universal, which is not to say that all people are the same. One cannot deny that notions about people and society and ways of consorting with others differ, as scholars like Geert Hofstede and David Pinto have

---

[31] Cf. Chinweizu, *The West and the rest of us: white predators, black slaves and the African elite*, Lagos 1987; L. Magesa, "Am I not a Human Being …", in: *African Ecclesial Review* 34(1992)1, 95-114.

[32] See e.g., J. Chipenda, *The church of Africa: towards a theology of reconstruction,* Nairobi 1991; C. Villa-Vicencio, *A theology of reconstruction,* Cambridge 1992; Kä Mana, *Foi Chrétienne, crise africaine et reconstruction de l'Afrique,* Nairobi 1992; J. Mugambi, *From liberation to reconstruction,* Nairobi 1995; M. Getui et al., *Theology of reconstruction,* Nairobi 1999.

shown, even though one cannot treat their dichotomies as absolute.[33] But the main difference lies in the style of reasoning. Africans are constantly pointing out to their European dialogue partners that African rationality differs from Western rationality and that the Aristotelian 'principle of contradiction' and Cartesian 'pure concepts' are too easily universalised.[34]

It is against this notion that 'all people are like us' that many Africans in the Netherlands are objecting. And it is on the same grounds that African theologians have problems with 'universal', 'global' and 'cross-cultural' theology, because they harmonise the differences between people.[35] They, together with many missionaries, defend the 'right to be different'. Hence intercultural hermeneutics is a balance between universality and particularity. In this regard missiology stresses the differentness of people and views every claim to universality with a hermeneutics of suspicion, whether the claim is that of central doctrinal authority or of modern rationality.[36]

What we have here is a paradigm shift in missionary and missiological thinking. Many missionaries working abroad today were still trained in a missiology that was firmly convinced of the malleability of the world. This applies to both the evangelical movement and liberation

---

[33] Cf. G. Hofstede, *Allemaal andersdenkenden: omgaan met cultuurverschillen,* Amsterdam 1991; D. Pinto, *Interculturele communicatie,* Houten 1990; W. Shadid, *Grondslagen van interculturele communicatie*, Houten 1998.

[34] Cf.M. Kirwen, *The Missionary and the Diviner. Contending Theologies of Christian and African Religions*, Maryknoll, New York 1987; Bujo, *The ethical dimension of community,* 225; Magesa, *African religion*, 14; Nkufu Nkemnkia, *African vitalogy,* 104-106. Universalists like K. Wiredu, K. Anthony Appiah and P. Houtondji relativise the difference between African and Western philosophies.

[35] See e.g., Magesa's criticism of R. Schreiter, *The new catholicity. Theology between the global and the local*, Maryknoll, New York 1997, in: L. Magesa, The global and the local: an African view, in: M. Amaladoss (ed.), *Globalization and its victims,* Delhi 1999, 188-189.

[36] Cf. W. Eggen and R. Van Rossum, *Waken bij de eigenheid van de ander: evangelisering in hedendaags perspectief*, Aalsmeer 1992; P. Turkson and F. Wijsen (eds.), *Inculturation. Abide by the otherness of Africa and the Africans,* Kampen 1994.

theology. In Africa and elsewhere there arose a missionary science of liberation operating on the borderline between missiology and pedagogics.[37] Given the right techniques, 'the world' could be improved. Recent experience has taught that the world has not improved.

For a long time mission was understood mainly in terms of communication and the science of communication was embraced as a major ancillary science of missiology. Given the right packaging of the contents and using the correct channels, the 'message' was sure to reach the 'recipient'.[38] Studies of and reflections on intercultural and interreligious dialogue have revealed a 'communication crisis'. It is to the credit of Theo Sundermeier (former missionary in South Africa) that he made this point and advocated the return of hermeneutics to missiology.[39]

Like Heinrich Balz (former missionary in Cameroun, currently in Tanzania) and Richard Friedli, I believe that the return of hermeneutics should not be exaggerated and that hermeneutics can find a place in a

---

[37] Cf. J. Nyerere, *Education for self-reliance,* Dar es Salaam 1967; P. Freire, *Pedagogy in process: the letters to Guinea-Bissau,* New York 1978; E. Mock, *Afrikanische Pedagogik,* Wuppertal and Aachen 1979; A. Hope, S. Timmel and C. Hodzi, *Training for transformation,* Gweru 1985; J. Crowley, *Go to the people,* Eldoret 1985; F. Wambua, *Participation of the poor,* Eldoret 1987; J. Kronenburg, *Empowerment of the poor,* Amsterdam and Nijmegen 1986; D. Kyeyune (ed.), *New trends for the empowerment of the poor*, Nairobi 1997.

[38] The Dutch missiologist H. Kraemer was the first scholar to reflect systematically on mission as communication. But it was mainly Eugene Nida and his pupils David Hesselgrave and Charles Kraft who cast this reflection in a technical mould. See H. Kraemer, *The communication of the Christian faith*, Philadelphia 1956; E. Nida, *Message and mission: the communication of the Christian faith,* New York 1960; D. Hesselgrave, *Communicating Christ cross-culturally,* Grand Rapids 1978; C. Kraft, *Communicating the gospel in God's way,* Pasadena 1979.

[39] Cf. T. Sundermeier, *Konvivenz und Differenz: Studien zu einer verstehende Missionswissenschaft,* Erlangen 1995; *Den Fremden verstehen: eine praktische Hermeneutik,* Göttingen 1996; T. Sundermeier and W. Ustorf (eds.), *Die Begegnung mit dem Anderen: Plädoyer für eine interkulturelle Hermeneutik,* Gütersloh 1991; D. Becker (ed.), *Mit dem Fremden leben: Perspektiven einer Theologie der Konvivenz,* Erlangen 2000.

broader conception of communication science. After all, mission is not just a matter of understanding the other but also of transmitting the faith.[40] Communication relates to faith from the perspective of the sender, hermeneutics relates to faith from the perspective of the recipient. As mentioned already, however, communication is not concerned with senders and recipients but with participants in a process. Hence communication and hermeneutics refer to two sides of the same coin.[41]

7.7 Integration or adaptation?

It remains a question whether, and if so, for how long migrants can and may maintain their 'differentness' in their new environment. Here there are diverse theories. One is that migrants worldwide need three generations to adapt. The first generation maintains the values and norms of their country of origin; the second generation lives in two worlds; and the third has largely adapted to their new country. Another theory is that adaptation starts with a phase of confusion, followed by a spell of acculturation, whereafter there is swing back to earlier norms and values.

From missiological research into the position of African Christians in the Netherlands we know that both theories contain some truth, and that it matters a great deal which group is under discussion, in which place and at what time. Are we talking about Cape Verdians in Rotterdam, Ghanaians in Amsterdam, or Somalians – at present the fastest

---

[40] See H. Balz, *Theologische Modelle der Kommunikation,* Gütersloh 1978, 98-124; Krise der Kommunikation Wiederkehr der Hermeneutik?, in: T. Sundermeier (ed.), *Die Begegnung mit dem Anderen,* 39-65, R. Friedli, Kultur und kulturelle Vielfalt, in: T. Sundermeier (ed.), *Die Begegnung mit dem Anderen,* 29-38. Also see G. Collet, Bekehrung, Vergleich, Anerkennung: die Stellung des Anderen im Selbstverständnis der Missionswissenschaft, in: *Zeitschrift für Missions- und Religionswissenschaft* 77(1993)3, 205-251.

[41] That is why in the department of empirical practical theology at Nijmegen, where the chair of missiology is at present located, speak of 'hermeneutic communication' as the broad function of ministry. The distinctive feature of missionary communication is that it is always intercultural and interreligious. See J. Van der Ven, *Education for reflective ministry,* Louvain 1998, 123-132.

growing group of migrants in the Netherlands –in the East of the country? Apart from the size of the group and the duration of their residence, religion is another important factor, something that is often overlooked in studies of new migrants in the Netherlands. Cape Verdians and Ghanaians are usually Christians. They prefer to present themselves as such. By so doing they want to promote their integration (without forfeiting their identity) with Dutch society. But the Dutch see them as primarily African, thus stigmatising them and keeping them at arm's length. In reaction to this condemnatory attitude on the part of the Dutch, and not out of choice, African Christians isolate themselves in their own communities.[42]

Studies based on extensive field research contradict each other on fundamental points, for example the research into the integration and secularisation of migrants, especially Islamic youths. For this reason many missiologists have serious problems with quantitative studies of migrants in the Netherlands and their religious experience. Often these studies are so general that they no longer come to grips with anything and hence contradict each other when it comes to concrete issues.[43] It is

---

[42] Cf. J. Maaskant, *Afrikaan en katholiek in Rotterdam,* Nijmegen 1999; F. Wijsen, "Een vreemdeling is twee dagen gast ...". Afrikaanse Katholieken in Nederland en hun uitdaging aan theologie en pastoraat, in: L. Boeve and J. Haers (eds.), *God ondergronds,* Averbode 2001, 161-174. See also J. Cohen, *Grenzen: over de verhouding van autochtonen en migranten*, Amsterdam 2001.

[43] A report of the Social Cultural Planning Bureau, J. Becker and J. de Wit, *Secularisatie in de jaren negentig,* Den Haag 2000, claims that secularisation is also happening among minority groups. In the same year a report of the European Research Centre on Migration and Ethnic Relations, K. Phalet, C. Van Lotringen and H. Entzinger, *Islam in de multiculturele samenleving,* Utrecht 2000, indicates that nearly 100% of Islamic youths call themselves Muslim and that 90% of them attach great value to it. A report of the Verwey-Jonker Institute, also based on research in Rotterdam, claims that migrants are less active religiously and that there are signs of extensive assimilation especially among second generation Turks and Moroccans. See H. Van Daal, *Het middenveld als smeltkroes,* Utrecht 2001. The discrepancies in diagnoses and prognoses is partly a result of different definitions of religion and religious institutions.

only through solidarity in a common cause, the abundance of life (John 10:10), that one gains the kind of knowledge that missiology is about. That is why missiology prefers presence and participation to observation and intervention. That is also why missiologists have problems with the methodological atheism or agnosticism in (religious) anthropology.

Many Africans in the Netherlands ask themselves despairingly what the Dutch expect of them when they say that 'foreigners' have to integrate. In effect integration usually means adaptation. This exposes the much vaunted 'tolerance' of the Dutch to criticism. Recently it has been stated by various candidates of political parties – albeit in the heat of their election campaigns – that the Dutch are 'far too tolerant'. Several studies, including ones conducted at the Radboud University Nijmegen, call such statements into question.[44] The same candidates also hold that foreigners simply have to adapt to our way of life. This is strongly reminiscent of the combatting of maladjusted behaviour of antisocial and socially deficient families and their religious upliftment in 'social planning' and 'folk missions' in the 1950s. Of course, these 'folk missions' did have the advantage that they took the religious factor seriously, something which has disappeared from modern welfare work, with the result that it fails to strike a chord with many Africans in the Netherlands.[45]

---

[44] Cf. M. Lubbers, *Nationalistic attitudes and ethnic exclusionism in a comparative perspective*, Nijmegen 2001; M. Coenders, *Exclusionistic electorates*, Nijmegen 2001; P. Essed, *Everyday racism,* Claremont 1990; G. Verberk, *Attitudes towards ethnic minorities,* Amsterdam 1999; H. Ghorashi, *Ways to survive, battles to win,* Nijmegen 2001; W. Shadid and P. Van Koningsveld (eds.), *Beeldvorming en interculturele communicatie,* Tilburg 2000; W. Shadid and P. Van Koningsveld (eds.), *Religie, cultuur en minderheden,* Tilburg 2000.

[45] Cf. F. Wijsen, *Geloven bij het leven: missionaire presentie in een volkswijk,* Baarn 1997, 146-148. Also see J. Jacobs et al., Vier ijkpunten geijkt, in: *Trajecta* 10(2001)4, 273-309, especially the contribution by L. Winkeler, Welvaart in zwart-wit, 302-309. For an African conception of welfare work see Shorter, *Jesus and the witchdoctor,* 125-136.

Missionaries who have worked in Africa can teach us a great deal in this regard. They have seen that people can cooperate very well even though they do not agree in every respect. Of course Africa is not paradise and is having its share of bloody conflicts. But these conflicts are not caused by ethnic and religious differences, as is commonly thought. In fact, there are signs pointing the other way: the greater the ethnic and religious diversity in a country, the smaller the chance of conflict. 'Integration without loss of identity' is perfectly feasible.[46]

7.8 There is no 'culture in between'

As we all know, anthropologists and missionaries had and still have a love-hate relationship.[47] Hence it is remarkable to see anthropologists starting to behave like a new kind of missionary. Thus Wim van Binsbergen sees himself as a bridge builder between cultural orientations and advocates a 'metaculture'. Wouter van Beek, again, advocates a 'culture in between'.[48]

By and large there are four strategies for dealing with enculturation. Some missionaries continue to identify with home and adhere rigidly to their familiar norms and values. Others try to 'go native' by identifying with the culture of the country where they are working. Yet others go

---

[46] See E. Elbadawi and N. Sambanis, Why are there so many civil wars in Africa? Understanding and preventing violent conflict, in: *Journal of African Economies* 9(2000)3, 254, 265. That Africans can cooperate even when they are not in agreement is evident in the recently published diaries of two Dutch missionaries: T. Haumann, *Vrede langs het oorlogspad: ontmoetingen in Zuid-Sudan,* Heeswijk Utrecht 1998; H. Tullemans, *Tussen twee werelden: brieven uit Afrika,* Nijmegen 2002.

[47] Cf. R. Bonsen, H. Marks and J. Miedema (eds.), *The ambiguity of rapprochement: reflections of anthropologists on their controversial relationship with missionaries,* Nijmegen 1990; A. Borsboom and J. Kommers (eds.), *Anthropologists and the missionary endeavour,* Saarbrücken 2002.

[48] Cf. W. Van Binsbergen, "*Culturen bestaan niet". Het onderzoek van interculturaliteit als een openbreken van vanzelfsprekendheden,* Rotterdam 1999, 34; W. Van Beek, The culture-in-between. Anthropologist and missionary as partners, in: Bonsen et al. (eds.), *The ambiguity of rapprochement*, 109.

for a dual identification, taking the best from their own culture and the best of African culture. Finally there are missionaries who identify with neither of the two cultures, thus creating a kind of cultural no-man's land.

I have seen many missionaries who have gone native, but this is not what their African dialogue partners expect of then. "Why do you make fun of us?", they say when they see a European walking around in sandals made from old car tyres or living in a mud hut. Missionaries who adhere rigidly to their own values and norms will get along well with Africans with 'white hearts', but they never manage to get intercultural communication going. What they end up with is monologue rather than dialogue. The attitude of settling for the trouble-free zone of a cultural no-man's land is considered untrustworthy, neither fish nor flesh. Only a few missionaries have been tempted to adopt Jürgen Habermas' theory of exchanging perspectives, in which the I-perspective and the you-perspective converge in a he-perspective, a theory which was hailed as a panacea in early forms of dialogic catechesis.

The best approach to intercultural (religious) communication is a dual identification: an attitude in which missionaries are not ashamed of having a (religious) culture of their own whose limitations they are aware of, and are able to appreciate what is good and beautiful in Africa and Africans without glorifying all things African.[49] It strikes me that some anthropologists are too much inclined to put the spiritual traditions of Africa on a pedestal. To the missionary participation goes hand in hand with confrontation, as Max Warren aptly put it in his introduction to John Taylor's *The primal vision*; and, allowing for the different context, his words apply equally to communication with Africans in the Netherlands:

---

[49] "Nur wo beides da ist, die tiefe Faszination durch eine andere Religion und die feste Verwurzelung in der eigenen, kommt es zum Verstehen," according to T. Sundermeier, *Was ist Religion?,* Gütersloh 1999, 204-205. W. Van Binsbergen struggles with his dual identification. See W. Van Binsbergen, Sangoma in Nederland, in: M. Elias and R. Reis (eds.), *Getuigen ondanks zichzelf,* Maastricht 1998, 14.

> Our first task in approaching another people, another culture, another religion, is to take off our shoes, for the place we are approaching is holy. We have then to ask what is the authentic religious content in the experience of the Muslim, the Hindu, the Buddhist, or whoever he may be. We may, if we have asked humbly and respectfully, still reach the conclusion that our brothers have started from a false premise and reached a faulty conclusion. But we must not arrive at our judgement from outside their religious situation.[50]

7.9 A moderate constructivism

Some anthropologists have said that cultures do not exist. There is a multiplicity of overlapping cultural orientations, with the result that everybody is committed to many orientations, none of which coincide with a particular group or territory, as Wim van Binsbergen put it somewhat provocatively in his inaugural lecture. Cultural orientations are associated with language, gender, religion, ethnicity, nationality, education, profession and social background. In public life people are situated at the intersection of ever changing cultural orientations with no systematic connection between them. Even in their private lives people have diverse cultural orientations which cannot be integrated. An individual is a fragmented subject. Cultures in a holistic sense are simply an illusion of the participants.[51]

I persist in using the terms 'culture' and 'cultural identity', not only because I do not think that dispensing with a problematic term will get us much further, but also because I believe that some anthropologists take constructivism too far. Many ethnic groups in former colonies

---

[50] Cf. Warren, General Introduction, 10-11. This typically Anglican approach is inspired by the French worker-priests. See A. Lande and W. Ustorf (eds.), *Mission in a pluralist world*, Frankfurt am Main 1996, 28.

[51] Cf. Van Binsbergen, "*Culturen bestaan niet*", 12-14. Also see R. Keesing, Theories of culture revisited, in: R. Borofsky (ed.), *Assessing cultural anthropology,* New York 1994, 301-312; R. Brightman, Forget culture: replacement, transcendence, relexification, in: *Cultural Anthropology* 10(1995)4, 509-546.

strive for liberation by invoking practices and notions that anthropologists describe as essentialist. Dismissing these as 'popular' or 'prescientific' knowledge that should make way for a more profound anthropological insight, namely that any talk of cultural identity is a product of construction, an 'illusion of the participants' with no correlate in the real world, is expressive of scientific self-overestimation which is also not very helpful to the emancipatory strivings of subalternate movements. To a Sukuma the statement, "I am a Sukuma", does not refer merely to his or her inner self, but very definitely to an external reality.

Actors in multicultural societies have various identities at their disposal, each with its own cultural orientations. These are perfectly real. They are what Victor Turner calls root paradigms and what Pierre Bourdieu calls *habitus*, a tendency to behave in a particular way.[52] A *habitus* is inculcated by education and training, is more or less stable and structured and, up to a point, corporeal. But it depends on the specific time and place, what Bourdieu calls 'the market', which mix of cultural orientations is selected to interpret experience and generate behaviour.

Radical constructivism also ignores the dialectic relation between reality and representation, as Pierre Bourdieu shows in his debunking of 'objective science'. Classifications produce differences and are themselves products of differentiation. Calling the language Sukuma, spoken by people called the Sukuma, and calling the area in which they live Sukumaland was not ineffective. Whereas up to about 1945 the name 'Sukuma' was not used to indicate an ethnic group, there are now eight million people calling themselves Sukuma occupying a territory almost as big as the Netherlands. But the effectiveness of the designa-

---

[52] See V. Turner, *Dramas, fields, metaphors,* Ithaca 1974; P. Bourdieu, *Le sense pratique,* Paris 1980. A proper balance between structure perspective and actor perspective, of which essentialism and constructivism are reflections is worked out in U. Hannerz, *Cultural complexity: studies in the social organization of meaning*, New York 1992.

tion depends on the authority of the people who use it and the extent to which this name for the group corresponds with its reality.[53]

7.10 Epilogue

Van Binsbergen has destroyed several 'sacred cows' of Africanists and anthropologists. In the public debate on 'multicultural drama' and the 'multicultural illusion' Paul Scheffer and Paul Schnabel are doing much the same, by claiming that the Netherlands is far too tolerant and that this tolerance has helped to influence the disadvantaged position of many members of ethnic minorities. They proclaim assimilation as a panacea: down with the ideal of 'integration without forfeiting identity'.

What contribution are missionaries and missiologists who have worked with Africans in Africa making to this debate? There is a false impression that for a theology of dialogue one has to go to Asia and that Africa has nothing to offer in this field. Africa is the most pluralistic continent on earth and, for all its bloody conflicts in recent times, it has a long tradition of peaceful coexistence.[54]

I have shown that the 'expansionist' paradigm in missiology has gradually made way for a paradigm of 'exploration', modelled on the old missionary ideal of 'pilgrimage to God'. But exploration does not

---

[53] Cf. P. Bourdieu, *Ce que parler veut dire,* Paris 1992, 135-148; F. Wijsen and R. Tanner, *"I am just a Sukuma". Globalization and identity construction in northwest Tanzania,* Amsterdam and New York 2002. To my mind the famous Africanist Terence Ranger goes too far in his constructivism. See T. Ranger, The invention of tradition in colonial Africa, in: E. Hobsbawm and T. Ranger (eds.), *The invention of tradition,* Cambridge 1983, 216-254; The invention of tradition revisited, in: T. Ranger and O. Vaughan (eds.), *Legitimacy and state in twentieth-century Africa*, London 1993, 62-111.

[54] Cf. C. Van 't Leven, Africa's tradition of peaceful co-existence, in: G. Speelman, J. Van Lin and D. Mulder (eds.), *Muslims and Christians in Europe,* Kampen 1993, 14-27; A. Byaruhanga Akiiki, African traditional values for human development, in: J. Agbasiere and B. Zabajungu (eds.), *Church contribution to integral development*, Eldoret 1989, 45-62; Olupona et al., *Religious plurality in Africa.*

preclude evaluation. Unlike postmodern cultural relativists, missiologists do not hesitate to question norms and values, especially in places where people are being enslaved and human rights are trampled upon. It would seem than in some sectors of society there is a taboo on standing up for one's opinions and, on that basis, judging what cannot be tolerated. In this respect Schnabel and Scheffers are quite right.

But judgments of cultural differences must be based on inside knowledge gained at grassroots level; in the process Africans' anger about European imperialism, past and present, and their desire to be liberated from it, must be taken into account. Participant observation is a method used by both anthropologists and missiologists, but missiologists put more emphasis on participation, including religious participation, than on observation. Those who have striven alongside others and prayed with them for 'abundant life' know that this ideal crystallises in diverse norms and values that simply do not amount to the same thing. This tends to be overlooked by cultural universalists who strive for social consensus and a global ethics. In this respect missiologists remain poised between universalism and particularism, and their preferential option for the poor for now translates into a preferential option for others, for guarding the African-ness of Africa and Africans.

There is still another fundamental question: does cultural particularism also imply moral particularism? I have argued that there is an alternative somewhere between universalism and particularism, namely pluralism. This pluralism is limited by communication, communication in which people not only seek to convert each other but are also prepared to learn from each other and for which the African palaver could serve as a model.[55] To return to some contentious issues from the election campaigns mentioned earlier in this chapter – head scarves, arranged marriages, female circumcision – missiologists insist that there

---

[55] Cf. Bujo, *Foundations of an African ethic*, 45-71. An example of such a communication is M. Kirwen, *The missionary and the diviner*. For the debate on particularism and religion see G. Ter Haar, *Rats, cockroaches and people like us*, Den Haag 2000; A. De Jong (ed.), *Ethnicity: blessing or curse?*, Nairobi 1999.

are no simple, uniform answers. In any case the people involved, usually African women, have very different views on the subject. Here, too, the principle of reciprocity, of comment and response, applies.

But there is a more fundamental issue at stake. Many Dutch people choose not to discuss these practices. They are seen merely as assaults on the lessons of modernity, lessons that may, if necessary, be enforced by the judiciary. The criminal case against the Rotterdam imam El-Moumni is a case in point. Hence the communication between Europeans and Africans that I am speaking about is a battle against modernity, a battle fought not between cultures but within cultures. Ultimately it is a battle about one of the fundamentals of modern society, the separation of rationality and religion. Many Africans, along with many missionaries and missiologists, believe that on this issue Europeans have gone too far. But the matter is still under discussion, also in our faculty, and missiology will be making itself heard.[56]

[56] To people like Paul Cliteur and Pim Fortuyn 'Yemenisation' and 'Islamisation' constitute a threat to 'modern' society. See P. Fortuyn, *Tegen de islamisering van onze cultuur,* Utrecht 1997; P. Cliteur, Jemen in Nederland, in: P. Cliteur and V. Van den Eeckhout (eds.), *Multiculturalisme, cultuurrelativisme en sociale cohesie,* Den Haag 2001, 17-64. For a missiological reflection on miscommunication see L. Hoedemaker, Reflecties over contextualiteit, in: L. Hoedemaker (ed.), *Theologiseren in context,* Kampen 1997, 263-319.

7.11 Further readings on mission as cross-cultural Christian communication

- F.-J. Eilers, *Communicating in Community. An introduction to social communication*, Manilla 2002.
- K. Krämer and K. Vellgutt (eds.), *Mission und Dialog. Ansätze für ein kommunikatives Missionsverständnis*, Freiburg, Basel and Wien 2012.
- C. Van Engen, D. Whiteman and J. Dudley Woodberry (eds.), *Paradigm shifts in Christian witness: insights from anthropology, communication, and spiritual power*, Maryknoll, New York 2008.
- F. Verstraelen, *Christianity in a new key. New voices and vistas through intercultural communication*, Gweru 1996.
- A. Walls, *The cross-cultural process in Christian history. Studies in the transmission and appropriation of Faith*, Maryknoll, New York 2002.

7.12 Questions for further comprehension

1. What is the significance of missionary experiences for coping with multiculturalism in European societies?
2. According to the author, why is there no ‘culture in between’ cultures?
3. What does the author mean by ‘moderate constructivism’?
4. According to the author, is ‘integration without loss of identity’ feasible?
5. Comment on the statement, “Our first task in approaching another people, another culture, another religion, is to take off our shoes, for the place we are approaching is holy”.

Epilogue From social to discursive analysis

Shortly after I defended and published my doctoral dissertation in 1994 (translated into Bahasa Indonesia and published in 2010 as *Buah Buah Roh*[1]) I was invited to participate in a team of Dutch scholars which was to set up a post-graduate (S-2) program in practical theology at the Universitas Kristen Duta Wacana in Yogyakarta. My first visit to Yogyakarta was in 1995.

My contribution to the program was to introduce and supervise internships together with the staff of the Pusat Pastoral. For this purpose I used the method that I had developed in my doctoral dissertation, namely the so called pastoral circle, later renamed the practical-theological spiral, rooted in the see-judge-act method of the Catholic social action movement and later developed in Latin American liberation theology comprising four steps: observation, interpretation, evaluation and innovation.

For the first and second step I used a specific way of conducting social-scientific research, namely ethnographic semantics of James Spradley.[2] My lecture notes were published by the Pusat Pastoral.[3] Later, Spradley's books were translated into Bahasa Indonesia. These books reflected a shift which I framed, in harmony with John Beattie,[4] as a shift from 'functional' to 'cognitive' anthropology. It defined culture in a cognitive way as the shared knowledge that people used to interpret experience and to generate behavior. It was concerned with the use of concepts, categories and classifications (or cognitions) in human practices.

---

[1] F. Wijsen, *Buah Buah Roh. Menjalankan Riset Social Partisipatif di Belahan Dunia Selatan*, Yogyakarta 2010.

[2] J. Spradley, *The ethnographic interview*, New York 1979; *Participant observation*, New York 1980.

[3] F. Wijsen, *Lingkaran pastoral dalam pendidikan pelayanan. Seri Pastoral 296*, Yogyakarta 1999.

[4] J. Beattie, *Other cultures. Aims, methods and achievements in social anthropology*, London and Henley 1982, xi.

Spradley assumed that cultural meaning systems were encoded in symbols; that language was the primary symbol system that encoded cultural meanings; that the meaning of a symbol was its relationship to other symbols in a particular culture; and that the task of the ethnographer was to discover the semantic relationships among the cultural symbols.[5]

The relational theory of meaning, characteristic of structuralism, was obvious. This was the way I myself was trained for conducting fieldwork in Tanzania, where newcomers to the field were prepared in so called Language and Inculturation Centers in Kipalapala and Musoma, starting from the assumption: to learn a culture is to learn its language.

Looking back at this period it is safe to say that I shared the assumption of the 'golden age of American anthropology',[6] summarised in Malinowski's definition of the aim of ethnography, quoted by Spradley, "to grasp the native's point of view".[7] It assumed that a 'native's point of view' exists, and that the researcher has access to it in objective ways. But the questions are: Who is this native? And what is the researcher's contribution to the generation of data?

In harmony with multi-dimensional model of meaning of Victor Turner,[8] namely the exegetical, the positional and the operational meaning, the third level of my analysis looked at how the meaning-systems were used by the participants. And although I was critical of pure structuralism, seeing it in harmony with Pierre Bourdieu[9] as formal and a-historical, I did not yet take into account the dialectical relationship between the symbol-system and its users, or the reproduction and transformation of the symbol-system through its use. This has be-

---

[5] Spradley, *The ethnographic interview*, 99.

[6] U. Hannerz, *Cultural complexity. Studies in the social organization of meaning*, New York 1992, 12.

[7] Spradley, *The ethnographic interview*, 3.

[8] V. Turner, *The forest of symbols. Aspects of Ndembu ritual*, Ithaca 1967, 50-52.

[9] P. Bourdieu, *In other words. Essays towards reflexive sociology*, Cambridge 1990.

come the main focus of my later research, as indicated in the new foreword to the Indonesian translation of my doctoral dissertation.[10]

When I edited a volume commemorating twenty-five years using the pastoral circle,[11] Gerrit Singgih wrote a contribution to it titled 'Punishment and liberation. How the Pastoral Circle transforms our theologies'.[12] In this contribution Singgih linked social analysis and cultural analysis to reflect on tacit assumptions underlying his own and his students' theologies. It clearly shows our common concern. The aim of the present contribution is to elaborate on the above mentioned shift from functional to cognitive anthropology, and to introduce a different way of looking at theology and 'science' of religion, both in terms of their object and in terms of methods, which can serve as the second step in the practical-theological spiral.

For the sake of clarity I do not go into the complexities of the relation between theology and science of religion; it suffices to say that in the practical-theological spiral they are combined in an interdisciplinary way; steps one and two are social scientific, steps three and four are theological. In my view, theology and science of religion do not have different objects or methods, but different views of science. Science of religion has an empirical view of science, operating from methodical agnosticism; theology has a hermeneutic view of science, operating from methodical conversion.[13]

---

[10] Wijsen, *Buah Buah Roh*, 3-5.

[11] F. Wijsen, P. Henriot and R. Mejía (eds.), *The Pastoral Circle revisited. A critical quest for truth and transformation*, Maryknoll, New York 2005.

[12] G. Singgih, Punishment and liberation, in: F. Wijsen, P. Henriot and R. Mejía (eds.), *The Pastoral Circle revisited*, Maryknoll, New York 2005.

[13] J. Cox, *Rational ancestors. Scientific rationality and African Indigenous Religions*, Cardiff 1998, 93-96.

Discursive study of religion

Malinowski's definition of the aim of ethnography expressed clearly the positivistic mode of thinking in the social sciences of his time. Phenomenology in Dutch science of religion shared the same positivistic mode. In the spirit of Husserl, phenomenologists wanted to go back to the "things as they are in themselves".[14]

Phenomenology of religion

From its very beginning as an academic discipline (Cornelius Tiele in The Netherlands competes with Max Müller in the United Kingdom for being the 'founding father' of science of religion), roughly between the First and the Second World War (of course, there were scholars of religion before this period) the dominant way of practicing 'science' of religion was phenomenological.

Phenomenology was a reaction against the influence of Darwin's evolution theory in other disciplines (Tylor, Frazer, Marett). After the so called 'intellectualism', which saw religion basically as a logical error, functionalism saw religion as an epiphenomenon of something else, society and economy (e.g., Durkheim), or biology and mind (e.g., Freud).

Instead, phenomenology wanted to do justice to religion as it was in itself, *sui generis*. It borrowed a framework from philosophy, based on the Enlightenment distinction between the thing as it is in itself and 'its appearance in the mind'.

More or less inspired by Husserl's 'return to the things themselves', the Dutch phenomenologist of religion, Gerardus Van der Leeuw's used three analytic concepts in his *Religion in manifestation and essence.*[15] First, *epoché* or bracketing, i.e., suspension of all judgments

---

[14] G. Flood, *Beyond phenomenology. Rethinking the study of religion*, London and New York 1999, 29-33.

[15] G. Van der Leeuw, *Religion in essence and manifestation. A study in phenomenology*, London 1973.

concerning the objective world. Second, empathy; through bracketing we are able to enter into the life of the other. Third, eidetic reduction, i.e., to grasp the essence of a religious manifestation and grouping together (typology) phenomena which share the same essence.

By doing so, phenomenology wanted to acquire objective knowledge of religion, the belief of the believers, or in terms of Malinowski's ideal of ethnography, 'the native's point of view'. Even Clifford Geertz's definition of religion as system of symbols was phenomenological because he saw the symbol system as existing independently of actors. For this reason, Talil Asad accused Geertz of being a theologian more than an anthropologist.[16]

Post-colonial and post-modern critique

From a post-colonial and post-modern perspective the phenomenological approach is problematic for ontological and epistemological reasons. The first is the objectivist understanding of 'religion'. Phenomenologists claim that there is 'something' outside there, sui generis. It exists independent of the scholar and it appears to him/her in his/her experience. The second is the positivist understanding of 'science'. By bracketing our preconceptions, it is possible to see reality as it is in itself, in a neutral or objective way.

But post-colonial and post-modern critics say that religion does not 'exist', at least not in the way phenomenologists thought that it existed. Religion is a Western construct, that was used for polemical purposes in the Reformation and was rooted in the Enlightenment distinction between the thing as it is in itself and it appearance in the mind. Moreover, there is no neutral or objective knowledge. Science does not describe something out there but constitutes (at least partly) the thing that is described.[17]

---

[16] T. Asad, Anthropological conception of religions. Reflections on Geertz, in: *Man* (1983)18, 237-259; C. Geertz, *The interpretation of cultures*, London 1993.
[17] Bourdieu, *In other words*.

Jonathan (not to be confused with Wilfred Cantwell) Smith said, "there is no data for religion. Religion is solely the creation of the scholar's study. It is created for the scholar's analytic purposes by his imaginative acts of comparison and generalisation. Religion has no existence apart from the academy".[18] From a post-colonial perspective it is added that knowledge of religion is constituted by power. The concept of religion is a European invention that was used to oppress other people's beliefs. Hinduism is a clear example, but also the Indonesian concept of *agama*.[19]

From phenomenological to discursive study of religion

In order to overcome the pitfalls of phenomenology scholars of religion go into two directions, social sciences and humanities. A social science approach gives a definition of the research object (the reality that is studied, in our case: religion), translates it in operational terms that can be observed (values, characteristics, properties) and measured by quantitative methods that produce – in most cases – statistical results.

The problem is that after more than 100 years of its existence science of religion has not been able to come up with a generally accepted definition of its object: religion. And this is exactly where discursive study of religion starts. Human practices and artifacts are not religious because of some intrinsic values or primordial properties that can be measured by objective criteria. Human practices and artifacts are religious because believers place them in a narrative context or a speech community. This is why people outside this speech community do not recognise them as religious. And this is why the boundary between what is considered to be religious and not religious shifted in history.

We can give many examples to show that the boundaries between belief and unbelief, or between religion and superstition, are not fixed

---

[18] J. Smith, *Imagining religion. From Babylon to Jonestown*, Chicago 1982.
[19] W.C. Smith, *The meaning and end of religion. A new approach to the religious traditions of mankind*, New York 1963, 59, 249-250.

but fluid. For Catholics, Marian devotion is religion, for Protestants it is idolatry. For Muslims associated with NU, going to the shrines of the saints is religion; for Muslims associated with Muhammadiyah this practice is superstition. For discursive study of religion the object of study is not religion, because religion does not 'exist', at least not in the way phenomenologists thought that it existed, but the discourses about religion, or why and how religion is constituted through discourse.[20]

Bourdieu's theory of practice

The dominant social science approach does not solve the pitfalls of phenomenology as it shares the objectivist view of religion and positivistic view of science.[21] Thus I looked for an alternative framework and found it in Bourdieu's theory of practice. This also explains why I put 'science' of religion in inverted commas. According to Bourdieu, 'science' of religion and social science in general is not an 'exact' science in the same was as natural sciences.

Pierre Bourdieu's life history

It is good to place Bourdieu's theory of practice in the context of his life history, in harmony with his own principle of self-reflexivity. Theories do not come 'from heaven'. Bourdieu studied philosophy in Paris in the early 1950s. In those days the dominant trend in philosophy was Jean Paul Sartre's existentialism which stressed people's freedom to determine their own destiny.

After his studies Bourdieu was sent to Algeria where he served as a soldier in the colonial war. There he experienced that existentialism was too individualistic and that people's freedom was bounded by power relations. He converted from philosophy to sociology; and from existentialism to Marxism.

---

[20] R. McCutcheon, *Studying religion. An introduction*, London and Oakville 2007.

[21] Flood, *Beyond phenomenology*.

After his military service he worked at the University of Algiers where he conducted large-scale statistical research. But he became suspicious about the exactitude of the 'exact' sciences. The social reality in a country such as Algeria was too complex to be grasped in clear-cut categories. He became interested in Weber's interpretative approach. But he went with Weber beyond Weber.[22]

In the early 1960 Bourdieu moved back to France where he met a new fashion: Claude Lévy-Strauss's structuralism. But here again, Bourdieu was not satisfied with structuralism. According to him it was a-historical and de-contextual. And it did not take into account the social position of the researchers and their own contributions to the production of their research material. Bourdieu always stressed self-reflexivity of the researchers.

Bourdieu's life project can be seen as an attempt to bridge the polarities between subjectivism and objectivism. His work can be situated in the center of two axes with two poles. First, there is the actor versus structure polarity. Second, there is the polarity between surface structures of society (functionalism) and deep structures of the mind (structuralism).

According to Bourdieu, subjectivists (e.g., Max Weber) reduce social reality to the interpretation of the actors. They postulate continuity between reality and experience of reality. On the other hand, objectivists claim that the experience of the actors does not represent 'real' reality; they postulate a discontinuity between reality and experience of reality. The 'real' reality is in behind reality, in the structures of the mind (e.g., Claude Lévy-Strauss) or in the structures of society (e.g., Karl Marx).

---

[22] P. Bourdieu, Genesis and structure of the religious field, in: C. Calhoun (ed.), *Comparative social research*. Vol. 13, London 1991, 1-44.

Bourdieu is interested in the dialectic relation between what is in the mind (concepts, classifications) and the structure of society (social positions, social relations). He sees the society as a pluralistic space of more or less autonomous fields (or 'markets') where groups of actors struggle to meet their interests (or make 'profit') using various resources (or 'capital'), in collaboration or in competition with each other. Thus almost always there is inclusion and exclusion at the same time

Bourdieu's key concept is 'habitus'. The habitus is a set of dispositions which incline agents to act and react in certain ways. Dispositions are inculcated, structured, durable, generative, embodied. The habitus gives people a practical sense ('sense pratique'), a feeling for what they should or should not do. Therefore he disagrees with Habermas who says that practice is rational. People act and react on the basis of a practical sense or feeling.

Particular practices are not the product of the habitus as such, but of the relationship between the 'habitus' on the one hand and the social context, 'field' or 'market', on the other. A field or market is a structured space of positions. And the positions are determined by the different kinds of recourses or 'capital': economic, social or cultural capital.

A 'field' or 'market' is always the site of struggles in which individuals seek to maintain or transform the distribution of the forms of capital specific to it. The individuals who participate in these struggles may have different aims, but they share in common some fundamental presuppositions. They must believe in the game they are playing, e.g., they know how to do business, politics.

Although Bourdieu borrows the concepts 'market', 'profit' and 'capital' from the language of economics, in his vocabulary these terms are not 'economic' in the narrow sense of the word. Though practices may not be governed by a strictly economic logic (they may not be oriented towards financial gain) – some even may be illogical in a strict economic sense – they may have a logic that is economic in a broader sense of the word: the maximisation of some kind of capital, e.g., cultural or symbolic capital, or some kind of 'profit', e.g., honour or prestige.

Bourdieu assumes a link between actions and interests. While he rejects that interests are always narrowly economic, they never cease to comply with an economic logic. This is the basic assumption about human action, Bourdieu's theory of practice. People do not 'invest' in activities if there is no return, if they are not 'profitable' in one way or another.

This is a heuristic principle. It calls upon the researcher to explore the interests that are at stake in the practices which take place in certain fields. What the interests are can only be determined through a careful empirical and historical inquiry. The fact that some actions appear to be disinterested (in a narrow economic sense) does not mean that they are interest-free.

Bourdieu's approach requires a systematic reconstruction of the field within which religious speech is produced and reproduced and its relation to the broader social space: a rigorous analysis of the social positions of the speakers, the social relations between them and the specific interests they might have.

The problem of structuralism is that its analyses remain too internal. They fail to take into account the socio-historical conditions within which the object of analysis is produced and reproduced. The problem with Marxists, on the other hand, is that they reduce the object of study to socio-economic processes. Here again, Bourdieu stresses the dialectic relation between the two.

Pierre Bourdieu's notion of 'identity'

Bourdieu's concept of 'habitus' brings us to another concept that is crucial to our research, namely 'identity'.[23] The confusion about the

---

[23] P. Bourdieu, *Language and symbolic power*, Cambridge 1991, 220-228.

concept 'identity', whether 'identities' are to be understood in the sense of 'essentialism' or 'constructivism', stems in part from the fact that one tends to forget that cognitive classifications are always subordinated to practical functions and oriented towards the production of social effects.

In most cases identities are not based on 'intrinsic values' that could serve as objective criteria, but they are the products of our classification. Therefore, they are not 'natural' or 'primordial' but 'social' or 'circumstantial' realities. Human practices or beliefs are not 'religious' because of intrinsic values but because believers classify them as religious. And as we already noted, the boundary between religious and not religious shifted during history.[24]

But, identities can be used strategically according to the material but also the symbolic interests of those who bear them. Identity (ethnic, social, or religious) is a resource or 'capital' by which people or groups of people try to serve their own interests, this is to gain material (financial) or symbolic (prestige) 'profit'. Thus there is a strategic or functional essentialism.

There are very few criteria capable of founding 'natural' classifications separated by 'natural' frontiers. The frontiers are always arbitrary or circumstantial, the product of a 'vision' and thereby of a 'di-vison' of the world.

Thus, identity discourse is a performative discourse which aims to impose a new definition of the frontiers. Bourdieu is inspired by the religious field in two ways. First, he takes the notion of performative language from the liturgy. The sacrament is what it is because believers say that it is what it is. But, contrary to speech act theory, Bourdieu said that speech is not by itself performative, but by the authority of the speaker, who addresses real life issues, and who is recognised as an authority by the listeners. Second, defining the frontiers of a region, culture identity is a religious act, dividing interior and exterior, sacred and profane, clean and unclean, indigenous and foreign.

---

[24] Asad, Anthropological conception of religions.

According to Bourdieu the main function of religion was to formulate visions of the world and thereby sanctify di-visions, and thus consecrate social reality; a function which in the modern situation has been taken over by the state. These practical classifications do not describe 'realities' out there but to a large extent they contribute to the production of what they apparently describe.

Once again, one can avoid the alternative of 'objectivism' versus 'subjectivism' by taking into account that 'reality' is the site of a permanent struggle to define 'reality', and that classifications produce differences as much as they are produced by them.

From here one can understand Bourdieu's critique of 'exact' science. Scientific classifications contribute to the production of what they apparently describe. Sociologists did not discover 'social classes' but they created them by their classification. Anthropologists did not discover 'ethnic groups' but they created them. By naming ethnic groups the colonial administrators created them, in most cases to serve their divide-and-rule policies. In the same way we can say: scholars of religion did not discover 'religions' but they created them, again in many cases to oppress them. 'Agama' in Indonesia can serve as example.[25]

Critical discourse analysis

Bourdieu did not translate his theory of symbolic power of language into research methods.[26] Critical or socio-cognitive discourse analysts have taken up his spirit and developed conceptual and technical frameworks for research.[27] Although Norman Fairclough only seldom refers to Bourdieu, he combined critical theory (macro sociology) with linguistic analysis and micro sociology.[28]

---

[25] Smith, *The meaning and end of religion*, 59, 249-250.

[26] Bourdieu, *Language and symbolic power*.

[27] M. Jørgensen and L. Phillips, *Discourse analysis as theory and method*, London 2002.

[28] N. Fairclough, *Discourse and social change*, Cambridge 1992; *Language and power*, London and New York 2001.

Fairclough starts with the following assumptions.[29] First, discourse is a practice just as any other practice. The only difference with other practices is its linguistic form. Second, there is a dialectic relation between discourse (the discursive) and reality (the non-discursive). Third, the relation between discourse and reality is mediated through discursive practice. Thus, discursive practice is crucial in linking language and reality, texts and context.

With other qualitative research methods (e.g., content analysis, conversation analysis) critical discourse analysts are interested in participants' perspectives. But, unlike these other approaches they are not interested in participants' perspectives as such. They are interested in how the perspectives of the participants are linked to their social positions, and more particularly, in their interests to reproduce or transform the societal order.[30]

Critical discourse analysts distinguish different dimensions of one and the same practice or level of analysis: the individual (micro) dimension; the institutional (mezzo) dimension; and the societal (macro) dimension.[31] For example, the interactions between teachers and pupils, doctors and patients, or parents and children (micro level) are not only related to images of what specific institutions such as school, hospital and family are (mezzo level), but also to processes in the wider society (macro level) such as democratisation or commercialisation.[32] These examples also show different units of analysis: the cognitive or ideational (i.e., images) unit and the social or inter-personal units (i.e., subject positions and social relations); and these units go together.

The same applies to interactions between husband and wife in marriage, employers and employees in labour organisations, shop attendants and customers in super markets, politicians and electorate in election campaigns, civil servants and citizens in a municipality. This way of looking at social positions in specific fields can easily be trans-

---

[29] Fairclough, *Discourse and social change*, 71-72.
[30] Fairclough, *Discourse and social change*, 65.
[31] Fairclough, *Discourse and social change*, 69.
[32] Fairclough, *Discourse and social change*, 65-66, 200-224.

lated to studies of interactions between lay people and clerics in the religious field,[33] between preachers and their audiences, between catechists and catechumens, or between militant and moderate believers.[34]

Whereas radical post-structuralists tend to assume that discourse positions the speakers, and discursive psychologists tend to assume that speakers position themselves through discourse, Fairclough and other critical discourse analysts assume that it is both.[35] Speakers position themselves but they are also positioned by the discourse. It is assumed that the relation between the discursive (text) and the non-discursive (context) is a dialectical one.

But how does one go about it? In harmony with the three assumptions mentioned above, critical discourse analysts distinguish three stages in which they use various methods of analysis. These methods are given different names. Fairclough speaks about the analysis of linguistic practice, the analysis of discursive practice, and the analysis of social practice.[36] Alternative names are the analysis of text, interaction and context,[37] or simply description, interpretation and explanation.[38]

Description

As was said above, according to critical discourse analysts, discourse is a practice just as any other practice. The only difference with other practices is its linguistic form.[39] Language use is not only a way of saying things; it is a way of doing things. In other words, language use is a 'speech act'.

---

[33] Bourdieu, Genesis and structure.

[34] F. Wijsen and S. Cholil, "I come from a *Pancasila* Family". Muslims and Christians in Indonesia, in: V. Küster and R. Setio (eds.), *Muslim Christian Relations Observed. Comparative Studies from Indonesia and The Netherlands*, Leipzig 2014, 29-46.

[35] Fairclough, *Discourse and social change*, 65.

[36] Fairclough, *Discourse and social change*.

[37] Fairclough, *Language and power*, 21.

[38] Fairclough, *Language and power*, 21-22; *Discourse and social change*, 199.

[39] Fairclough, *Discourse and social change*, 71.

Thus the first method is description, or the analysis of the linguistic features of the text. At this stage, Fairclough suggests various tools, e.g., grammar, vocabulary, cohesion and structure.[40] In harmony with linguistic anthropologists,[41] Fairclough says that it "is sometimes useful for analytic purposes to focus upon a single word" and that "there are certain culturally salient 'keywords' which are worth focussing on in social research".[42] This is what 'ethnography of speaking' called 'names for things', and discursive psychologists 'identity labels'.[43] Wierzbicka, for example, studied the shift in the use of the word 'dialogue'.[44] She hypothesises that the word 'dialogue' was first used in the context of negotiations between East and West during the Cold War era, and shifted to other fields, e.g., interreligious or inter-faith dialogue as proposed at the Second Vatican Council and at the World Council of Churches during the late 1960s.

Words are not neutral. They carry a hidden, ideological or political agenda. For example, it does make a difference whether we speak about Palestine 'terrorists' or 'freedom fighters'.[45] And, it does make a difference whether scholars of religion speak about 'religious studies' or 'science of religion'. These terms are not neutral but ideological. There is an overlap with the third stage where we look at the ideological function of language use.

Words are ideological when they fix meaning. This is standardisation or naturalisation of text. Often the meanings of words are taken for granted, and thereby become common sense. The fixed meaning is

---

[40] Fairclough, *Discourse and social change*, 73-78.

[41] J. Fabian, *Language and colonial power: the appropriation of Swahili in the former Belgian Congo, 1880-1938*, New York 1986.

[42] Fairclough, *Discourse and social change*, 185-186.

[43] C. Antaki and S. Widdicombe (eds.), *Identities in talk*, London and Thousand Oaks 1998.

[44] A. Wierzbicka, The concept of 'dialogue' in cross-linguistic and cross-cultural perspective, in: *Discourse Studies* 8(2006)5, 680.

[45] Fairclough, *Discourse and social change*, 75; McCutcheon, *Studying religion*, 66.

an effect of a power struggle,[46] a closure of the multiplicity of meanings. Therefore it is useful to "focus on *alternative* wordings and their political and ideological significance".[47]

"The full account of the variability of a word ... would require *comparison* of meaning systems".[48] This is what Van Dijk calls "discourse variations, in different situations".[49] Fairclough speaks in terms of the relational theory of meaning.[50] The meaning of a single word depends on semantic relations such as similarity, contrast, overlap and inclusion. Thus, "it is useful *to compare* the wording of particular domains".[51] Constant comparative analysis is used to find alternative wordings and the possible socio-cognitive effects of their use.[52]

Interpretation

According to critical discourse analysts, linguistic practice and social practice are mediated through discursive practice. The discursive practice (i.e., interaction) is crucial as the dialectic relation between linguistic practice (i.e., text) and social practice (i.e., context) is based on it.[53] This stage makes materialist models different from other, e.g., cognitivist or mentalist models of discourse analysis.[54] Through the discursive practice, language use and social reality are linked.

---

[46] Fairclough, *Language and power*, 27, 73; *Discourse and social change*, 77-81.
[47] Fairclough, *Discourse and social change*, 77, see also 190.
[48] Fairclough, *Language and power*, 78, italics are mine.
[49] T. Van Dijk, *Discourse and context. A sociocognitive approach*, Cambridge 2008, 107.
[50] Fairclough, *Language and power*, 78.
[51] Fairclough, *Discourse and social change*, 193, italics are mine.
[52] G. Strauss and J. Corbin, *Basics of qualitative research. Grounded theory. Procedures and techniques*, Newbury Park 1998.
[53] Fairclough, *Discourse and social change*, 72, 80.
[54] J. Blommaert and J. Verschueren, *Debating diversity. Analysing the discourse of tolerance*, London and New York 1998, 26-27.

Consequently, the second stage is interpretation, or the analysis of the production, distribution and consumption of text.[55] Here again, Fairclough proposes various tools.[56] Also discourse styles and genres come in. Inter-discursivity is what Foucault calls the 'order of discourse'. This refers to hegemony of certain discourses over other discourses. For example, political and economic discourse rules over cultural and religious discourse (e.g., Habermas), or the other way round (e.g., Huntington).

When participants produce (communicate) or consume (interpret) text and talk they draw upon 'mental maps',[57] their 'cognitive apparatus',[58] 'members' resources'[59] or 'mental models'[60] stored as texts in their long-term memory.[61] For example, participants may refer to narratives about 12th-century Christian crusades, about 15th-century Western imperialism, or about the 19th-century Arab slave trade. These resources are cognitive in the sense that they are in people's heads; they are social in the sense that they are socially constructed and have social effects.[62] Recipients can only make sense of (or understand) texts if they can relate them to texts which they already have in their heads.

Distribution of text takes place through discourse genres in specific fields with social relations and subject positions. "A genre implies not only a particular text type, but also particular processes of producing, distributing and consuming texts", says Fairclough.[63] As was noted above, classroom communication is a specific genre[64] or discourse type.[65] It positions the teacher as teacher and the student as student. The

---

[55] Fairclough, *Discourse and social change*, 71, 86.
[56] Fairclough, *Discourse and social change*, 78-86.
[57] Fairclough, *Discourse and social change*, 82.
[58] Fairclough, *Language and power*, 133.
[59] Fairclough, *Language and power*, 20, 118.
[60] Van Dijk, *Discourse and context*, 75.
[61] Fairclough, *Language and power*, 8-9, 20, 118.
[62] Fairclough, *Language and power*, 19-20.
[63] Fairclough, *Discourse and social change*, 126.
[64] Fairclough, *Discourse and social change*, 232.
[65] Fairclough, *Language and power*, 24-25, 122.

actors in classroom communication cannot change their positions but they can fulfill them in different ways.

In the same way, a medical interview implies interaction between doctor and patient; buying things involves interaction between customer and shop assistant; an election campaign involves interaction between politicians and electorate, and so on.[66] These interactions (texts) take place in concrete contexts such as hospital, school, family, municipality, neighbourhood or society at large.[67] They shape them and are shaped by them.

Explanation

Critical discourse analysts moreover assume that there is a dialectic relation between language use and social reality. What participants say is shaped by and shapes social structures, either by reproducing them or transforming them.[68] Discourses "can be *expected* to have long-term *effects* on the knowledge and beliefs, social relationships, and social identities of an institution or society", says Fairclough.[69]

For example, the school system presupposes a specific discourse type (e.g., lecture or seminar) and specific social relations (e.g., authoritarian or democratic) and subject positions (e.g., teacher and pupil). The social system of school determines to a large extent the discourse. By using it, teachers and pupils reproduce the school system without change, or they transform it.[70] For example, teachers and pupils may reproduce a hierarchical relation, or develop an egalitarian relation. By taking the positions the participants become teacher or pupil. So reproduction may serve conservation or transformation of the existing order. It is not only rigid but also creative.[71]

---

[66] Fairclough, *Discourse and social change*, 124-130.
[67] Fairclough, *Discourse and social change*, 69.
[68] Fairclough, *Discourse and social change*, 72.
[69] Fairclough, *Language and power*, 62, italics are mine.
[70] Fairclough, *Language and power*, 31-32.
[71] Fairclough, *Language and power*, 24, 32.

The third stage is explanation; this is the analysis of the socio-cognitive effects of the text. Also at this stage Fairclough mentions a variety of tools.[72] In our research we focus on hegemony and ideology, and we notice the overlap with he first stage where we spoke about alternative wordings and their ideological significances. By analysing social practice, discourse analysis becomes a form of ideology critique. Unlike Foucault, who holds that there is no reality beyond discourse, or at least that scholars do not have access to it and thus lack instruments to assess what is 'true' or 'un-true', Fairclough is convinced that ideology critique is possible.[73] Against Foucault's determinism, he places a dialectic relation between discourse and reality.

Fairclough speaks about effects at three levels: knowledge or belief, social identities and social relations.[74] In other words, language constitutes 'identities', 'relations' and 'ideas'.[75] These are the ideational and interpersonal (identity in relation) effects of language use.

Fairclough is particularly interested in social change, i.e., whether language use reproduces or transforms the societal order.[76] Ideology is fixation of meaning so that social reality appears to be natural, and thus taken for granted. When participants continue to say that "women are weak", or "blacks are inferior", sexism and racism are reproduced. Or, in our disciplines, when scholars of religion say that religious studies is "science of religion", they reduce the diversity and complexity of this field of study to exact science.

Conclusion and discussion

Some theologians may argue that this way of looking at religion is 'scientific' and not 'theological'. Here again I would argue that these theologians reduce the meaning of theology to one form of theology,

[72] Fairclough, *Discourse and social change*, 86-96.
[73] Fairclough, *Discourse and social change*, 58.
[74] Fairclough, *Discourse and social change*, 64-65.
[75] Fairclough, *Language and power*, 62, 93-94.
[76] Fairclough, *Discourse and social change*, 65.

namely confessional or ecclesiastical theology, whereas there is also a tradition of 'scientific' theology.[77] This is why I find the distinction between 'methodical agnosticism' and 'methodical conversion' so important.[78] Methodical conversion can become or can be based on 'confessional conversion'. But within the academic language game or speech community conversion should remain methodical.

Looking back at my own development it is clear that 'discursive' (critical or socio-cognitive) analysis fits the emancipation aim of the practical-theological spiral better than old-style 'social' analysis, as it focuses on power. It has implications for the first stage of the practical-theological spiral, namely the way the interviewer puts questions. In harmony with Ludwig Witgenstein it is better not to ask for the meaning of words, but ask how words are used, as the meaning of words is their use. Thus the researcher should ask: How do you describe? What words do you use? But interview technique goes beyond the focus of this article which focused on the second stage of the practical-theological spiral only. In this stage we advocated a shift from 'social' (focus the surface structures of society) over 'cultural' (focus on shared meaning-systems) to 'discursive' (analysis of discursive practices) analysis.

---

[77] Flood, *Beyond phenomenology*, 20-25.
[78] Cox, Rational ancestors, 93-96.

Acknowledgement of sources

Chapter 1

F. Wijsen, New wine in old wineskins? Intercultural theology instead of missiology, in: M. Frederiks, M. Dijkstra and A. Houtepen (eds.), *Towards an intercultural theology*, Zoetermeer 2003, 39-54.

Chapter 2

F. Wijsen, The practical-theological spiral. Bridging theology in the West and the rest of the world, in: F. Wijsen, P. Henriot and R. Mejía (eds.), *The Pastoral Circle revisited. A critical quest for truth and transformation*, Maryknoll, New York 2005, 108-126.

Chapter 3

F.J.S. Wijsen, 'I have all kinds of medicines.' Dialogue and syncretism in African Christianity, in W. Valkenberg and F. Wijsen (eds.), *The polemic dialogue*, Saarbrücken 1997, 123-145.

Chapter 4

F. Wijsen, The resurgence of religion in today's world, in: F. Stenger and J. Wandera (eds.), *Christian-Muslim co-existence in Eastern Africa*. Nairobi 2008, 41-58.

Chapter 5

F. Wijsen, Popular Christianity in East Africa. Inculturation or syncretism?, in: *Exchange. Journal of Missiological and Ecumenical Research* 29(2000)1, 37-60.

Chapter 6

F. Wijsen, Mission in a new key. From inculturation to interculturation, in: *SMA Bulletin*, June 2007(125), 41-53.

Conclusion

F. Wijsen, Mission and multiculturalism. On communication between Europeans and Africans, in: *Exchange. Journal of Missiological and Ecumenical Research* 32(2003)3, 260-277.

Epilogue

F. Wijsen, The Practical-Theological Circle revisited. From social to discursive analysis, in: R. Setio, W. Wibowo and P. Widjaja (eds.), *Teks dan Konteks yang Tiada Bertepi*, Semarang 2012, 73-91

Bibliography

Adeney, B., *Strange virtues. Ethics in a multicultural world*, Downers Grove 1995.

Adeyemo, T., The Salvation Debate and Evangelical Response, in: *East Africa Journal of Evangelical Theology* 2(1984)2, 4-19.

All Africa Press Service, Virgin Mary visits Tanzania, in: *News and Features Bulletin*, July 13, 1987.

All Africa Press Service, Religious Plays Promote Inculturation of Gospel in Tanzania, in: *News and Features Bulletin*, July 20, 1987.

All Africa Press Service, Bujora Village leads in blending culture and faith, in: *News and Features Bulletin*, January 29, 1990.

Allen, T., *Trial justice. The International Criminal Court and the Lord's Resistance Army*, London and New York 2006.

Amaladoss, M. (ed.), *Globalization and its victims as seen by its victims*, Delhi 1999.

Anderson, G., *Witness to World Christianity. The international association of Missions Studies, 1972-2012*, New Haven 2012.

Antaki, C. and S. Widdicombe (eds.), *Identities in talk*, London and Thousand Oaks 1998.

Appiah, K., *In my father's house. Africa in the philosophy of culture*, Oxford 1992.

Arinze, F., *Meeting other believers,* Nairobi 1997.

Asad, T., Anthropological conception of religion. Reflections on Geertz, in: *Man* 18(1983), 237-259.

Association of the Universities in the Netherlands, *Assessment of research quality*, Utrecht 2000.

Bagir, Z., Islam, science and 'Islamic science', in: Z. Bagir (ed.), *Science and religion in a post-colonial World. Interfaith Perspectives*, Hindmarsh 2005, 37-61.

Balina, A., A. Mayala and J. Mabula, *Sukuma expression of traditional religion in life*, Kipalapala 1971. (mimeographed).

Balz, H., *Theologische Modelle der Kommunikation,* Gütersloh 1978.

Balz, H., Krise der Kommunikation – Wiederkehr der Hermeneutik?, in: T. Sundermeier and W. Ustorf, *Die Begegnung mit dem Anderen. Plädoyer für eine interkulturelle Hermeneutik*, Gütersloh 1991, 39-65.

Banawiratma J. and J. Müller, *Contextual social theology. An Indonesian model*, Manila 1999.

Barber, B., *Jihad vs. McWorld*, New York 1995.

Barrett, D. (ed.), *World Christian Encyclopedia. A Comparative study of Churches and Religions in the Modern World*, Nairobi, Oxford and New York 1982.

Barth, F., *Ethnic groups and boundaries. The social organization of difference*, London 1969.

Beattie, J., *Other cultures. Aims, methods and achievements in social anthropology*, London and Henley 1982.

Becker, D., Der Westen gegen den Rest?, in: D. Becker (ed.), *Globaler Kampf der Kulturen*, Stuttgart 1999.

Becker, D. (ed.), *Mit dem Fremden leben: Perspektiven einer Theologie der Konvivenz,* Erlangen 2000.

Becker, D., *Mission verstehen. Themen und Thesen interkultureller Forschung*, Neuendettelsau 2012.

Becker D. and A. Feldtkeller (eds.), *Es begann in Halle ... Missionswissenschaft von Gustav Warneck bis heute*, Neuendettelsau 1997.

Becker, J. and J. de Wit, *Secularisatie in de jaren negentig,* Den Haag 2000.

Bellagamba, A., *Mission and ministry in the global Church*, Maryknoll, New York 1992.

Berger, P., *The Heretical Imperative. Contemporary Possibilities of Religious Affirmation*, New York 1979.

Berger, P., *The desecularization of the world. Resurgent religion and world politics*, Grand Rapids 1999.

Berner, U., Synkretismus und Inkulturation, in: Siller (ed.), *Suchbewegungen. Synkretismus, kulturelle Identität und Kirchliches Bekentnis*, Darmstadt 1991, 130-144.

Bettscheider, H. (ed.), *Reflecting mission, practising mission,* Nettetal 2001.

Bevans, S., *A century of Catholic mission*, Oxford 2013.

Bevans, S. and R. Schroeder, *Constants in context. A theology of mission for today*. Maryknoll, New York 2004.

Bevans, S. and R. Schroeder, *Prophetic dialogue. Reflections on Christian Mission today*, Maryknoll, New York 2011.

Biernatski, W., *Roots of Acceptance. The Intercultural Communication of Religious Meanings*, Rome 1991.

Bitterli, U., *Die 'Wilden' und die 'Zivilisierten'*, München 1976.

Blomjous, J., Development in Mission Thinking and Practice, 1959-1980. Inculturation and Interculturation, in: *African Ecclesial Review* 22(1980)6, 293-298.

Blommaert, J. and J. Verschueren, *Debating diversity. Analysing the discourse of tolerance*, London and New York 1998.

Boff, C., *Theologie und Praxis. Die erkenntnistheoretische Grundlagen der Theologie der Befreiung*, München 1983.

Boff, L. and C. Boff, *Introducing liberation theology*, Maryknoll, New York 1987.

Bonsen, R., H. Marks and J. Miedema (eds.), *The ambiguity of rapprochement: reflections of anthropologists on their controversial relationship with missionaries,* Nijmegen 1990.

Borgman, E., Theology as the art of liberation. Edward Schillebeeckx's response to the theologies of the EATWOT, in: *Exchange. Journal of Missiological and Ecumenical Research* 32(2003)2, 98-108.

Borsboom, A., and F. Jespers (eds.), *Religion and identity*, Saarbrücken 2003.

Borsboom, A. and J. Kommers, *Anthropologists and the missionary endeavour*, Saarbrücken 2002.

Bosch, D., *Transforming mission. Paradigm shifts in theology of mission* , Maryknoll, New York 1992.

Bourdieu, P., *Outline of a Theory of Practice*, London 1977.

Bourdieu, P., *Le sense pratique,* Paris 1980.

Bourdieu, P., *In other words. Essays towards reflexive sociology*, Cambridge, 1990.

Bourdieu, P., Genesis and structure of the religious field, in: C. Calhoun (ed.), *Comparative social research*. Vol. 13, London 1991, 1-44.

Bourdieu, P., *Language and symbolic power*, Cambridge 1991.

Bourdieu, P., *Ce que parler veut dire*, Paris 1992.

Bourdieu, P., *Das religiöse Feld*, Konstanz 2000.

Bourdieu, P., *Ein soziologischer Selbstversuch*, Franfurt am Main 2002.

Bredero, A., *De ontkerstening der Middeleeuwen,* Baarn 2000.

Brightman, R., Forget culture. Replacement, transcendence, relexification, in: *Cultural Anthropology* 10(1995)4, 509-546.

Bühlmann, W., *The coming of the third church. An analysis of the present and the future of the church*, Maryknoll, New York 1978.

Bujo, B., *The ethical dimension of community. The African model and the dialogue between North and South.* Nairobi 1998.

Bujo, B., *Foundations of an African ethic: beyond the universal claims of Western morality,* New York 2001.

Bünker, A. and L. Weckel (eds.), *"ihr werdet mein Zeige sein .." Rückfragen au seiner störrischen theologischen Disziplin*, Freiburg, Basel and Wien 2005.

Buono, G., *Missiology. Theology and praxis*, Nairobi 2000.

Burama, I. and A. Margalit, *Occidentalism. The West in the eyes of its enemies*, New York 2004.

Busch, D., *Interkulturelle Mediation. Eine theoretische Grundleging triadischer Konfliktbearbeitung in interkulturell bedingten Kontexten*, Frankfurt am Main 2005.

Busch, D. and H. Schröder (eds.), *Perspektiven interkultureller Mediation. Grundlagentexte zur kommunikationswissenschaftlichen Analyse triadichen Verständigung*, Frankfurt am Main 2005.

Byaruhanga Akiiki, A., African traditional values for human development, in: J. Agbasiere and B. Zabajungu (eds.), *Church contribution to integral development*, Eldoret 1989, 45-62.

Camps, A., Vier sleutelbegrippen voor een meer empirische missiologie, in: *Vox Theologica* 42(1972), 218-231.

Camps, A., Four key-notes of an empirical missiology, in: *Neue Zeitschrift für Missionswissenschaft* 29(1973) 135-142.

Camps, A., *Partners in dialogue. Christianity and other world religions*, Maryknoll, New York 1983.

Castillo Guerra, J., F. Wijsen, Multiculturele of interculturele liturgie? In: D. Broersen, G. Smit, H. Luyten (red.), *Ik loop hier stage*, Heeswijk 2005, 85-102.

Castillo Guerra, J., F. Wijsen, M. Steggerda, *Een gebedshuis voor alle volken. Kerkopbouw en kadervorming in room-katholieke allochtonengemeenschappen*, Zoetermeer 2006.

Castillo Guerra, J. and F. Wijsen, Katholieke Migranten tussen folklore en het recht om bestaan, in: E. Burgmans and P. Minderhoud (eds.), *Mythen en misverstanden over migratie,* Nijmegen 2007, 274-308.

Chinweizu, *The West and the rest of us. White predators, black slavers and the African elite*, Lagos, 1987.

Chipenda, J., *The church of Africa: towards a theology of reconstruction,* Nairobi 1991.

Clément, D., The Research Committee at Bujora, in: B. Flou, B. Knudsen, G. Pedersen and D. Clement, *Folk Research in Mwanza Region*, in: *Tanzania Notes and Records* (1977)81 and 82, 75-78.

Cliteur, P., Jemen in Nederland, in: P. Cliteur and V. van den Eeckhout (eds.), *Multiculturalisme, cultuurrelativisme en sociale cohesie,* Den Haag 2001.

Cliteur, P., *Moderne Papoea's. Dilemma's van een multiculturele samenleving*, Amsterdam 2002.

Clooney, F., The emergent field of comparative theology, in: *Theological Studies* 56(1995), 521-550.

Coenders, M., *Exclusionistic electorates*, Nijmegen 2001.

Cohen, J., *Grenzen: over de verhouding van autochtonen en migranten*, Amsterdam 2001.

Collet, G., Mission und Kommunikation, in: *Zeitschrift für Missions- und Religionswissenschaft* 74(1990)1, 1-18.

Collet, G., Bekehrung, Vergleich, Anerkennung: die Stellung des Anderen im Selbstverständnis der Missionswissenschaft, in: *Zeitschrift für Missions- und Religionswissenschaft* 77(1993)3, 205-251.

Collet, G., *'Bis an die Grenzen der Erde'. Grundfragen heutiger Missionswissenschaft*, Freiburg 2002.

Comoro, C. and J. Sivalon, The Marian Faith Healing Ministry, in: T. Spear and I. Kimambo (eds.), *East African Expressions of Christianity*, Nairobi 1999, 275-295.

Cory, H., Religious beliefs and practices of the Sukuma / Nyamwezi tribal group, in: *Tanganyika Notes and Records,* 54(1960), 14-26.

Cox, H., *Fire from heaven. The rise of Pentecostal spirituality and the reshaping of religion in the twenty-first century*, London 1996.

Cox, J., *Rational ancestors. Scientific rationality and African Indigenous Religions*, Cardiff 1998.

Crowley, J., *Go to the people,* Eldoret 1985.

Daneel, I., C. van Engen and H. Vroom (eds.), *Fullness of Life for All. Challenges for Mission in Early 21st Century*, Amsterdam and New York 2003.

Davie, G., *Europe: The Exceptional Case. Parameters of Faith in the Modern World*, London 2002.

De Bekker, N., *Hand in hand met Afrika,* Tilburg 2000

Degrijse, O., *Going forth. Missionary consciousness in Third World Catholic churches*, Maryknoll, New York 1984.

De Jong, A., *De missionaire opleiding van Nederlandse missionarissen,* Kampen 1995.

De Jong, A. (ed.), *Ethnicity: blessing or curse?*, Nairobi 1999.

De Jong, A., Africans viewed in the missionary mirror, in: *Exchange. Journal of Missiological and Ecumenical Research* 30(2001)1, 49-77.

De Mesa, J., Making salvation concrete and Jesus real, in: *Exchange. Journal of Missiological and Ecumenical Research* 30(2001)1, 1-17.

De Schrijver, G. (ed.), *Liberation theologies on shifting grounds*, Leuven 1998.

Donavan, V., *Christianity rediscovered,* Notre Dame 1978.

Dorr, D., *Mission in today's world*, Maryknoll, New York 2000.

Droogers, A., De minimale religiositeit van de meerderheid, in: R. Bakker, R. Fernhout, J. Gort and A. Wessels (eds.), *Religies in nieuw perspectief. Studies over interreligieuze dialoog en religiositeit op het grondvlak*, Kampen 1985, 88-108.

Droogers, A., Syncretism. The problem of definition. The definition of the problem, in: J. Gort, H. Vroom, R. Fernhout and A. Wessels (eds.), *Dialogue and Syncretism. An Interdisciplinary Approach*, Grand Rapids 1989, 7-25.

Dussel, E., *The Invention of the Americas. Eclipse of 'Other' and the Myth of Modernity*, New York 1995.

Du Toit, C., Secular spirituality versus secular dualism, in: C. du Toit and F. Mayson (eds.), *Secular spirituality as a contextual critique of religion*, Pretoria 2006.

Eboh, S., *African communalism. The way to social harmony and peaceful co-existence*, Frankfurt am Main and London 2004.

Eggen, W. and R. van Rossum, *Waken bij de eigenheid van de ander: evangelisering in hedendaags perspectief*, Aalsmeer 1992.

Eilers, F.-J., *Communicating between cultures*, Manila 1987.

Eilers, F.-J., *Communicating in Community. An introduction to social communication*, Manilla 2002.

Elbadawi, I. and N. Sambanis, Why are there so many civil wars in Africa? Understanding and preventing violent conflict, in: *Journal of African Economies* 9(2000)3, 224-269,

Elliston, E., *Introduction to missiological research design*, Pasadena 2011.

Essed, P., *Everyday racism,* Claremont 1990.

Estermann, J., Missiological Instititute Missio, in: S. Karotemprel et al., *Promoting mission studies*, Shilling 2000, 43-73.

Evans-Pritchard, E., *Nuer religion*, Oxford 1956.

Exeler, A., Vergleichende Theologie statt Missionswissenschaft? Provozierende Anfrage eines nichtfachmannes, in: H. Waldenfels (ed.), *"...denn ich bin bei euch"*, Zürich 1978, 199-211.

Exeler, A., Wege einer vergleichenden Pastoral, in: L. Bertsch and F. Schlösser (eds.), *Evangelisation in der dritten Welt*, Freiburg 1981, 92-121.

Fabella, V. and S. Torres, *The emergent gospel*. Maryknoll, New York 1977.

Fabian, J., *Language and colonial power: the appropriation of Swahili in the former Belgian Congo, 1880-1938*, New York 1986.

Fairclough, N., *Discourse and social change*, Cambridge 1992.

Fairclough, N., *Language and power*, London and New York 2001.

Flood, G., *Beyond phenomenology. Rethinking the study of religion*, London and New York 1999

Fortuyn, P., *Tegen de islamisering van onze cultuur,* Utrecht 1997.

Fox, H., *Listening to the world. Cultural issues in academic writing*, Urbana 1994.

Freire, P., *Pedagogy of the oppressed*, New York 1971.

Freire, P., *Pedagogy in process: the letters to Guinea-Bissau,* New York 1978.

Freitag, A. (ed.), *Emigranten voor God: wereldbetekenis van het Nederlandse missiewerk.* Parts 1 and 2, SteijlTegelen 1949.

Friedli, R., *Fremdheit als Heimat. Auf der Suche nach einem Kriterium für den Dialog zwischen den Religionen*, Zürich 1974.

Friedli, R., Kultur und kulturelle Vielfalt, in: T. Sundermeier and W. Ustorf, *Die Begegnung mit dem Anderen. Plädoyer für eine interkulturelle Hermeneutik*, Gütersloh 1991, 29-38.

Friedli, R.. Mission, Religionen, Religionswissenschaft. Erfahrungen mit universitären Neukompositionen, in: D. Becker (ed.), *Mit dem Fremden Leben*, Erlangen 2000, 185-191.

Geertz, C., *The religion of Java*, London 1960.

Geertz, C., *The interpretation of cultures*, New York 1993.

Geertz, C., *Available light. Anthropological reflections on philosophical topics*, Princeton 2000.

Gerloff, R. (ed.), Open Space. The African Diaspora in Europe and the Quest for a Human Community, in: *International Review of Mission* (2000)354.

Getui, M. et al., *Theology of reconstruction,* Nairobi 1999.

H. Ghorashi, *Ways to survive, battles to win,* Nijmegen 2001.

Giles, L., Possession Cults on the Swahili Coast. A re-examination of Theories of Marginality, in: *Africa* 57(1987)2, 234-258.

Gittins, A. (ed.), *Life and death matters: the practice of inculturation in Africa,* Nettetal 2000.

Gittins, A., *Mission at the margins. Strategy and spirituality for mission*, Maryknoll, New York 2002.

Gort, J., H. Janssen and H. Vroom, *Religion, conflict and reconciliation*, Amsterdam and New York 2002.

Gutiérrez, G., *Theology of liberation*, Maryknoll, New York 1973.

Gyekye, K., *Tradition and modernity. Philosophical reflection on African experience*, New York 1997.

Habermas, J., *Erkentnis und Interesse*, Frankfurt am Main 1968.

Habermas, J., *Theorie des kommunikativen Handeln* II, Frankfurt 1982.

Hall, S., The West and the rest. Discourse and power, in: S. Hall and B. Gieben (eds.), *Formations of modernity*, Cambridge 1992.

Hanga, S., Kenyan Pilgrims Flock to Meet Tanzania's Priest of the Sick, in: *The East African*, Dec. 26, 1994 - Jan 1, 1995, 1-2.

Hannerz, U., *Cultural complexity. Studies in the social organization of meaning*, New York 1992.

Hastings, A., *Church and mission in modern Africa,* London 1967.

Hastings, A., *African Catholicism. Essays in Discovery*, London 1989.

Hastings, A., *The Church in Africa. 1450-1959*, Oxford 1994.

Haumann, T., *Vrede langs het oorlogspad: ontmoetingen in Zuid-Sudan,* Heeswijk Utrecht 1998.

Healey, J., *A fifth Gospel. The experience of black Christian values,* Maryknoll, New York 1981.

Healey, J. and D. Sybertz, *Kamati ya Utafiti wa Utamaduni, Imani za jadi za kisukuma katika misemo, hadithi, methali na desturi za maisha*, Nantes 1988.

Healey, J. and D. Sybertz, *I Pointed out to you the stars. An African narrative Theology of Inculturation*, Nairobi 1996.

Heijke, J. et al., *In elkaars spiegel. Westers Christendom in Afrika,* Baarn 1993.

Hendriks, J., *Brieven uit Afrika, Witte Paters*, n.p. n.d. [Boxtel: Prokuur der Witte Paters, 1948].

Hendriks, J., *Strijd en Hoop*, n.p. n.d. [Sumve 1947-1949; Nyegezi: Regional's House, White Fathers]. (type-written manuscript).

Hendriks, J., *Ha Kikome*, St. Justin 1959.

Hendriks, J., *Liwelelo*, Tabora 1960.

Hendriks, J., Adaptation [Paper presented at the Pastoral Formation Centre], Kipalapala 1962. (mimeographed).

Henriot, P., Grassroots analysis. The emphasis on culture, in: G. De Schrijver (ed.), *Liberation theologies on shifting grounds*, Leuven 1998, 333-350.

Hermans, H. and H. Kempen, *The dialogical self. Meaning as movement*, San Diego 1993.

Hesselgrave, D., *Communication Christ cross-culturally. An introduction to Missionary Communication*, Grand Rapids 1978.

Hesselgrave, D. and E. Stetzer (eds.), *Missionshift. Global mission issues in the third millennium*, Nashville 2010.

Hillman, E., *Many paths. A Catholic approach to religious pluralism*, Maryknoll, New York 1989.

Hock, K., *Einführung in die Religionswissenschaft*, Darmstadt 2002.

Hoedemaker, L., The people of God and the ends of the earth, in: F. Verstraelen (general editor), *Missiology. An ecumenical introduction*, Grand Rapids 1995, 157-171.

Hoedemaker, L. (ed.), *Theologiseren in context,* Kampen 1997.

Hoekendijk, J., *De kerk binnenste buiten,* Amsterdam 1964.

Hofstede, G., *Allemaal andersdenkenden: omgaan met cultuurverschillen,* Amsterdam 1991.

Holland, J. and P. Henriot, *Social analysis. Linking faith and justice*, Maryknoll, New York 1983.

Hollenweger, W., Kultur und Evangelium, Das Thema der interkulturellen Theology, in: *Jahrbuch Evangelische Mission*. Band 17, 1985, 52-60.

Hope, A. and S. Timmel, *Training for transformation*. Handbooks 1, 2, 3, Gweru 1984.

Hountondji, P., *African philosophy. Myth an reality*, London 1983.

Hudson, K., *Museums of Influence*, Cambridge 1987.

Huinder, C., P. Schnabel, R. Gowricharn and R. Mok, *De multiculturele illusie. Een fikse ruzie waard*, Utrecht 2000.

Huizer, G., Research-through-action, in: G. Huizer and B. Manheim (eds.), *The politics of anthropology*, The Hague and Paris 1979, 395-420.

Huizer, G., *Folk spirituality and liberation in Southern Africa*, Bourdeaux 1991.

Huntington, S., *The clash of civilizations and the remaking of the world order*, New York 1996.

Huntington, S. and L. Harrison (eds.), *Culture matters: how values shape human progress,* New York 2001.

Idinopulos, T. and B. Wilson, *What is religion?* Leiden 1998.

Illich, I., *Mission and midwifery. Essays on missionary formation*, Gwelo 1974.

Jacobs, J. et al., Vier ijkpunten geijkt, in: *Trajecta* 10(2001)4, 273-309.

Janssen, H. , Der pastorale Zirkel – eine Einführung, in: M. Pankoke-Schenk and G. Evers (eds.), *Inkulturation und Kontextualität*, Frankfurt am Main 1994, 221-230.

Jenkins, P., *The next Christendom*, New York 2002.

Jenkins, P., Christianity moves South, in: F. Wijsen and R. Schreiter (eds.), *Global Christianity. Contested claims*, Amsterdam and New York 2007, 15-33.

Joinet, B., I am a stranger in my father's house: the insertion of the missionary into a local community, in: *Pastoral Orientation Service* No. 8-9, 1972, 17-28.

Joinet, B., *The challenge of modernity in Africa*, Nairobi 2000.

Jongeneel, J., *Philosophy, Science and Theology of Mission*, Frankfurt am Main 1995.

Jongeneel, J., Is Missiology an academic discipline?, in: *Exchange. Journal of Missiological and Ecumenical Research* 27(1998)3, 1-14.

Jørgensen, K., *Equipping for service. Christian leadership in Church and society*, Oxford 2012.

Jørgensen, M. and L. Phillips, *Discourse analysis as theory and method*, London 2002.

Kalilombe, P., Evangelisation and the Holy Spirit, in: *African Ecclesial Review* 18(1976)1, 8-18.

Kalilombe, P., The salvific value of African religions, in: *African Ecclesial Review* 21(1979)3, 143-157.

Kalilombe, P., Spirituality in the African perspective, in: R. Gibellini (ed.), *Paths of African Theology*, London 1994, 115-135.

Kalilombe, P., *Doing theology at the grassroots*, Gweru 1999.

Kä Mana, *Foi Chrétienne, crise africaine et reconstruction de l'Afrique,* Nairobi 1992.

Kamati ya Utafiti wa Utamaduni, *Imani za jadi za kisukuma katika misemo, hadithi, methali na desturi za maisha*, Nantes 1988.

Kamstra, J., Een moeilijke keuze: de godsdienst van de gewone man, in: *Tijdschrift voor Theologie* 20(1980)269, 253-279.

Kanyandago, P. (ed.), *Marginalized Africa. An international perspective*, Nairobi 2002.

Karotemprel, S. (ed.), *Following Christ in mission,* Nairobi 1995, 21-36

Karotemprel, S. et al., *Promoting mission studies*, Shillong 2000.

Kasper, W., Geest – Christus – Kerk, in: J. Lescrauwaet et al. (eds.), *Leven uit de Geest. Theologische Peilingen aangeboden aan E. Schillebeeckx*, Hilversum 1974, 46-64.

Keesing, R., Theories of culture revisited, in: R. Borofsky (ed.), *Assessing cultural anthropology*, New York 1994, 301-312.

Kibicho, S., *The Kikuyu Conception of God, Its Continuity into the Christian Era and the Question it raises for the Christian Idea of Revelation*. Doctoral Dissertation, Nashville 1972.

Kibicho, S., The Teaching of African Religion in our Schools and Colleges and the Christian Attitude towards this Religion, in: *Africa Theological Journal* 10(1981)3, 29-37.

Kibicho, S., The mission of the church of Jesus Christ today from the perspective of the younger churches, in: A. Ngindu Mushete, *The mission of the Church today. Reports of the Yaoundé meeting (4-11 April, 1984). Special Issue of the Bulletin of African Theology* 7(1985)13-14, 17-27.

Kibicho, S., *God and revelation in an African contexts*, Nairobi 2006.

Kim, K. and A. Anderson (eds.), *Mission today and tomorrow*, Oxford 2011.

Kimmerle, H., *Mazungumzo. Dialogen tussen Afrikaanse en Westerse filosofieën,* Amsterdam 1995.

Kiogora, T., Angels, Demons and Spirits in African Christianity, in: A. Nasimiyu-Wasike and D. Waruta (eds.), *Mission in African Christianity*, Nairobi 1993, 52-66.

Kirk, A., *What is mission? Theological explorations*, London 1999.

Kirwen, M., *The Missionary and the Diviner. Contending Theologies of Christian and African Religions*, Maryknoll, New York 1987.

Kirwen, M., *African cultural themes*, Nairobi and Minnesota 2004.

Klare, M., *Resource wars. The new landscape of global conflict,* New York 2001.

Knitter, P., *No other name? A Critical Survey of Christian Attitudes Toward the World Religions*, Maryknoll, New York 1985.

Knitter, P., *One earth many religions. Multifaith dialogue and global responsibility*, Maryknoll, New York 1995.

Kobia, S., *The courage to hope. A challenge to the churches in Africa*, Nairobi 2003, 103-150.

Kraemer, H., *The Christian message in a Non-Christian world,* London 1938.

Kraemer, H., *The communication of the Christian faith*, Philadelphia 1956.

Kraemer, H., *World cultures and world religions: The coming dialogue*, London 1960.

Krämer, K. and K. Vellgutt (eds.), *Mission und Dialog. Ansätze für ein kommunikatives Missionsverständnis*, Freiburg, Basel and Wien 2012.

Kraft, C., *Communicating the gospel in God's way,* Pasadena 1979.

Kraft, C., *Anthropology for Christian Witness*, Maryknoll, New York 1996.

Kramm, T., Was ist von einer 'vergleichende Theologie' zu erwarten?, in: *Zeitschrift für Missionswissenschaft und Religionswissenschaft* 68(1984)69-73.

Kramm, T., Vergleichende Theologie statt Missionswissenschaft, in: *Zeitschrift für Missionswissenschaft und Religionswissenschaft* 70(1986)101-111.

Krieger, D., *The new universalism. Foundations for a global theology*, Maryknoll, New York 1991.

Kristin Arat, M., Die nichtamtliche Religiosität als dialogisches Element der Religionen am Beispiel von Christentum und Islam, in: *Zeitschrift für Missionswissenschaft und Religionswissenwissenschaft* 76(1992)2.

Kroeger, J. (ed.), *The gift of mission. Yesterday, today, tomorrow*, Maryknoll, New York 2013.

Kronenburg, J., *Empowerment of the poor*, Amsterdam and Nijmegen1986.

Küng, H., What is true religion? Toward an Ecumenical Criteriology, in: L. Swidler (ed.), *Toward a Universal Theology of Religion*, Maryknoll, New York 1987, 4-23.

Küng, H., *Projekt Weltethos,* München and Zürich 1990.

Küng, H., *Global responsibility. In search of a new world ethic*, New York 1991.

Küster, V., *The many faces of Jesus Christ. Intercultural Christology*, London 2001.

Küster, V., *Mission revisited. Between mission history and intercultural theology*, Münster and Zürich 2011.

Kyeyune, D. (ed.), *New trends for the empowerment of the poor*, Nairobi 1997.

Lande, A. and W. Ustorf (eds.), *Mission in a pluralist world*, Frankfurt am Main 1996.

Lawson, E. and R. McCauley, *Rethinking religion. Connecting Cognition and Culture*, Cambridge 1990.

Lewin, K., *Resolving social conflicts*, New York 1948.

Linden, I., The Churches and genocide. Lessons from the Rwandan tragedy, in: *The Month*, July 1995, 256-263.

Lobinger, F., *Towards non-dominating leadership. Aims and methods of the Lumko-series*, Delmenville 1983.

Lovett, B., *For the joy set before us. Methodology of adequate theological reflection on mission*, Oxford 2008.

Lubbers, M., *Nationalistic attitudes and ethnic exclusionism in a comparative perspective*, Nijmegen 2001.

Lupande, J., *The Sukuma of Tanzania. Bujora cultural centre*, Denmark 1994; A. Bessire and M. Bessire, *Sukuma*, New York 1997.

Luzbetak, L., *The Church and Cultures. New Perspectives in Missiological Anthropology*, Maryknoll, New York 1989.

Maaskant, J., *Afrikaan en katholiek in Rotterdam,* Nijmegen 1999.

Magesa, L., Some critical theological and pastoral issues facing the Church in East Africa today, in: *African Christian Studies* 4(1988)4, 43-60.

Magesa, L., Politics and theology in Africa, in: *African Ecclesial Review* 31(1989)3, 131-142.

Magesa, L., Overview of 100 Years of Catholicism in Kenya, in: *African Ecclesial Review* 32(1990)1, 42-50.

Magesa, L., Assessing pastoral ministry in a parish situation, in: *African Ecclesial Review* 33(1991)5, 281-287.

Magesa, L., "Am I not a Human Being …", in: *African Ecclesial Review* 34(1992)1, 95-114.

Magesa, L., The Church in Eastern Africa, in: A. Radoli (ed.), *How local is the local Church? Spearhead 126-128*, Eldoret 1993, 3-35.

Magesa, L., The present and the future of inculturation in East Africa, in: P. Turkson and F. Wijsen (eds.), *Inculturation. Abide by the Otherness of Africa and the Africans*, Kampen 1994, 57-71.

Magesa, L., *African religion. The moral traditions of abundant life*. Maryknoll, New York 1997.

Magesa, L., The global and the local: an African view, in: M. Amaladoss (ed.), *Globalization and its victims,* Delhi 1999, 187-192.

Magesa, L., African Renaissance, in: P. Kanyandago (ed.), *Marginalized Africa*, Nairobi 2002, 13-27.

Magesa, L., Being honest about inculturation in Africa, in: *Service* (2006)5.

Malishi, L., *Introduction to the history of Christianity in Africa*, Tabora 1987.

Mall, R., *Intercultural philosophy*, Lanham 2000.

Maluleke, T., A rediscovery of the agency of Africans, in: P. Kanyandago (ed.), *Marginalized Africa*, Nairobi 2002, 165-190.

Mannheim, K., *Ideology and utopia. An introduction to the sociology of knowledge*, London 1960.

Massaar, J. and L. Spruit, 'Kerncijfers uit de kerkelijke statistiek 2000 van het R.K. Kerkgenootschap in Nederland', KASKI memorandum no. 321, October 2001.

Mayer, C.-H., *Intercultural Mediation and Conflict Resolution*, Stuttgart 2005.

Mazrui, A., *Islam between globalization and counter-terrorism*, Oxford 2006.

Mbigi, L., *Ubuntu. The African dream in management*, Randburg 1997.

Mbiti, J., Our Saviour as an African experience, in: B. Lindars and S. Smalley (eds.), *Christ and Spirit in the New Testament*, Cambridge 1973, 398-414.

Mbogoni, L., *The cross versus the crescent. Religion and politics in Tanzania from the 1880s to the 1990s*, Dar es Salaam 2004.

McCutcheon, R., *Studying religion. An introduction*, London and Oakville 2007.

McLuhan, M., *The Gutenberg galaxy*, Toronto 1962.

Mejía, R., The new understanding of pastoral theology, in: C. McGarry, R. Mejía and V. Shirima (eds.), A new light on our path, Nairobi 1993, 27-37.

Mejía, R., Pastoral Theology and the Pastoral Circle: The Methodology and Dynamics of the Pastoral Circle, in P. Ryan (ed.), *New Strategies for a New Evangelization in Africa,*Nairobi 2002, 111-128.

Mercy Amba Oduyoye, *Daughters of Anowa. African women and patriarchy*, Maryknoll, New York 1995.

Meyer, B., If you are a Devil, you are a Witch and, if you are a witch, you are a Devil, in: *Journal of Religion in Africa* 22(1992)2, 98-132.

Meyer, B., Beyond syncretism. Translation and diabolization in the appropriation of Protestantism in Africa, in: C. Stewart and R. Shaw (eds.), *Syncretism/Anti-Syncretism. The politics of religious synthesis*, London and New York 1994, 60-63.

Millroth, B., *Lyuba. Traditional Religion of the Sukuma*. Doctoral Dissertation, Uppsala 1965.

Mock, E., *Afrikanische Pedagogik,* Wuppertal and Aachen 1979.

Mosha, R., The prophetic role of the Church in Tanzania today, in: L. Magesa (ed.), *The prophetic role of the Church in Tanzania today. Spearhead 115*, Eldoret 1991, 13-32.

Mugambi, J., *African heritage and contemporary Christianity*, Nairobi 1989.

Mugambi, J., *From liberation to reconstruction. African Christian theology after the Cold War*, Nairobi 1995.

Mugambi, J., *Christian theology and social reconstruction*, Nairobi 2003.

Mugenda, O. and A. Mugenda, *Research methods*, Nairobi 2003.

Müller, K., *Mission theology. An introduction*. Nettetal 1987.

Müller, K., Missiology, in: S. Karotemprel (ed.), *Following Christ in mission*, Bombay 1995, 21-36.

Müller, K. (ed.), *Dictionary of Mission. Theology, History, Perspectives*, Maryknoll, New York 1997.

E. Mveng, *L'Afrique dans l'église,* Paris 1985.

G. Mwageni, The Church in the African society, in: *Pastoral Orientation Service* (1980)1, 36-46.

Mwoleka, C., *Do this. The Church of the Third Millennium*, Ndanda and Peramiho 1988.

Neckebrouck, V., *De stomme duivelen. Het anti-missionair syndroom in de westerse kerk*, Brugge 1990.

Neckebrouck, V., Westerse weerstanden tegen de kerkelijke leer over missie en ontwikkeling in kensociologisch perspectief, in: J. Bulckens, P. Cooreman (eds.), Kerkelijk leven in Vlaanderen anno 2000, Leuven 1989.

Ngindu Mushete, A., *Les thèmes majeurs de la théologie Africaine,* Paris 1989.

Nida, E., *Customs and cultures. Anthropology for Christian Missions*, New York 1954.

Nida, E., *Customs, culture and Christianity*, London 1954.

Nida, E., *Message and mission: the communication of the Christian faith,* New York 1960.

Niebuhr, H., *Christ and culture*. New York 1951.

Njozi, H., *Mwembechai killings and the political future of Tanzania*, Ottawa 2000.

Nkufu Nkemnkia, M., *African vitalogy: a step forward in African thinking*, Nairobi 1999.

Nyamiti, C., A critical assessment on some issues in today's African theology, in: *African Christian Studies* 5(1989)1, 5-18.

Nyamiti, C., My approach to African theology, in: *African Christian Studies* 7(1991)4, 35-53.

Nyasani, J., The Ontological Significance of I and We in African Philosophy, in: *African Christian Studies* 7(1991)1, 13-25.

Nyerere, J., *Education for self-reliance,* Dar es Salaam 1967.

Oborji, F., *Concepts of Mission in the evolution of contemporary missiology*, Rome and Lagos 2005.

Okure, T. (ed.), *To cast fire upon the earth. Bible and mission in today's multicultural global context*, Pietermaritzburg 2000.

Olupona, J. and S. Nnyang (eds.), *Religious plurality in Africa,* Berlin and New York 1993.

Ott, C. and J. Payne (eds.), *Missionary methods. Research, reflections and realities*, Passadena 2013.

Pals, D., *Seven theories of religion*, Oxford 1996.

Pambe, I., *Symbols and Change in African Beliefs. Religious Symbols and the Leader-specialist among the Sukuma-Nyamwezi of Tanzania*. Doctoral Dissertation, Rome 1978.

Pambe, I., Religious symbols, inter culture communication and change in Africa, in: *Pastoral Orientation Service* (1980)5-6.

Pambe, I., Christianity and meaning, in: *Pastoral Orientation Service* (1982)4-6, 21-27.

Pannenberg, W., *Wissenschaftstheorie und Theologie*, Frankfurt 1973.

p'Bitek, O., *African religions in Western scholarship,* Nairobi 1970.

Peel, J., Syncretism and Religious Change, in: *Comparative Studies in Society and History* 10(1967-1968)2, 121-141.

Petersen, D. and J. Aallman (eds.), Africans meeting missionaries: rethinking colonial encounters, in: *Journal of Religious History,* 23(1999)1.

Phalet, K., C. van Lotringen and H. Entzinger, *Islam in de multiculturele samenleving,* Utrecht 2000.

Phiri, I., D. Govinden and S. Nadar (eds.), *Her-stories. Hidden histories of women of faith in Africa*, Pietermaritzburg 2002.

Piepel, K., *Lerngemeinschaft Weltkirche. Lernprozesse in Partnerschaften zwischen Christen der Ersten und der Dritten Welt*, Aachen 1993.

Piepke, J. (ed.), *Anthropology and mission,* Nettetal 1988.

Pinto, D., *Interculturele communicatie,* Houten 1990.

Platvoet, J. and A. Molendijk (eds.), *The pragmatics of defining religion*, Leiden 1999.

Pontifical Council for Interreligious Dialogue, Dialogue and Proclamation, in: *Bulletin of the Pontifical Council for Interreligious Dialogue* 26(1991)2, 210-250.

Pontifical Council for promoting Christian Unity, Traditions regarding the procession of the Holy Spirit, in: *Eastern Churches Journal* 2(1995)3, 35-46.

Pontifical Council for promoting Christian Unity, *Catechism of the Catholic Church*, Dublin 1994, No. 248.

Pope John Paul II, Encyclical Letter 'Redemptoris Missio', nos. 21 and 29.

Pope John Paul II, International Theological Commission, Christianity and the religions, Nos. 81 and 94.

Pope John Paul II, Congregation for the Doctrine of the Faith, Declaration 'Dominus Jesus'. Vatican City 2000, No. 12.

Pope Paul VI, Apostolic Exhortation *Africae terrarum*, No. 17, published in *African Ecclesial Review* 10(1968)71-84.

Pope Paul VI, Address at the closing of the all African Bishop's symposium, in: *African Ecclesial Review* 11(1969)4, 402-405.

Portier, W., Interpretation and method, in: R. Schreiter and M. Hilkert (eds.), *The praxis of Christian experience. An introduction to the theology of Edward Schillebeeckx*, San Francisco 1989, 19-36.

Rahner, K., Einzigkeit and Dreifaltigkeit Gottes, in: A. Bsteh (ed.), *Der Gott des Christentums and des Islam*, Mödling 1978, 129-147.

Ramambason, L., *Missiology: its subject-matter and method. A study of mission-doers in Madagascar,* Frankfurt am Main 1999.

Ranger, T., Movement of ideas, in: I. Kimambo and A. Temu (eds.), *A history of Tanzania*, Nairobi 1969.

Ranger, T., *The African Churches of Tanzania*, Nairobi 1974.

Ranger, T., The invention of tradition in colonial Africa, in: E. Hobsbawm and T. Ranger (eds.), *The invention of tradition*, Cambridge 1983, 216-254.

Ranger, T., The invention of tradition revisited, in: T. Ranger and O. Vaughan (eds.), *Legitimacy and state in twentieth-century Africa*, London 1993, 62-111.

Reed, L., *Preparing missionaries for intercultural communication*, Pasadena 1985.

Ritzer, G., *The McDonaldization of society*, Thousand Oaks 1993.

Ritzer, G., *The McDonaldization thesis. Exploration and extension*, London 1997.

Robert, D., *Christian mission. How Christianity became a world religion*, Malden 2009.

Robertson, R., Glocalization. Time - space and homogeneity - heterogeneity, in: M. Featherstone, S. Lash and R. Robertson (eds.), *Global modernities*, London 1995, 25-44.

Roest Crollius, A. and T. Nnkeramihigo, *What is so new about inculturation?* Rome 1984.

Rommen, E. and G. Corwin, *Missiology and the social sciences*, Pasadena 1996.

Rütti, L., *Theologie der Mission*, München 1972.

Rütti, L., Mission – Gegenstand der Praktischen Theologie oder Frage der Gesamttheologie?, in: F. Klostermann and R. Zerfass (eds.), *Praktische Theologie Heute*, München and Mainz 1974, 288-307.

Rweyemanu, P. and G. Akilimali, *Si kiwete tena. Aonana na Bikira Maria*, Mshindi 1986.

Salemink, T., *De Afrikaanse mythe,* Kampen 1997.

Sanneh, L., *Translating the message. Missionary impact on culture,* Maryknoll, New York 1989.

Sanneh, L., *Disciples of all nations. Pillars of world Christianity*, Oxford 2008.

Sardar, Z., *Postmodernism and the Other. The new imperialism of Western culture*, London 1997.

Scannone, J., "Axial" shift instead of "paradigm shift". In: G. De Schrijver (ed.), *Liberation theologies on shifting grounds*, Leuven 1998, 85-105.

Schäfer, T., P. Schallenberg and U. Zzelinka (eds.), *Zur Mission herausgefordert,* Paderborn 1999.

Scharer, M. and B. Hilberath (eds.), *Kommunikative Theologie*, Mainz 2002.

Scheuerer, F., *Interculturality. A challenge for the mission of the Church*. Bangalore 2001.

Schillebeeckx, E., *Geloofsverstaan: interpretatie en kritiek*, Bloemendaal 1972.

Schillebeeckx, E., *The understanding of faith. Interpretation and criticism*, London 1974.

Schillebeeckx, E., *Jesus. An experiment in Christology*, New York 1979.

Schillebeeckx, E., Theologie als bevrijdingskunde, in: *Tijdschrift voor Theologie* 24(1984)4, 388-402.

Schipani, S. and A. Wessels (eds.), *The promise of hope*, Elkhart and Amsterdam 2002.

Schmidt, W., *The Origin and Growth of Religion. Facts and theories*, New York 1972.

Schoonenberg, P., *De geest, het Woord en de Zoon*, Averbode 1991.

Schreijack, T. (ed.), *Religionsdialog im Kulturwandel. Interkulturelle und interreligiöse Kommunikations- und Handlungskompetenzen auf dem Weg in die Weltgemeinschaft*, Münster 2002.

Schreiter, R., *Constructing local theologies*, Maryknoll, New York 1985.

Schreiter, R., *The new Catholicity. Theology between the Global and the Local*, Maryknoll, New York 1997.

Schweigman, C., Ujamaa. A phantom, in: *Quest. International African Journal of Philosophy* 15(2001)1-2, 113-125.

Secretariat for non-Christian religions, attitudes of the church toward the followers of other religions, in: *Bulletin of the Secretariat for Non-Christian Religions* 19(1984)2,126-241.

Shadid, W. , *Grondslagen van interculturele communicatie*, Houten 1998.

Shadid, W. and P. van Koningsveld (eds.), *Beeldvorming en interculturele communicatie,* Tilburg 2000.

Shadid, W. and P. van Koningsveld (eds.), *Religie, cultuur en minderheden,* Tilburg 2000.

Shorter, A., Symbolism, ritual and history. An examination of the work of Victor Turner, in: T. Ranger and J. Kimambo (eds.), *The historical study of African religion*, London 1972, 139-149.

Shorter, A., *African culture and the Christian Church*, London 1973.

Shorter, A., *Priest in the village: experiences of African community,* London 1979.

Shorter, A., Symbol, ritual and history. An examination of the work of Victor Turner, in: T. Tanger and I. Kimambo (eds.), *The historical study of African religion*, London 1979, 139-150.

Shorter, A., *Jesus and the Witchdoctor. An Approach to Healing and Wholeness*, London and Maryknoll, New York 1985.

Shorter, A., *Toward a theology of inculturation*, Maryknoll, New York 1988.

Shorter, A., *African culture. An overview*, Nairobi 1998.

Shorter, A., *Christianity and the African imagination*, Nairobi 1999.

Sievernich, M., *Die christliche Mission. Geschichte und Gegenwart*, Darmstadt 2009.

Siller, H., Synkretismus. Bestandsaufnahme und Problemanzeigungen, in: H. Siller (ed.), *Suchbewegungen. Synkretismus, kulturelle Identität und Kirchliches Bekentnis*, Darmstadt 1991, 1-17.

Singgih, G., Punishment and liberation, in: F. Wijsen, P. Henriot and R. Mejía (eds.), *The Pastoral Circle revisited*, Maryknoll, New York 2005.

Skreslet, S. (ed.), *Comprehending Mission. The questions, methods, themes, problems and prospects of missiology*, Maryknoll, New York 2012.

Smalley, W. (ed.), *Readings in Missionary Anthropology*, Tarrytown 1967.

Smith, J., *Imagining religion. From Babylon to Jonestown*, Chicago 1982.

Smith, W. C., *The meaning and end of religion. An approach to the religious traditions of mankind*, New York 1963.

Smith, W. C., *Towards a world theology*, Philadelphia 1981.

Søgaard, V., *Research in Church and Mission*, Pasadena 1996.

Sperber, D. and D. Wilson, *Relevance. Communication and Cognition*, Cambridge 1986.

Spradley, J. (ed.), *Culture and cognition*, San Francisco 1972.

Spradley, J., *The Ethnographic Interview*, New York 1979.

Spradley, J., *Participant observation*, New York 1980.

Statement of the bishops of Africa, in: *African Ecclesial Review* 17(1975)1, 56-59.

Stevens, L. , Religious change in a Haya Village, Tanzania, in: *Journal of Religion in Africa* 21(1991)1, 2-25.

Stewart, C. and R. Shaw (eds.), *Syncretism/Anti-Syncretism. The politics of religious synthesis*, London and New York 1994.

Stewart, C. and R. Shaw, Introduction. Problematizing syncretism, in: C. Stewart, R. Shaw (eds.), *Syncretism/Anti-syncretism. The Politics of Religious Synthesis*, London and New York 1994, 1-26.

Strauss, G. and J. Corbin, *Basics of qualitative research. Grounded theory. Procedures and techniques*, Newbury Park 1998.

Sundermeier, T., *Nur gemeinsam können wir leben. Das Menschenbild schwarzafrikanischer Religionen,* Gütersloh 1988.

Sundermeier, T., Begegnung mit dem Fremden. Plädoyer für eine verstehende Missionswissenschaft, in: *Evangelische Theologie* 50(1990)5, 390-400.

Sundermeier, T., *Konvivenz und Differenz. Studien zu einer verstehende Missionswissenschaft*, Erlangen 1995.

Sundermeier, T., *Den Fremden Verstehen. Eine praktische Hermeneutik*, Göttingen 1996.

Sundermeier, T., *Was ist Religion? Religionswissenschaft im theologischen Kontext*, Gütersloh 1999.

Sundermeier, T. and W. Ustorf, *Die Begegnung mit dem Anderen. Plädoyer für eine interkulturelle Hermeneutik*, Gütersloh 1991.

Sundermeier, T., *Konvivenz und Differenz: Studien zu einer verstehende Missionswissenschaft,* Erlangen 1995.

Sundermeier, T., *Den Fremden verstehen: eine praktische Hermeneutik,* Göttingen 1996.

Sundermeier, T., Aspects of interreligious hermeneutics, in: M. Frederiks, M. Dijkstra and A. Houtepen (eds.), *Towards an intercultural theology*, Zoetermeer 2003.

Sundermeier, T. and W. Ustorf (eds.), *Die Begegnung mit dem Anderen: Plädoyer für eine interkulturelle Hermeneutik,* Gütersloh 1991.

Taber, C., *To understand the world, to save the world. The interface between missiology and the social sciences*, Harrisburg 2000.

Tanner, K., *Theories of culture. A new agenda for theology*, Minneapolis1973.

Tanner, R., An Introduction to the Spirit Beings of the Northern Basukuma, in: *Anthropological Quarterly* 29(1956)3, 69-81.

Tanner, R., *Transition in African Beliefs. Traditional Religion and Christian Change. A Study in Sukumaland, Tanzania, East Africa*, Maryknoll, New York 1967.

Tanner, R. and F. Wijsen, Christianity in Usukuma. A working misunderstanding, in: *Neue Zeitschrift für Missionswissenschaft* 49(1993)3, 177-193.

Tanzania's renegade priest - Felician Nkwera, in: *New African*, May 1992, 26.

Tarimo, A., *Human rights, cultural differences and the church in Africa*, Morogoro 2004.

Taylor, J., *The primal vision. Christian presence amid African religion,* London 1963.

Taylor, J., *The go-between God: The Holy Spirit and Christian mission,* London 1972.

Tcherkézoff, S., *Dual classification reconsidered. Nyamwezi sacred kingship and other examples*, Cambridge 1987.

Tempels, P., *Bantoe-filosofie,* Antwerp 1946.

Ter Haar, G., *Spirit of Africa. The Healing Ministry of Archbishop Milingo of Zambia*, London 1992.

Ter Haar, G., *Halfway to Paradise. African Christians in Europe*, Cardiff 1998.

Ter Haar, G. (ed.), *Strangers and sojourners. Religious Communities in the Diaspora*, Leuven 1998.

Ter Haar, G., *Rats, cockroaches and people like us*, Den Haag 2000.

Thomas, S., *The global resurgence of religion and the transformation of international relations*, New York 2005.

Tillich, P., *Systematic theology*. Vol. 1, Chicago 1951.

Tirimanna, V., The church and the crossing of boundaries, in: F. Wilfred and O. Beozzo (eds.), Frontier Violations. *Concilium* 2(1990), 80-89.

Tirumanywa, C., *Christian religion on trial. The Good News is justice and peace for all on Earth*, Dar es Salaam 1991.

Tomecko, D. and J. Tomecko, in: *Sukuma*, n.p., n.d.

Tosolini, T., H. G. Gadamer and E. Levinas. Two philosophical approaches to the concept of dialogue, in: *Studies in Interreligious Dialogue* 12(2002)1, 37-62.

Tullemans, H., *Tussen twee werelden: brieven uit Afrika,* Nijmegen 2002.

Turkson, P. and F. Wijsen (eds.), *Inculturation. Abide by the Otherness of Africa and the Africans,* Kampen 1994.

Turner, V., *The forest of symbols. Aspects of Ndembu ritual*, Ithaca 1967.

Turner, V., *The ritual process. Structure and anti-structure*, London 1969.

Turner, V., *Dramas, fields, metaphors,* Ithaca 1974.

Turner, V., *Revelation and divination in Ndembu ritual*, Ithaca and London1975.

Ukpong, J. et al., *Reading the Bible in the global village*, Cape Town 2002.

Urban-Mead, W. and J. Cinnamon (eds.), *Missionaries and Ethnography. Social Sciences and Missions Nr. 19*, Leiden 2006.

Ustorf, W., Rethinking missiology, in: A. Houtepen and A. Ploeger (eds.), *World Christianity reconsidered*, Zoetermeer 2001, 67-78.

Valkenberg, W. and F. Wijsen, *The polemical dialogue; Chinweizu, The West and the rest of us. White predators, black slaves and the African elite*, Lagos 1987.

Van Beek, W., The culture-in-between. Anthropologist and missionary as partners, in: R. Bonsen, H. Mark and J. Miedema (eds.), *The ambiguity of rapprochement. Reflections of anthropologists on their controversial relationship with missionaries*, Nijmegen 1990, 101-120.

Van Binsbergen, W., Becoming a sangoma. Religious anthropological fieldwork in Francistown, Botswana. In: *Journal of Religion in Africa* 21(1991)4, 309-344.

Van Binsbergen, W., Sangoma in Nederland. Over integriteit en interculturele bemiddeling. In: M. Ellias and R. Reis (eds.), *Getuigen ondanks zichzelf*, Maastricht 1998, 1-29.

Van Binsbergen, W., *'Culturen bestaan niet'. Het onderzoek van interculturaliteit als een openbreken van vanzelfsprekendheden*, Rotterdam 1999.

Van Binsbergen, W., *Intercultural encounters. African and anthropological lessons towards a philosophy of interculturality*, Münster 2003.

Van Daal, H., *Het middenveld als smeltkroes,* Utrecht 2001.

Van den Eerenbeemt, A., *De missie-actie in Nederland. 1600 - 1940,* Nijmegen 1945.

Van der Leeuw, G., *Religion in essence and manifestation. A study in phenomenology*, London 1973.

Van der Ven, J., Practical theology. From applied to empirical theology, in: *Journal of Empirical Theology* 1(1988)1, 7-27.

Van der Ven, J., *Practical theology. An empirical approach*, Louvain 1998.

Van der Ven, J., *Education for reflective ministry*, Louvain 1998.

Van der Ven, J., Theologie beoefenen binnen een Instituut der Religiewetenschappen, in: *Tijdschrift voor Theologie* 42(2002)3, 244-267.

Van Dijk, T., *Discourse and context. A sociocognitive approach*, Cambridge 2008.

Van Engelen, J., *Langs een andere weg. Zoektocht naar een empirische missiologie van het Rijk Gods*, Nijmegen 1996.

Van Engelen, J., *Van kerk naar rijk Gods. Naar een empirische missiologie*, Nijmegen 2003.

Van Engen, C., N. Thomas and R. Gallagher, *Footprints of God. A narrative theology of mission*, Monrovia 1999.

Van Engen, C., D. Whiteman and J. Dudley Woodberry (eds.), *Paradigm shifts in Christian witness: insights from anthropology, communication, and spiritual power*, Maryknoll, New York 2008.

Van Kessel, I. and N. Tellegen (ed.), *Afrikanen in Nederland*, Leiden and Amsterdam 2000.

Van Leeuwen, A., *Christianity in world history. The meeting of the faiths of East and West*, London 1960.

Van 't Leven, C., Africa's tradition of peaceful co-existence, in: G. Speelman, J. van Lin and D. Mulder (eds.), *Muslims and Christians in Europe,* Kampen 1993, 14-27.

Van 't Spijker, G., Anthropology: a tool for missionary studies. In: K. Bediako et al. (eds.), *A new day dawning*, Zoetermeer 2004, 52-65.

Verberk, G., *Attitudes towards ethnic minorities,* Amsterdam 1999.

Verschuren, P., *Dogma's en ontwikkeling in wetenschap en methodologie*, Nijmegen 2002.

Verschuren, P. and H. Doorewaard, *Designing a research project*, Utrecht 1999.

Verstraelen, F. (ed.), *Oecumenische inleiding in de missiologie,* Kampen 1988.

Verstraelen, F., *Christianity in a new key. New voices and vistas through intercultural communication*, Gweru 1996.

Verstraelen, F., *Christianity in a new key. New voices and vistas through intercontinental communication*, Gweru 1996.

Villa-Vicencio, C., *A theology of reconstruction,* Cambridge 1992.

Von Sicard, S., Christian-Muslim relations in Africa, in: J. Olupona and S. Nyang (eds.), *Religious Plurality in Africa. Essays in Honour of John S. Mbiti*, Berlin and New York 1993, 273-283.

Waldenfels, H., On the hermeneutics of intercultural encounter, in: *Studies in Interreligious Dialogue* 2(1992)1, 31-50.

Waliggo, J.-M. et al., *Inculturation. Its meaning and urgency*, Nairobi 1986.

Walls, A., *The cross-cultural process in Christian history. Studies in the transmission and appropriation of Faith*, Maryknoll, New York 2002.

Walls, A. and C. Ross, *Mission in the twenty-first century. Exploring the five marks of global mission*, Maryknoll, New York 2008.

Wambua, F., *Participation of the poor,* Eldoret 1987.

M. Warren, General introduction, in: J. Taylor, *The primal vision. Christian presence amid African religion,* London 1963.

Weber, F., *Mission. Gegenstand der Praktische Theologie*, Frankfurt am Main 1999.

Westerlund, D., The study of African religions in retrospect from Westernization to Africanization, in: J. Olupona (ed.), *Religious plurality in Africa*, Berlin and New York 1993, 43-66.

Whiteman, D., *Missionaries, anthropologists, and cultural change*, Williamsburg 1983.

Wiedenman, L., Missionswissenschaft oder kontextuelle Theologie?, in: M. Pankoke-Schenk and G. Evers (eds.), *Inkulturation und Kontextualität. Theologien im Weltweiten Austausch*, Frankfurt am Main 1994, 231-240.

Wierzbicka, A., The concept of 'dialogue' in cross-linguistic and cross-cultural perspective, in: *Discourse Studies* 8(2006)5, 675-703.

Wiredu, K., *Cultural universals and particulars. An African perspective*, Indiana 1996.

Wijsen, F., Missionair pastoraat in de stad Maastricht, in: *Wereld en Zending. Tijdschrift voor missionaire informatie en bezinning* 14(1981)1, 48-54.

Wijsen, F., Geloof in een volksbuurt van Maastricht, in: M. Van Uden and J. Pieper (eds.), *Bij geloof. Over bedevaarten en andere uitingen van volksreligiositeit*, Hilversum 1991, 163-188.

Wijsen, F., *There is only one God. A Social-Scientific and Theological Study of Popular Religion and Evangelization in Sukumaland, Northwest Tanzania*, Kampen 1993.

Wijsen, F., Volksreligiositeit in Maastricht. Een semiotische analyse, in: J. Pieper, P. Post and M. van Uden (eds.), *Bedevaart en pelgrimage*, Baarn 1994, 155-200.

Wijsen, F., "The Gold and the spirits are close". Popular Religion and social transformation in Sukumaland, North-West Tanzania, in: *Exchange. Journal of Missiological and Ecumenical Research* 24(1995)1, 45-60.

Wijsen, F., "All People See the Same Sun". Liturgy in Africa between Inculturation and Syncretism, in: *Questions Liturgiques* 77(1996)1-2, 77-95.

Wijsen, F., Der Pastorale Zirkel in der Ausbildung im kirchlichen Dienst, in: H. Janssen (ed.), *Zeichen der Zeit. Pastoraler Zirkel, Gesellschaftsanalyse, Bibel-Teilen*, Aachen 1996, 45-56.

Wijsen, F., *Geloven bij het leven. Missionaire presentie in een volkswijk.* Baarn 1997.

Wijsen, F., 'I have all kinds of medicines.' Dialogue and syncretism in African Christianity, in: W. Valkenberg and F. Wijsen (eds.), *The Polemic Dialogue*, Saarbrücken 1997, 123-145.

Wijsen, F., 'Strive in competition for good deeds'. Christians and Muslims in Tanzania, in: *Studies in Interreligious Dialogue* 7(1997)2, 158-167.

Wijsen, F., The Pastoral Circle in the Training of Church Ministers, in: *African Ecclesial Review* 39(1997)4, 238-250.

Wijsen, F., Beyond the Fatal Impact Theory, in: M. Amaladoss (ed.), *Globalization and its victims as seen by its victims,* Delhi 1999, 122-131.

Wijsen, F., *Lingkaran pastoral dalam pendidikan pelayanan*. Seri Pastoral 296, Yogyakarta 1999.

Wijsen, F., Inculturation or Syncretism? Popular Christianity in East Africa, in: A. Kalliath (ed.), *Pilgrims in Dialogue. A new configuration of Religions for Millennium Community*. Bangalore 2000, 247-285.

Wijsen, F., "Een vreemdeling is twee dagen gast …". Afrikaanse Katholieken in Nederland en hun uitdaging aan theologie en pastoraat, in: L. Boeve and J. Haers (eds.), *God ondergronds,* Averbode 2001, 161-174.

Wijsen, F., Intercultural Theology and the Mission of the Church, *Exchange. Journal of Missiological and Ecumenical Research* 30(2001)3, 218-228.

Wijsen, F., 'When two elephants fight the grass gets hurt...' Muslim-Christian Relationships in Upcountry Tanzania, in: F. Wijsen and P. Nissen (eds.), *'Mission is a Must.' Intercultural Theology and the Mission of the Church*, Amsterdam and New York 2002, 235-248.

Wijsen, F., Mission and Multiculturalism. On Communication between Europeans and Africans, in: *Exchange. Journal of Missiological and Ecumenical Research* 32(2003)3, 260-277.

Wijsen, F., New Wine in Old Wineskins? Intercultural Theology instead of Missiology, in: M. Frederiks, M. Dijkstra and A. Houtepen (eds.), *Towards an Intercultural Theology,* Zoetermeer 2003, 39-54.

Wijsen, F., "…op zondag willen wij vooral onszelf zijn". Allochtone Christenen in Nederland, in: C. Hermans (ed.), *Is er nog godsdienst in 2050?*, Budel 2003, 92-111.

Wijsen, F., Religionism in Tanzania, in: A. Borsboom and F. Jespers (eds.), *Identity and Religion. A Multidisciplinary Approach*, Saarbrücken 2003, 121-137.

Wijsen, F., The Practical-Theological Spiral. Bridging Theology in the West and the Rest of the World, in: F. Wijsen, P. Henriot and R. Mejía (eds.),

The Pastoral Circle Revisited. A Critical Quest for Truth and Transformation, New York 2005, 108-126.

Wijsen, F., Mission in a new key. From inculturation to interculturation, in: *SMA Bulletin*, June 2007(125), 41-53.

Wijsen, F., *Seeds of conflict in a haven of peace. From religious studies to interreligious studies in Africa*, Amsterdam and New York 2007.

Wijsen, F., 'The future of the church is in our hands'. Christian migrants in the Netherlands, in: J. Haers and N. Hintersteiner (eds.), *Postcolonial Europe in the Crucible of Cultures. Reckoning with God in a World of Conflicts*, Amsterdam and New York 2007, 99-110.

Wijsen, F., The resurgence of religion in today's world, in: F. Stenger and J. Wandera (eds.), *Christian-Muslim Co-Existence in Eastern Africa*, Nairobi 2008, 41-58.

Wijsen, F., Global Christianity. A European Perspective, in: *Exchange. Journal of Missiological and Ecumenical Research* 39(2009) 2, 147-160.

Wijsen, F., *Buah Buah Roh. Menjalankan Riset Social Partisipatif di Belahan Dunia Selatan*, Yogyakarta 2010.

Wijsen, F., Discourse Analysis in Religious Studies. The Case of Interreligious Worship in Friesland, in: *Anthropos. International Review of Anthropology and Linguistics* 105(2010)2, 539-553.

Wijsen, F., Indigenous Spirituality and Sustainable Development. A Critical Appraisal of African Renaissance Rhetoric, in: J. Gort, H. Jansen and H. Stoker (eds.), *Crossroads Discourses between Christianity and Culture*, Amsterdam and New York 2010, 275-300.

Wijsen, F., Religion, Development and Security. A Mission Studies Perspective, in: *Exchange. Journal of Missiological and Ecumenical Research*, 40(2011) 2, 274-287.

Wijsen, F., From Religious to Interreligious Studies in East Africa, in: I. Mwase and E. Kamaara (eds.), *Theologies of Liberation and Reconstruction*. Nairobi 2012, 249-268.

Wijsen, F., The practical-theological spiral revisited. From social to discursive analysis, in: R. Setio, W. Wibowo and P. Widjaja (eds.), *Teks dan Konteks yang Tiada Bertepi*, Semarang 2012, 73-91.

Wijsen, F., *Religious Discourse, Social Cohesion and Conflict. Studying Muslim-Christian Relations,* Oxford 2013.

Wijsen, F., 'There are radical Muslims and normal Muslims': an analysis of the discourse on Islamic extremism, in: *Religion* 43(2013)1, 70-88.

Wijsen, F., Interkulturelle Theologie und Religionswissenschaft, in: *Interkulturelle Theologie. Zeitschrift für Missionswissenschaft* 40(2014)2-3, 219-229.

Wijsen, F., "Keep the conversation going". Regulating Islamic Revivalism in Tanzania, in: T. Ndaluka and F. Wijsen (eds.), *Religion and state in Tanzania revisited. Reflections from 50 years of independence*, Münster 2014, 198-205.

Wijsen, F., Theology as religious studies. A plea for methodological conversion, in: J. Mugambi (ed.), *Endless Quest. The Vocation of an African Christian Theologian*, Nairobi 2014, 290-302.

Wijsen, F., What is intercultural about Intercultural Theology?, in: *Gema Teologi. Jurnal Fakultas Theologia Universitas Kristen Duta Wacana*, 2014, 185-192.

Wijsen, F. and S. Cholil, 'I come from a Pacasila Family'. Muslims and Christians in Indonesia, in: V. Küster and R. Setio (eds.), *Muslim Christian Relations Observed. Comparative Studies from Indonesia and The Netherlands*, Leipzig 2014, 29-46.

Wijsen, F. and F. Husein, Dakwah and mission. Muslim - Christian encounters in Indonesia, in: C. Sterkens, M. Machasin and F. Wijsen (eds.), *Religion, Civil Society and Conflict in Indonesia*, Zürich and Berlin 2009, 135-152.

Wijsen, F. and S. Marcos, Indigeneity and sustainability. An introduction, in: F. Wijsen and S. Marcos (eds.), *Indigenous Voices in the Sustainability Discourse. Spirituality and the struggle for a better quality of life*, Münster 2010, 9-30.

Wijsen, F. and B. Mfumbusa, Seeds of conflict. Christian-Muslim relations in Tanzania, in: J. Gort, H. Jansen and H. Vroom (eds.), *Religion, conflict and reconciliation*, Amsterdam and New York 2002, 316-326.

Wijsen, F. and T. Ndaluka, Ujamaa is still alive. A sign of hope for Africa?, in: A.J. Bwangatto (ed.), *Africa is not Destined to die. Signs of hope and renewal*. Nairobi 2012, 240-253.

Wijsen, F. and P. Nissen (eds.), *'Mission is a Must'. Intercultural Theology and the Mission of the Church*. Amsterdam and New York 2002.

Wijsen, F. and R. Tanner, *'I am just a Sukuma'. Globalization and Identity Construction in Northwest Tanzania*, Amsterdam and New York 2002.

Wijsen, F. and R. Tanner, The Limitations of an Ecumenical Language. The case of Ki-Swahili, in: *Anthropos. International Review of Anthropology and Linguistics* 103(2008)2, 549-554.

Wijsen, F. and H. Tullemans (eds.), *Dictionary of Literary Swahili by Jan Knappert and Leo van Kessel,* Lewiston 2010.

Wijsen, F. and R. Schreiter (eds.), *Global Christianity. Contested claims*, Amsterdam and New York 2007.

Wijsen, F. and G. Singgih, Regulation on Houses of Worship. A Threat to Social Cohesion?, in: Sterkens, Machasin and Wijsen, *Religion, Civil Society*, 87-97.

Wijsen, F. and J. Vos, 'This is how we are at home'. Indonesian Muslims in The Hague, in: V. Küster and R. Setio (eds.), *Muslim Christian Relations Observed. Comparative Studies from Indonesia and The Netherlands*, Leipzig 2014, 15-28.

Wijsen, F., P. Henriot and R. Mejía (eds.), *The Pastoral Circle Revisited. A Critical Quest for Truth and Transformation*, New York 2005.

Winkeler, L., Welvaart in zwart-wit, 302-309. For an African conception of welfare work see Shorter, *Jesus and the witchdoctor,* 125-136.

Witvliet, T., Reponse to Werner Ustorf, in: A. Houtepen and A. Ploeger (eds.), *World Christianity reconsidered*, Zoetermeer 2001, 229-251.

Woodberry, J., C. Van Engen and E. Elliston (eds.), *Missiological education for the 21st century. The Book, the circle and the sandals*, Maryknoll, New York 1997.

Wrogemann, H. (ed.), *Missionstheologien der Gegenwart. Globale Entwicklungen, kontextuelle Profile und ökumenische Herausforderungen*, Gütersloh 2013.

Ziebertz, H.-G., Komplementarität von Forschungsmethoden, in: J. Van der Ven and H.-G. Ziebertz (eds.), *Paradigmenentwicklung in der Praktischen Theologie*, Kampen 1993, 225-260.

Ziebertz, H.-G., Normativity and Empirical Research in Practical Theology, in: *Journal for Empirical Theology* 15(2002)1, 5-18.

Index of Subjects

Index of names

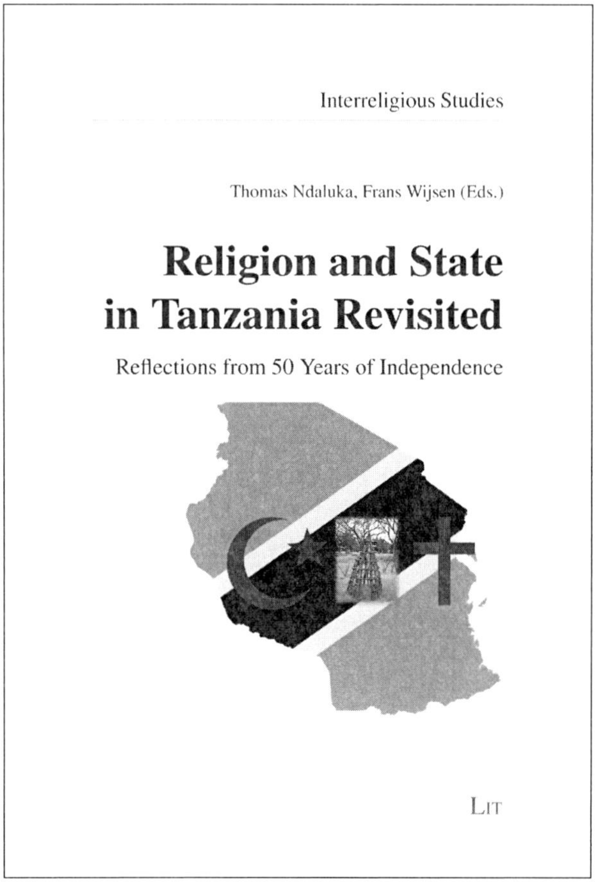

Thomas Ndaluka; Frans Wijsen (Eds.)
Religion and State in Tanzania Revisited
Reflections from 50 Years of Independence

This book looks at the relationship between religion and state in Tanzania as a feature of the Tanzanian social scene from pre-colonial and colonial to post colonial times. The authors examine the changes in the character of religion and state relations, especially after independence, and the way these changes are experienced in different communities (particularly by African traditionalists, Muslims and Christians). The book studies the nature of the relationship between religion and state, the way it is conceptualised and experienced, and the implications for the democratic aspirations of pluralist Tanzania.

Interreligious Studies, vol. 7, 2014, 224 pp., 29,90 €, br., ISBN-CH 978-3-643-90546-8

LIT Verlag Berlin – Münster – Wien – Zürich – London
Auslieferung Deutschland / Österreich / Schweiz: siehe Impressumsseite